GOD *and* REASON

An Invitation to Philosophical Theology

Second Edition

Ed. L. Miller
UNIVERSITY OF COLORADO, BOULDER

PRENTICE HALL *Upper Saddle River, NJ 07458*

Library of Congress Cataloging-in-Publication Data
Miller, Ed. L. (Eddie LeRoy)
    God and reason : an invitation to philosophical theology / Ed. L.
Miller. -- 2nd ed.
        p.   cm.
    Includes bibliographical references.
    ISBN 0-02-381261-3 (pbk.)
    1. Philosophical theology. 2. Faith and reason. I. Title.
BT40.M49   1995
210--dc20   93-46592
                                                         CIP

Acquisitions Editors: Maggie Barbieri and Ted Bolen
Editorial Production Supervision: John Travis and Shelly Kupperman
Editorial Production Manager: Alexandra Odulak
Text and Cover Designer: Eileen Burke

For old friends, from when it all began:

Jerry Campana
Cliff Holland
Eddie English
Gene Talley
and
Dave Graves

Printed in the United States of America

10 9 8 7 6

ISBN 0-02-381261-3

Prentice-Hall International (UK) Limited, *London*
Prentice-Hall of Australia Pty. Limited, *Sydney*
Prentice-Hall Canada, Inc., *Toronto*
Prentice-Hall Hispanoamericana, S.A., *Mexico*
Prentice-Hall of India Private Limited, *New Delhi*
Prentice-Hall of Japan, Inc., *Tokyo*
Editora Prentice-Hall do Brasil, Ltda., *Rio de Janeiro*

Contents

4. The Teleological Argument   69

5. The Moral Argument   89

6. Religious Experience   107

7. Faith and Reason   129

approach. While it is surely necessary to attend to recent developments, it would be a mistake to attempt a serious consideration of these topics except against the backdrop of the discussions that have converged over the centuries into a whole philosophical-theological tradition. Second, the reader will encounter here a heavy stress on the existence of God. For a time the question of God's existence and the traditional theistic arguments were eclipsed by allegedly more pressing issues, or simply laid aside as otherwise misguided. But the current literature suggests a renewed interest in evidence for God, and whether the arguments possess force or relevance is, I think, yet a good question and surely of interest to many readers. At any rate, a somewhat extended consideration of these arguments can be justified on the grounds that they continue to be, at the very least, useful vehicles for the introduction and discussion of fundamental theories, concepts, and distinctions that bear on much more than just the question of God.

If anything is distinctive about the approach taken in this book, it is, surely, these two concerns—the concern for the historical development of the issues, and for the central problem of the existence of God. But to these concerns might be added a third and more subtle one. It is the concern, suggested recurringly and in various ways, that the kinds of issues addressed here cannot be adequately dealt with by means of what might be called a "hammer and tongs" approach that thinks it can bang out all the answers in a crude, cold, and calculating way. For the issues often verge on the personal and subjective dimensions of our existence and invite the awareness that, at the end of the day, there are other factors that shape our perspectives—and legitimately so—than the purely objective and rational.

The second edition of *God and Reason* has provided, of course, an opportunity to update, expand, clarify, and otherwise improve the discussions. Although this has been done, the original character and tone of the book has been retained. An attempt has been made to broaden the horizon to give greater attention to the other Western traditions, as well as to some strains of the Eastern, though the book still addresses primarily the larger audience of those within the Judeo-Christian tradition. Naturally, considerations of space have dictated that not all relevant topics could be included, and in this respect I have been guided (I hope) by a sense for both what is essential and what makes for a coherent outline and discussion. As in the first edition, the footnotes provide clues for the reader who wishes to pursue the primary sources further, and I have appended a brief bibliographical note. (Relevant primary materials, as well as extended bibliographies on each topic, are collected in my book of readings, *Philosophical/Religious Issues: Classical and Contemporary Statements* [Englewood Cliffs, N.J.: Prentice-Hall, 1995], to which *God and Reason* is something of a companion.)

All Biblical quotations are from the New Revised Standard Version, copyright 1990 by the Division of Christian Education, the National Council of Churches of Christ in the U.S.A., and are used by permission.

I wish to acknowledge the helpful insights of Prof. Elias Baumgarten, Mr. William Carroll, and Prof. Thomas Quinn who contributed to the first edition, and with respect to the second edition, Prof. Lee Speer, Prof. Wes Morriston, Dr. Paul Keyser, Jeff Broome, Prof. Garry DeWeese and several assistants: Mr. Greg Johnson, Mr. Erik Hanson, Mr. Shawn Mather, and Mr. and Mrs. Glenn Ashton—especially Margaret, who bore the brunt of manuscript preparation. Thanks also to my wife Cynthia and son Sean for helping with the index.

E.L.M.

1

What Is Philosophical Theology?

One can hardly appreciate what philosophical theology really is unless one becomes personally related to its issues and involved in its debates. Still, a brief consideration of philosophy, religion, and theology—and, of course, *philosophical* theology—will provide a point of departure and a framework in terms of which our discussion may gain some momentum. Furthermore, even in this preliminary discussion, some important ideas will emerge that may illuminate the phenomenon of the human in relation to the world.

Philosophy: A Traditional View

Probably everyone has at least some idea of the nature of philosophy and philosophizing. Upon examination, however, our idea may turn out to be a rather obscure one, though we are certain that philosophy has something to do with thinking, and thinking on a grand scale.

The word itself derives from the Greek φιλοσοφία, which means "love of wisdom." (According to one tradition, Pythagoras first called himself a philosopher—lover of wisdom—insisting that wisdom itself is the proper possession of God alone.) A more inclusive statement would spell out the several fields of philosophic inquiry: metaphysics (the theory of reality or, in a more restricted sense, the theory of transcendent reality), epistemology (the theory of knowledge), axiology (the theory of value), ethics (the study of moral or

1

human values), aesthetics (the theory of art and beauty), and logic (the science of right thinking). If the first, etymological, definition suggests too little about philosophy, this one suggests too much, at least for the present purpose. What is required is a more practical definition, one that expresses concisely but as accurately as possible the character of philosophy.

I submit the following as a working definition of philosophy: Philosophy is the attempt to provide, within limits, a rational interpretation of reality as a whole. This is, more or less, a traditional view of philosophy inasmuch as it is suggested, I think, by the history of philosophy itself. It is also the conception of philosophy that will lie behind most of the discussion in this book. Let us then consider it more carefully.

The word "rational" is important. It emphasizes that philosophy, more obviously than other disciplines, rejects and condemns all forms of superstition, dogmatism, and uncritical opinion and seeks to replace them with concepts that are born of hard and coherent thinking. Philosophy is, in this broad sense of the word, rationalistic: Its principal tool is reason and its business is reflection; it is both critical and constructive; it is analytic (it takes ideas apart) and synthetic (it puts them together). In short, the philosopher believes, with Socrates, that "the unexamined life is not worth living."

But the phrase "within limits" suggests an important qualification. Though the philosopher eschews irrationalism and embraces reason, his or her thought necessarily gives way, at one point or another, to the nonrational (not to be confused with *ir*rational) contributions of presupposition, intuition, poetic vision, mystery, and the like. Does not every position or theory or argument begin, for instance, with assumptions about something or other? In fact, a strong case could be made for the nonrational and nonarguable foundations and features of the classical philosophical systems such as those propounded by Plato, St. Augustine, Descartes, Spinoza, Kant, and Hegel. It is for this reason (the inevitable presence of the nonrational or subjective element) that there can never be a definitive philosophy, one that will command unanimous consent.

Finally, the phrase "reality as a whole" suggests the encompassing or synoptic character of philosophic inquiry. Each of the specialized disciplines (for example, biology, psychology, astronomy, and anthropology) focuses on a particular aspect of reality, whereas the philosopher, surveying all facets of experience, seeks to formulate the *ultimate* principles. As Plato says, the philosopher is one who desires all wisdom, not only some part of it, one who is a spectator of all time and existence. Again, the encompassing scope of the philosopher's interest is suggested in Immanuel Kant's three famous questions reflecting the theoretical, practical, and personal dimensions of philosophical thought:

What may I know?

What must I do?

What may I hope?

In a sense, all other inquiries can be construed as subfields of philosophy inasmuch as they all contribute, ultimately, to answering the questions that philosophers ask, questions concerning the nature of knowledge, of value, of meaning, and of reality itself.

On this view, philosophical activity lies somewhere between that of the scientist and the poet. The philosopher attempts to speak rationally and systematically, but at the same time to speak of the things that matter most. The philosopher attempts to organize and systematize his or her encounters with existence and value, to articulate a *Weltanschauung* or "world view," a general impression and judgment about the whole of things. This view of the philosophical enterprise may be called the "speculative" view and is otherwise suggested by the American philosopher Alfred North Whitehead:

Speculative philosophy is the endeavour to frame a coherent, logical, necessary system of general ideas in terms of which every element of our experience can be interpreted. . . . Philosophers can never hope finally to formulate these metaphysical first principles. Weakness of insight and deficiencies of language stand in the way inexorably. Words and phrases must be stretched towards a generality foreign to their ordinary usage; and however such elements of language be stabilized as technicalities, they remain metaphors mutely appealing for an imaginative leap. . . . Rationalism is an adventure in the clarification of thought, progressive and never final. But it is an adventure in which even partial success has importance.[1]

---

[1]Alfred North Whitehead, *Process and Reality* (New York: Macmillan, 1929), pp. 4, 6, 14.

But, oddly, one of the most persistent issues in recent philosophy concerns the nature of philosophy itself! Thus we should have no illusion that the conception of philosophy represented here, though traditional, is embraced by all. It might be problematic, for example, for someone with an "analytic" orientation. In the earlier part of the twentieth century, it was maintained by an influential group of philosophers (mainly British) that the standard problems of the history of philosophy are not real problems at all but actually pseudoproblems, problems of language, and that the proper philosophical task is to clarify the subtleties and ambiguities of philosophical discourse through what was called "linguistic analysis," or, as someone expressed it, "talk about talk." In this way, traditional philosophical problems are not solved but *dis*solved. Nowadays, however, the analytic approach represents something somewhat broader and softer, though still exercising, primarily, an interest in definition, conceptual coherence, logical scrutiny, and, in a word, clarification. Our conception of philosophy might also be troublesome for those of a "phenomenological" bent. Phenomenology, also a twentieth-century movement but sponsored this time by continental thinkers, seeks knowledge of the structures of consciousness and the way in which reality is actually experienced. Likewise with existentialism, which has seen its heyday but still lingers as a philosophical force. Here the abstractions and speculations of traditional philosophizing are spurned in favor of a focus on the meaning, purpose, passions, and decisions of the concretely existing individual.

These, and still other perspectives, have staked legitimate claims in the contemporary philosophical territory. And each has an important agenda. But it is a mistake to confuse what is a part of the philosophical enterprise with the whole of it. And what the whole of it *is* is best understood from the broad sweep of our entire philosophical tradition.

The Essence of Religion

Our definition of philosophy was offered along with a concession that not everyone would buy it. It is even more difficult to agree on the nature of religion. On this matter the theologian, anthropologist, psychologist, Hindu, Jew, and Christian may each proffer radically different views. Either that, or a proposed definition will likely be so broad as to include beliefs and practices concerning almost everything short of the kitchen sink: God, superhuman realities, the cause and purpose of the universe, worship, rituals, symbols, hierarchies, social obligations, moral duties, and so on. "Religion" is indeed a squishy word. And rather than venturing into a quagmire, we may do well to focus upon one element that seems to be present in nearly every conception of religion and to ask whether it is not indeed the central and distinctive one.

The word "religion" is almost always associated with God and the supernatural. It might be argued, however, that religion itself has nothing necessarily to do with God at all. Certainly, if anything is the science or study of the divine, it is theology, not religion, and belief in God makes one a theist, not a religious person. Of course, if one thinks that "religion," "theology," and "theism" are simply different words for the same thing, that's the end of the matter. But it appears that we can identify "theology" with the pursuit of the knowledge of God (which is exactly what the word means, from the Greek θεός, "God") and "theism" with belief in God, and still find something important to which we can assign the word "religion."

Theology and theism, like cosmology and Platonism, are intellectual and cognitive affairs; they concern the *theory about* and *belief in* something. It is evident, though, that there is more to a position than the theory behind it. If someone claims to be a Christian or a Marxist or a Buddhist, I immediately understand something of this person's beliefs, how he or she thinks, what judgments have been made on certain theoretical questions. But I am also informed about this person's response or *commitment* to something. And it would appear that it is this latter aspect of someone's position—the more experiential, volitional, or existential aspect—that we have foremost in mind when we speak of someone's "religion"; it is primarily a matter of personal appropriation and devotion. (In fact, the word "religion" derives from the Latin verb *religare*, which originally meant "to tie" or "to bind" and, eventually, to be tied or bound in reverence and devotion to something.) Of course, we would not be inclined to call every commitment a religious one, but only that commitment to and appropriation of something acknowledged as *ultimate* or in some sense *holy*.

It must be noted that it is possible to be thus responsive and devoted to something ultimate, and to be in this sense religious, without entertaining even a belief in God, much less passionate commitment. An individual's religion may or may not be theological or theistic in character, that is, it may or may not involve a belief in God; for the Christian it will, for the Marxist it won't, and for the Buddhist it will depend on the brand of Buddhism (Therevada Buddhism, for example, is a wholly nontheistic religion). It has already been hinted that there can be no religious commitment in an intellectual vacuum and that it necessarily rests upon or involves some intellectual judgment or other; religious commitment presupposes reason, and reason is fulfilled in religious commitment. But to identify religion with any *particular* belief, such as belief in the Judeo-Christian God, would be to exclude a vast block of human experience that most of us simply cannot resist calling *religious*. According to a fragment of Aeschylus, the ancient Greek dramatist,

> Zeus is all, and more than all!

This is a religious response, whatever Zeus may symbolize; there are many gods with a small *g*, including wealth, political causes, humanitarian ideals, and pleasure.

The English philosopher F. H. Bradley (1846–1924) adopted this very conception of religion when he identified it as a

fixed feeling of fear, resignation, admiration or approval, no matter what may be the object, provided only that this feeling reaches a certain strength, and is qualified by a certain degree of reflection.[2]

This definition is a good one (at least for my purpose) inasmuch as it emphasizes (1) that the essence of religion lies in the existential appropriation or affirmation of an object; though (2) in order to qualify as religious, this affirmation must attain a distinctive power for the individual; (3) that the particular object of the commitment

---

[2]F. H. Bradley, *Appearance and Reality* (London: Sonnenschein, 1893), p. 439, n.

is purely secondary; and (4) that there is no religious commitment apart from reflection and intellectual judgment. I myself would hazard that religion is the experience of the Highest Good that we grasp and are grasped by, the response to an ultimate Power and Purpose confronting us and eliciting our devotion. It may be useful, by the way, to compare this with the kind of commitment demanded in the first lines of the Jewish *Shema* (Deut. 6:4–5): "Hear, O Israel: The LORD is our God, the LORD alone. You shall love the LORD your God with all your heart, and with all your soul, and with all your might."

If our previous characterizations of philosophy as concerned with critical reflection and of religion as concerned with ultimate commitment are accepted, we may ask further whether the distinction between the two is not a reflection of two very different (though in practice inseparable) factors of an individual's position, be it that of the Christian, Marxist, Buddhist, or whatever. Does not such a position necessarily involve, at the same time, intellectual assent to some doctrines and ideas, and personal appropriation or the actual *living* of those ideas? We may even ask whether the distinction between philosophy and religion is not a reflection of the very *nature* of the human being as at once a rational and volitional creature, a creature both of cognition and of decision.

The opening sentence of Aristotle's *Metaphysics* is a classic statement of the rational or philosophical nature of man: "All men by nature desire to know." There is no one who is not caught up to some degree in the world of ideas and reflection, no one who does not seek rational grounds for his or her commitment. Some are, of course, better philosophers than others, and some are more dominated by the intellectual impulse than others. Still, everyone reflects upon what concerns one most; everyone raises, in one's own way, what at least appear to be the ultimate questions.

On the other hand, we are more than creatures of intellect. We are also beings who will, approve, and sanction; we are creatures of commitment. Just as no one is altogether devoid of the philosophical impulse, so also there is no one whose life does not revolve around something, an ultimate Good that stirs one's deepest feelings, an object of worship, an integrating center of meaning, a highest cause. The German-American theologian Paul Tillich called it "ultimate concern." Naturally, one person's commitment may be more clearly defined, more consciously directed, more intense, or more elevated than another's, but everyone is committed, in one way or another, to something that (at least for the moment) is recognized as holding supreme worth and significance—one can usually tell what it is for a given individual by the way that person lives. For everyone there is a pearl of great price for which one would gladly sell all; and where one's treasure is, there will the heart be also.

Not everyone may agree that this twofold nature of humanity, as we might call it, is suggestive of the distinction between philosophy and religion, and some will surely balk at the reduction of religion to something like ultimate concern, pure and simple. That a passionate stamp collector is for that reason as much a religious individual as St. Francis of Assisi may strike us as ludicrous, and we feel thus compelled to distinguish (as Tillich will urge us later) between religious commitment that directs itself to an unworthy object and is, consequently, demonic and idolatrous, and commitment that realizes itself in that which is truly ultimate and worthy of our highest devotion. Be that as it may, I do insist that, as the French philosopher Blaise Pascal said, "the knowledge of God is very far from the love of Him,"[3] and that religion clearly has more to do with the latter than it does with the former.

We are by our very nature creatures of both reflection and commitment. About this we have no choice. We do, however, have a choice about what we believe and how we go about justifying its truth. That is why philosophical theology is important.

Theology: Philosophical and Revealed

As stated previously, theology concerns the knowledge of God. There are, however, two kinds of theology: revealed and philosophical. These represent radically different ways in which, it is thought, knowledge of God may be attained.

---

[3]Blaise Pascal, *Pensees*, no. 280, in *Pensees and the Provincial Letters*, tr. W. F. Trotter and Thomas M'Crie (New York: Modern Library, 1941).

One of the distinctive features of the Judeo-Christian tradition is its belief in a divine self-disclosure: God has intervened in human history and spoken; he has unveiled himself in a "special revelation." And the knowledge of God drawn from this revelation is an example of revealed theology. Such theology is sometimes called "dogmatic" (in the best sense of the word) or "confessional" theology because it seeks to elucidate the divinely bestowed articles of faith (dogmas) that it takes as its fundamental and nonnegotiable data. Not unlike the mathematician, the dogmatic theologian begins with certain givens, though in this case *revealed* givens; the system is bounded by revelation, self-contained, and offered as a package deal. Philosophical theology, on the other hand, is the attempt to attain knowledge of God and related matters through the *lumen naturale*, "natural light," independently of special revelation. It assumes a "general revelation" whereby at least some rudimentary knowledge of God is accessible to all. Further, in the

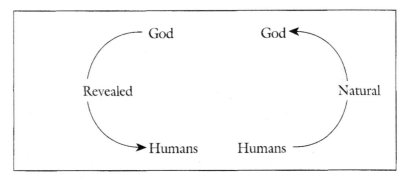

confrontation with special revelation, one is more or less a passive recipient, whereas a knowledge of God through general revelation involves the active employment of our natural faculties, including observation, inference, reflection, and interpretation. It is the difference between God's movement toward us and our movement toward God.

Philosophical theology is otherwise known as "natural" theology. The latter may suggest to some a knowledge of God through nature, though the term usually indicates the knowledge of God acquired through the intellect in its natural state, unaided by a supernatural illumination or grace. We shall soon see that some of the arguments for the existence of God have nothing whatever to do with the world of nature or sense experience.

In the end, distinctions and labels—such as those we have employed here—often prove woefully inadequate, if not downright misleading. We will see that most philosophical theologians have been in fact propelled, and to some degree controlled, by an interest in special revelation such that, in practice, the lines become blurred and it becomes difficult to sort things out. Still, the distinction we have drawn between the two kinds of theology gets at an important difference and, in practice, is broadly applicable.

We will return to philosophical theology presently. For the moment, we might dwell a bit on the concept of special revelation. If it is accepted that God has indeed been revealed through a supernatural self-disclosure, then there are open to us at least two different interpretations of that special revelation. The more traditional of the two is often called the "propositional" view. As the word suggests, this view holds that divine revelation is contained in the language, statements, or propositions of a text, such as the Bible or Koran. And it involves a certain conception of the way in which God has revealed himself. In the case of the Koran, for example, God spoke to his Prophet who, in turn, wrote down what he said.

Often associated with the propositional view of revelation is the traditional doctrine of the inspiration of the Holy Scriptures, for it is the supernatural inspiration that is thought to guarantee the truth of the statements contained in those Scriptures. In the Christian tradition, adherents of this doctrine usually defend it with the Biblical claim that "All scripture is inspired by God" (2 Tim. 3:16), and that "no prophecy ever came by human will, but men and women moved by the Holy Spirit spoke from God" (2 Peter 1:21). They then proceed to explain inspiration in one of several ways. One extreme view, sometimes called the "dictation theory," holds that the writers of the Bible were, like typewriters, completely passive (or even oblivious) to the promptings of the Spirit who articulated through them the divine and infallible message. This interpretation, or at least one version of it, was unmistakably embraced by Pope Leo XIII in his 1893 encyclical *Providentissimus Deus*:

All of the books, and the whole of each, which the Church receives as sacred and canonical were written down at the dictation of the Holy Spirit;

and, in fact, so far from there possibly being any error present in divine inspiration, this latter of itself not only excludes but rejects it with the same necessity that God himself, who is the supreme Truth, cannot be the author of any error whatever. . . . For the Holy Spirit himself with supernatural power so stirred and moved them to write, and so assisted as they wrote, that they both conceived correctly in mind, and wished to write down faithfully, and expressed aptly with infallible truth, all and each of those things which he directed; otherwise he himself would not be author of the entire Holy Scripture.[4]

Other theories of inspiration attempt more obviously to account for the differences in the various writers' vocabulary, style, experience, recollections, and reflection. In some theological circles, many battles have been waged, sometimes bitterly, over questions concerning the inspiration and infallibility of the Biblical writings. This preoccupation is, however, understandable, for if the propositional view of revelation is correct, then the proposition is everything.

In contemporary theology this conception of revelation has largely given way to a nonpropositional view. This includes Roman Catholics, who, following the Second Vatican Council in the 1960s, scrapped anything resembling the dictation theory just mentioned. What could it mean to say that God has revealed himself otherwise than in the statements contained, for example, in the Bible? The nonpropositional understanding of revelation, too, takes several forms. A good example conceives revelation to be (as it is called in German) *Heilsgeschichte*, "redemptive history." This view directs our attention from what God has said to what he has done and is doing, to his "mighty acts" in the unfolding of history. For the Jewish tradition, for example, God is revealed throughout the history of Israel in his repeated and continuing interventions on behalf of his Covenant People; and in all of this a decisive significance is accorded Moses, the Exodus story, and the giving of the Law. For the Christian, divine revelation would be epitomized in the cluster of redeeming events associated with Jesus Christ: his incarnation, ministry, death, and resurrection. Revelation is thus not so much a collection of canonical books, or a system of theological assertions

---

[4]Pope Leo XIII, in Heinrich Denzinger *et al.* (eds.), *Enchiridion Symbolorum*, secs. 1951f., 31st ed. (Freiburg/Breisgau: Herder, 1957) (my translation).

concerning God, people, and salvation, as it is revelatory *acts*, God himself acting even yet in history and bringing to completion his redemptive purpose.

Both the propositional and *heilsgeschichtlich* views of revelation result in unfortunate distortions when pushed to extremes. If the former tends to degenerate into a literalistic "bibliolatry," or Bible worship, the latter may slip into an overly subjective interpretation of the divine will. The truth is, of course, that these are not mutually exclusive views of revelation, and many theologians have managed to steer between the two, allowing each to make its legitimate contribution.

The Swiss theologian Emil Brunner (1889–1966) represents such a mediating position. After attacking the "fatal equation" of revelation with propositions, a misunderstanding that, as he says, dates from the Apostolic Fathers and hangs like a dark shadow over the whole history of the Christian Church, Brunner interprets revelation primarily as the unrepeatable, unique, absolute, and personal *event* of Jesus Christ:

In the time of the Apostles, as in that of the Old Testament Prophets, "divine revelation" always meant the whole of the divine activity for the salvation of the world, the whole story of God's saving acts [*Heilsgeschichte*], of the "acts of God" which reveal God's nature and His will, above all, Him in whom the preceding revelation gains its meaning, and so therefore is its fulfillment: Jesus Christ. He Himself is the Revelation. Divine revelation is not a book or a doctrine; the Revelation is God Himself in His self-manifestation within history. Revelation is something that *happens*, the living history of God in His dealings with the human race. . . .

But the Bible, for Brunner, is nonetheless indispensable as a witness to and *interpretation* of God's dealing with the world: "The Bible is the word of God because in it, so far as He chooses, God makes known the mystery of His will, of His saving purpose in Jesus Christ."[5] On this understanding, then, the Bible is

---

[5]Emil Brunner, *Revelation and Reason*, tr. Olive Wyon (Philadelphia: Westminster Press, 1946), pp. 8, 135.

not a body of theological information but rather the response of those to whom it was vouchsafed to be witnesses to the acts of God; it is not itself the revelation of God, but rather the record of the revelation, necessary for an understanding of God's redemptive plan.

Still another important concept is that of "progressive revelation," an idea that is compatible with both propositional and non-propositional views, though usually associated more closely with the latter. Progressive revelation denies that revelation drops out of heaven, complete and intact. Rather, it understands God's self-manifestation over the ages of human history as apprehended and represented in a way that is appropriate to the developing stages of our evolving intellectual, moral, and spiritual consciousness. Thus, in the case of the Biblical tradition, we should not be surprised that God is represented as dealing crudely with the primitive people of Israel's early history, though later dealing with them on more exalted planes, commensurate with their developing response. The ethical monotheism (belief in one God) of the later prophets is far removed from the henotheism (belief in a supreme god) of the First Commandment: "You shall have no other gods before me." Ezekiil's promise that the sins of the father will not be visited on the sons reflects, ethically, a considerable advance on the Exodus promise that they will. And does not Jesus's Sermon on the Mount, with its recurring distinction, "You have heard that it was said to those of ancient times. . . . But I say to you. . . .," exemplify a radical reinterpretation and elevation of earlier revealed principles?

It should be stressed that on this view it is not God himself who changes and progresses but, rather, our responses to him. It should also be seen that revelation is, therefore, two-dimensional, involving the divine initiative and human response; in a sense, without either one of these, nothing has actually been revealed, no revelation has really occurred. On the other hand, it does not follow that all revelation must be relativized in terms of a certain people, a particular place, a particular time, and a given level of intellectual, moral, and spiritual attainment. "You shall not murder" is as universally binding now as ever, and even "You shall have no other gods before me" can be easily translated into a timeless religious principle.

It is still another question whether revelation has achieved some kind of finality, or *exclusive authority*, in Jesus Christ, or Moses, or . . .

The Spirit of Xenophanes

Though our main concern is not with revealed theology but with philosophical theology, historically these two approaches to the knowledge of God have been closely though sometimes unhappily allied.

Xenophanes of Colophon, an early Greek philosopher of the fifth century B.C., is an excellent example of the spirit and concern of philosophical or natural theology. There is even some justification for calling Xenophanes the father of philosophical theology in the West. He, more emphatically and articulately than any other early philosopher, repudiated the old mythological and superstitious theology propagated by the ancient Greek poets Homer and Hesiod. Consider his attack upon their naive, anthropomorphic concept of the gods: "If oxen or horses or lions had hands, or could draw the forms of their gods like horses, and the oxen like oxen; and they would make their bodies in accordance with the body that they themselves each posses." Or consider his distress over the way the poets impiously attributed immoral acts to the gods: "Both Homer and Hesiod have ascribed to the gods all the things which are among men reproachful and a disgrace: stealing, committing adultery, and deceiving one another." But Xenophanes' theologizing is not wholly negative and critical. He does appear also to have propounded a positive and philosophically more adequate theory of the divine than his Greek predecessors: "There is one God, greatest among both gods and men, who resembles mortals not at all in body or in mind." Again, "He always remains in the same place, not moving at all. Nor does it befit him to move about at different times to different places."[6]

---

[6]Xenophanes, Fragments 15, 11, 23, and 26, tr. Ed. L. Miller, in "Xenophanes: Fragments 1 and 2," *The Personalist*, 51 (1970), pp. 143f.

Xenophanes reflects the theological and philosophical revolution from which the Western intellectual tradition was born, and he himself anticipated many of the ideas of subsequent theology. But the main reason for mentioning Xenophanes is that he represents so well the rationalist (both critical and constructive) bent of all philosophical theology.

It would be a mistake, however, to conclude that all philosophical theologians have, like Xenophanes, opposed and rejected traditional authority. The thirteenth-century thinker St. Thomas Aquinas, for example, though certainly one of the greatest philosophical theologians ever, repeatedly emphasized the necessity of special revelation:

Even as regards those truths about God which human reason can investigate, it was necessary than man be taught by a divine revelation. For the truth about God, such as reason can know it, would only be known by a few, and that after a long time, and with the admixture of many errors; whereas man's whole salvation, which is in God, depends upon the knowledge of this truth. Therefore, in order that the salvation of men might be brought about more fitly and more surely, it was necessary that they be taught divine truths by divine revelation.[7]

In this way, philosophical and dogmatic interests have often been amiable partners in the theological enterprise. The problem, when it has arisen, has usually come from the other side. Not all theologians who acknowledge the authority of divine revelation acknowledge also the authority of natural reason, at least in the sphere of spiritual of theological truth. Thus there have been some trying moments. The Protestant reformer Martin Luther, for example, declares that no one can be saved who is unwilling to tear out the eyes of reason, kill it, and bury it. Further:

If all the smart alecks on earth were to pool their wits, they could not devise a ladder on which to ascend to heaven . . . he who would deal with

---

[7]St. Thomas Aquinas, *Summa Theologica*, Part I, Qu. 2, Art. 1, in *Basic Writings of Saint Thomas Aquinas*, ed. Anton C. Pegis (New York: Random House, 1945), I.

the doctrines of the Christian faith [should] not pry, speculate, and ask how it may agree with reason, but, instead, merely determine whether Christ said it. If Christ did say it, then he should cling to it, whether it harmonizes with reason or not, and no matter how it may sound.[8]

This does not mean that Luther had no respect for reason when relegated to its proper realm or illuminated by divine grace:

I don't say that men may not teach and learn philosophy; I approve thereof, so that it be within reason and moderation. Let philosophy remain within her bounds, as God has appointed, and let us make use of her as a character in a comedy; but to mix her up with divinity may not be endured.[9]

But even with his concession to philosophy, Luther clearly represents a very different attitude toward the natural reason than does St. Thomas.

There has been, in fact, an anti-intellectualist or at least antiphilosophical undercurrent throughout the history of Christian thought. A more recent example may be drawn from Neo-orthodox theology, so prominent in the 1950s, 60's, and 70's, sponsored by yet another Swiss theologian, Karl Barth, on all counts the most influential theologian of the twentieth century. Barth gave a dogmatic "No!" (the title of one of his essays) to natural theology, denying (against Brunner) that there is any *Anknüpfungspunkt*, "point of contact," between God's Word and human consciousness in its fallen state, and denying that there is any "other task" of theology either before or beyond the proclamation of God's special revelation. He held, in fact, that even one's "Yes!" to the revelation in Christ is wholly the work of God, concurring with the Lutheran formula, "I believe that not of my own reason and power do I believe in my Lord or am able to come to him. . . ." Such talk is often rooted in the Biblical teaching about the loss of the *imago Dei*, "image of God," in which we were,

---

[8]Martin Luther, "Tenth Sermon on John 6," tr. Martin H. Bertram, in *Luther's Works*, ed. Jaroslav Pelikan and Helmut T. Lehmann (St. Louis, Mo.: Concordia, 1959), XXIII.

[9]Martin Luther, *Table Talk*, tr. and ed. William Hazlitt (London: George Bell, 1884), p. 23.

according to Gen 1:26—one of the most important verses in the Bible—originally created: "Then God said, 'Let us make humankind in our image, according to our likeness. . . .'" In what way and to what degree this divine image was corrupted by the Fall and original sin is one of the bedrock questions of theology. However it is answered, it obviously holds implications for any doctrine of natural knowledge of God. It is clear what the implications are for Luther and Barth.

Many insist that the Bible itself witnesses to a general revelation, a knowledge of God accessible, at least in principle, to all people. Others, including many contemporary Evangelicals, think that the Bible urges upon us, more specifically, the task of apologetics, the rational defense of the Faith. The favorite text is Rom. 1:19-20. It has been cited repeatedly by apologists throughout the centuries, and we will return to it on numerous occasions.

. . .what can be known about God is plain to them, because God has shown it to them. Ever since the creation of the world his invisible nature, namely, his eternal power and deity, has been clearly perceived being understood through the things that have been made. So they are without excuse.[10]

Barth responds that, far from being a proof text for natural theology, this passage is actually a proof text against it, as a careful reading reveals: Nature itself testifies to the invisibility, hiddenness, and *in*accessibility of God and directs us instead to the divine self-disclosure in Jesus Christ. And as for Christian apologetics, Barth calls it "Christian theology that has lost its nerve." My own view is that both sides have missed the real point of Rom. 1:19–20. These verses do teach that God is apparent in nature but, when taken with what follows, are clearly part of a scathing indictment of those who nonetheless wilfully spurn this knowledge in favor of sinful self-indulgence and idolatry—not good news but bad news. I think, though, that Barth was right about the general Biblical indifference to, if not outright disdain for, apologetics. Certainly the allegedly relevant passages are few and far between and, like Rom. 1:19–20, are often capable of alternative interpretations.

---

[10]My translation.

At any rate, this tension, and even conflict, between natural and revealed theology raises, obviously, the crucial issue of the relation between faith and reason, a problem to be considered later.

More on Philosophical Theology

The labels "philosophy of religion"[11] and "philosophical theology" are often used interchangeably, though they do not necessarily mean the same thing. Philosophical theology is a certain subject matter, namely, God or the divine, approached in a certain way, namely, philosophically. But philosophy of religion is, strictly speaking, what is called a "second-order" study. It is important to know what this means since second-order inquiry has been thought by some to be the main task of philosophy, and everyone would acknowledge at least its relevance.

To ask a second-order question is to ask a question about a question. Thus that older style of analytic philosophy we mentioned earlier, concerned as it is with the analysis of language, is essentially a second-order study. Now philosophy *of* religion is philosophizing in a more or less analytic manner *about* religion. It should be apparent that this is something quite different from, and considerably more restricted than, the broader concerns of actual theologizing. Similarly, philosophy of science is not science itself but the critical analysis of scientific language, concepts, and methods. It engages in no scientific research and requires no laboratory. In the same way, one can entertain all sorts of discussion *about* religion and theology without being a religious person or without actually theologizing.

On the other hand, philosophical theology (as I am using the term) by no means excludes the second-order concerns of philosophy of religion. In fact, at certain points the two are inseparable. All important philosophers have been to some degree, in this sense, analytic in their methodology inasmuch as they have been forced, at one point or another, to grapple with problems of meaning and language. St. Thomas Aquinas, for example, contributed much to the understanding of the nature of religious language and concepts. Still, Thomas knew—or thought he knew—what was meant by a

---

[11]Here, and in many places throughout our discussion, it will be most convenient to use the word *religion* in its more usual, though more ambiguous, sense rather than in the special and refined sense suggested earlier.

question such as "Does God exist?," whereas many recent philosophers have declared a moratorium on all God talk or theological discourse until the meaning and status of such language can be clarified. In fact, some thinkers have found more interest in the question "What does it mean to ask 'Does God exist?'?" than in the primary question itself. It is not a simple matter to suggest all that is involved in philosophical theology, but clearly it is a more comprehensive concept, both in its interests and in its methods, than philosophy of religion taken in its strict sense.

Philosophical theology encompasses a great number of issues such as immortality, faith, and reason, the problem of evil, and so forth. For the most part, however, discussion centers on one topic: God. This should not be surprising since God is, after all, and in accordance with the meaning of the word, the proper object of *theological* inquiry. We might, thus, distinguish between philosophical theology proper, which centers specifically on God, and philosophical theology in general, which also addresses all those related issues. Further, and perhaps more important, it should be seen that the question of God is at least in some sense presupposed by many of the others. What is the problem of faith and reason if there can be no divine authority to have faith *in*? What is the problem of evil to the person who rejects the existence of a loving and just God anyway? Accordingly, St. Thomas announced, as he began to unfold his theological system, that

we must first establish, as the necessary foundation of the entire work, the investigation by which it is demonstrated that God exists. For if we do not demonstrate that God exists, all investigation of divine matters is impossible.[12]

Inasmuch as our discussion too will be directed first, and rather extensively, to the fundamental problem of God's existence, it may be helpful here to outline the whole domain of philosophical theology proper, even though such a summary must at many points be overly simplified and inadequate.

To begin, let us recall that theology is strictly the science or study of God. There are two different kinds of theology: revealed theology, which provides a supernatural knowledge of God, and

---

[12]St. Thomas Aquinas, *Summa Contra Gentiles*, I, 9 (my translation).

philosophical or natural theology, which ascends to a natural knowledge of God by way of the unaided intellect. Within the sphere of purely philosophical or natural knowledge of God, we can further distinguish two approaches, the rational and the nonrational. Under the nonrational, or noninferential, approach would fall, for example, the various sorts of religious experiences. The mystic, to be sure, claims to have a knowledge of God that transcends reason and possesses an experiential and self-authenticating certainty. On the other hand, the rational approach is argumentative and attempts to establish a knowledge of God in a logical, rational, inferential manner.

In defense of the odd-sounding division of philosophical theology into the rational and *non*rational categories, one might appeal to Plato, Kierkegaard, the mystics, and others as belonging to the philosophical tradition even though there is in their positions a strong strain of the nonrational, perhaps even the distinctive strain. Genuine philosophical activity need not be—indeed, cannot be— wholly discursive, as I suggested in the first section of this chapter. Further, we have a natural inclination to include under the nonrational certain kinds of religious experience that properly should be considered in relation to revealed theology. In this respect, it must be emphasized that everything on the side of philosophical theology represents a possible knowledge of God that is in principle accessible to *all*, not just to those favored by an active and specific self-disclosure by God, and this includes religious experience. Still, I will be the first to confess that such distinctions and classifications are, in the end, bound to be more or less artificial.

Under the rational approach to the knowledge of God fall the traditional theistic arguments, that is, arguments for God's existence. Because these arguments occupy an important place in the history of philosophy, and therefore also in the following chapters, we should grasp at the very beginning something of their nature, and this means making still another important distinction. There are two kinds of theistic arguments, the *a priori* and the *a posteriori*. *A priori* knowledge is knowledge acquired prior to or independently of sense experience. Simply stated, a person who believes in *a priori* knowledge is known as a "rationalist" (using the word now in a more technical or restricted sense than before), as opposed to an "empiricist," who believes that all knowledge is acquired *a posteriori*, that is, through sense experience. Accordingly, the *a priori* arguments seek to demonstrate God's existence without any reference to the sense world. These arguments are completely rationalistic, in

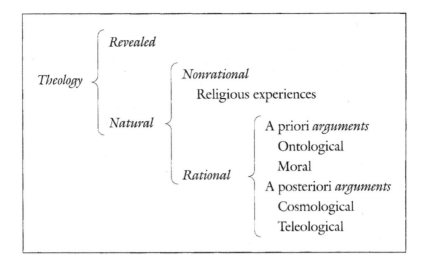

the narrower meaning of the word. By contrast, the *a posteriori* arguments attempt to infer the existence of God from sense experience. These arguments are empirical.

Of the many theistic arguments, we will consider four that are truly classical and representative. Both the Ontological Argument and the Moral Argument claim to prove the existence of God *a priori*, apart from sense experience: the Ontological Argument through an analysis of the concept of God or the idea of the most perfect being; the Moral Argument on the basis of moral experience or the universal sense of duty.

Both the Cosmological and Teleological arguments, on the other hand, attempt to demonstrate the existence of God *a posteriori*, from the evidence of sense experience. The Cosmological Argument begins with the sheer existence of the universe and concludes that God must exist as its ultimate cause. According to the Teleological Argument, God must exist in order for us to account for a certain feature of the universe, namely, its apparent design and intelligibility.

What Is God?

One last matter and our preliminaries are over. We can hardly prove the existence of God or otherwise talk about him unless we have some idea of what we're talking about. So what *is* God? While this question is impossible to answer given the limitations of our present task, some foray, however feeble, should be made in the direction of a definition; as we have just emphasized, God *is*, after all, the central topic of philosophical theology. But what a bewildering complex of concepts immediately confronts us! To get an idea of this array, just consider some of the ways in which God has been characterized: Supreme Being, The All, The Nothing, The Absolute, That Than Which Nothing Greater Can Be Conceived, Most Perfect Being, Ground of Being, Heavenly Father, Heavenly Mother, Ultimate Principle, Unmoved Mover, Eternal Thou, Great Architect, Primordial Unity. Or consider some of the names ascribed to this Reality, reflecting widely differing cultural settings and differing roles, relations, activities and modes of worship: Brahman, Allah, Yahweh, Zeus, Marduk, Odin, Osiris.

In the attempt to cut through all this for the sake of a manageable topic, we first focus on *theism*, which, as we have already seen, simply means the belief in God or gods. In this loose sense, theism includes several other "isms," such as monotheism, the belief in one God; pantheism, the belief that everything is God; polytheism, the belief in many gods; henotheism, the belief in a tribal god; and deism, the belief in a God who, after creating the world, ceased to show any interest in it—sometimes called the "absentee God." Usually, however, "theism" is used in the more restricted sense of *classical* theism, which involves the conception of God as embraced by the dominant Jewish, Islamic, and Christian thinkers of the Western tradition—St. Thomas Aquinas is often cited as the obvious example of a classical theist.

What, then, is the God of classical theism? It is a matter of spelling out the divine attributes, that is, those features that, taken together, constitute his nature. A long list of these attributes could be given, but we mention here just the most obvious. The God of classical theism was inherited largely from Greek philosophy. For Plato and Aristotle especially, multiplicity and change necessarily involve relativity, ambiguity, and other sorts of metaphysical deficiency and thus cannot possibly be predicated on, or be features of, the Fullness of Being; the twin ideas of unity and immutability become, then, necessary marks, or attributes, of the wholly Real, God. (One can see this emerging already in the pre-Socratic fragments of Xenophanes, quoted earlier.) Other attributes represent God as omnipotent (all-powerful), omniscient (all-knowing), omnibenevolent (all-loving), personal (a conscious being who cares, feels, etc.), eternal (timeless), and morally perfect (sinless, or unfailing in every virtue). And then there is the really big one, the divine *aseity*. This comes from the Latin *a se*, which means "in," "from," or "because of" (*a*) "himself," "herself," or "itself" (*se*). In application to God, this expression thus stresses the independence, absoluteness, freedom, and sovereignty of the divine Being. We will see later, in Chapter 10, that on the classical view there actually can be no real plurality of attributes in God since he is necessarily and absolutely one, as we have just said; thus the several attributes are really just various ways in which the single nature of God is grasped and expressed.

A great deal of discussion focuses on the divine attributes. Even among those who generally embrace classical theism it is debated, to take but one example, whether it is conceptually coherent to affirm of God that he is eternal, in the sense of existing outside of time. How can such a being relate to or intervene in history? How can such a being be concerned, pleased, displeased, or responsive? Can such a being be a person at all? How can one pray passionately to or worship what amounts to a metaphysical iceberg? And can this concept of God be squared with the great Scriptural traditions of Christianity, Judaism, and Islam? Notwithstanding the problems and continuing discussions concerning the divine attributes, classical theism occupies a fairly secure position even on the current scene. It is not, however, the only game in town.

A wholesale rejection of classical theism is urged by the radical alternative called "Process Theology," a major contemporary movement. This is a theological spin-off of Process Philosophy, sponsored in its twentieth-century version by Alfred North Whitehead, whom we have already encountered as an example of a speculative philosopher. It's not called "process" philosophy for nothing. Its central idea is that ultimate reality is dynamic, active, on the move. The theological application of this vision was worked out largely in several books by Charles Hartshorne, one with the provocative title *Omnipotence and Other Theological Mistakes*.[13] On this view, and in brash contrast to classical theism, God is viewed not as independent of the world but as standing in a reciprocal relation to it, in which

---

[13]Charles Hartshorne, *Omnipotence and Other Theological Mistakes* (Albany: State University of New York Press, 1984).

he is actually in some way *conditioned* by it. There is a give-and-take between God and the world such that the reality and future of each is dependent on the other. Reality is thus bipolar, and it *unfolds*—God along with it.

Such a view might appear, initially, to accord best with our actual experience, pervaded as it is with temporality and, indeed, with the Biblical portrayal of God who intervenes in history, responds to his people, and the like. On the other hand, we must not be naive in regard to the considerations that have compelled virtually the whole of the Western theological tradition in the direction, rather, of classical theism. A real explanation and justification of radically different conceptions of God cannot be provided here. Our only purpose has been to hint at the problem of defining "God," and to suggest that, for better or for worse, it is the classical theistic conception that has dominated our intellectual tradition and thus lies more or less behind the discussions in this book. In a word, it is the conception of God as the ultimate and personal Being—all-powerful, all-knowing, and all-good—who is the cause and goal of all things.

And with that, we can really begin.

2

The Ontological Argument

Of all traditional proofs for the existence of God, none is more enigmatic than the Ontological Argument. Originally formulated over 800 years ago, it has always been the subject of much perplexity, and in recent years it has once again gravitated to the forefront of philosophical discussion. In every age, including our own, some have regarded the Ontological Argument as an example of philosophical sleight-of-hand, others as the most profound and certain demonstration of God's existence. Whatever else may be decided about the Ontological Argument, it is no doubt the best example of a purely *a priori* proof, unfolding as it does without any reference whatsoever to the world of sense experience. The argument begins with the concept or idea of God as the most perfect being ("ontological" derives from the Greek participle ὄν, ὄντος, "being") and through an analysis of this mere concept deduces God's objective reality.

St. Anselm and Descartes

St. Anselm (1033–1109), Archbishop of Canterbury, first conceived this demonstration of God's existence. It is important to notice that Anselm's Ontological Argument was part of an extended prayer that included a contrite confession of sin along with a plea for illumination. Far from a piece of detached academicia, Anselm's argument is imbued with a deep piety and motivated by a desire to enrich the spiritual life by demonstrating through reason what one already believes and is committed to as an article of faith:

I do not endeavor, O Lord to penetrate thy sublimity, for in no wise do I compare my understanding with that; but I long to understand in some degree thy truth which my heart believes and loves. For I do not seek to understand that I may believe, but I believe in order to understand.[1]

Anselm thus disarms at the very beginning those, usually skeptics, who delight in pointing out that the people who seek to demonstrate the existence of God are usually believers already. Not only is this true (nobody ever pretended otherwise), but most religious thinkers themselves would insist that the real nature of their proofs concerning God, his attributes, and so forth can be appreciated only against the background of faith, that is, as a rational unfolding of revealed truths.

   Anselm begins his argument with a reference to Psalms 14:1: "The fool says in his heart, 'there is no God.'" But what does "God" mean? Anselm answers that even the atheist understands "God" to mean—in Anselm's famous formula—*aliquid quo nihil maius cogitari possit*, "that than which nothing greater can be conceived." (It is important to appreciate that by this Anselm does not mean the greatest being that happens to exist, but the greatest *possible* being.) Now the atheistic fool agrees, of course, that the idea of God exists; otherwise, it could not be employed even in the denial, "God does not exist." The atheist does not therefore deny God's existence as an idea in the mind; what is denied is that God exists objectively, outside the mind, in reality. But Anselm counters that it is greater for a thing to exist in reality than for it to exist only as an idea in the mind. God (a being than which nothing greater can be conceived) must then exist in reality, not merely as an idea in the mind, for if he existed in the mind only he would not be God, because then something greater could be conceived. In Anselm's own words,

if that, than which nothing greater can be conceived, exists in the understanding alone, the very being than which nothing greater can be conceived, is one than which a greater can be conceived. But obviously this is

---

[1]St. Anselm, *Proslogium*, Ch. 1, in *St. Anselm: Basic Writings*, tr. Sidney Norton Deane, 2nd ed. (La Salle, Ill.: Open Court, 1962).

impossible. Hence, there is no doubt that there exists a being, than which nothing greater can be conceived, and it exists both in the understanding and in reality.[2]

By this reasoning, anyone who denies the existence of God is denying the existence of a being who must exist in order to be the very thing he is talking about. It is like saying: God—a being who must exist in order to be "God"—does not exist. Is this not a simple-minded self-contradiction? No wonder the atheist is called a fool!

Some readers, seeing that the argument turns on the notion of God as the greatest possible being, will invariably object that this is not in fact how they use the linguistic symbol "God." But obviously it is not the symbol "God" that is crucial to the argument but the *idea* that is usually associated with it, namely, the idea of the greatest possible being. If someone were to persist in an unorthodox use of "God," Anselm might simply ask, "Well, by what symbol do you denote the greatest possible being? *X*, you say? Now, if *X* is the greatest possible being, does it not follow that *X* must exist, since. . . .?" Even if one had *no* name for the greatest possible being, at least the idea of it would be understood; otherwise, all of the present discussion would be utterly unintelligible to that person, and that idea (even if it must be spelled out as "the greatest possible being" or "that than which nothing greater can be conceived") is all that Anselm requires.

René Descartes (1596–1650), a French philosopher and mathematician who is often called the father of modern philosophy, also argued the existence of God with a version of the Ontological Proof. Whereas St. Anselm begins with the formula "that than which no greater can be conceived," Descartes begins with "the most perfect being." It should be noted that Descartes is thinking of metaphysical perfection, that is, the full actualization of possible being, rather than moral perfection, though clearly the former implies the latter. There is a second and perhaps more important difference. Anselm, exemplifying the Augustinian principle of faith in search of understanding, derived his concept of God from Scripture. Descartes, on the other hand, proceeding in a purely philosophical manner, seizes the idea of God as a necessary deduction from the data of pure reason. Briefly, he moves by means of "clear

---

[2]*Ibid.*, Ch. 2.

and distinct ideas" from the indubitable reality of his own mind to a reflection on the fact that he doubts, to an awareness of his own limited or finite perfection, to the idea of infinite perfection. This is not to say that Descartes was, at the start, an unbeliever; he did in fact accept the authority of the Scriptures and of the Church, though in a manner unlike Anselm he distinguished philosophy from theology and sought to provide a philosophical demonstration of God's existence independently of revelation, one that proceeds solely in terms of intellectual intuition and deduction and that delivers a conclusion as certain as the conclusion of any mathematical demonstration.

Descartes begins with the philosophical concept of the most perfect being and then asks what this concept involves or, in other words, what is included in the attributes of the most perfect being. We must say, of course, that God possesses all perfections: omniscience, omnipotence, justice, benevolence, and so on. Now since it is more perfect to exist than not to exist, existence too is a perfection. (Clearly, an actually existing thing possesses more metaphysical power than an imaginary one; if someone doubts this, he or she should try sweeping the house with a nonexistent broom.) If, then, we neglect to ascribe existence to God, he cannot be the most perfect being or the sum of all perfections. God must therefore exist because actual existence is a necessary attribute or perfection of the most perfect being, one of his defining properties, "that crown of perfections without which we cannot comprehend God," and (as Anselm had argued) a property that can be found in the concept of no other thing.[3] The very concept of God entails his real existence, says Descartes, just as the idea of a triangle entails the equality of its angles to two right angles, or the idea of a sphere or circle entails the equidistance of all its parts from its center. But whereas it does not follow from the nature of triangles or circles that they must exist,

I cannot conceive of a God without existence, anymore than of a mountain without a valley. . . . from the fact alone that I cannot conceive God except

---

[3]René Descartes, "Notes Against a Programme," in *The Philosophical Works of Descartes*, tr. Elizabeth S. Haldane and G. R. T. Ross, rev. ed. (Cambridge, England: Cambridge University Press, 1934), I, p. 445.

as existing, it follows that existence is inseparable from him, and consequently that he does, in truth, exist.[4]

This form of the Ontological Argument may be represented in the following reasoning, where "perfection" means an attribute free of any deficiency whatsoever—for example, unlimited goodness, unlimited power, and so on.

God possesses all perfections.

Existence is a perfection.

_____

Therefore, God possesses the perfection of existence

The argument is valid. But must we accept that God therefore actually exists?

Two Early Rebuttals

Anselm had no sooner propounded his proof than it was challenged by Gaunilon, a monk of the monastery of Marmoutier near Tours. Though Gaunilon was, of course, a believer, he was persuaded that Anselm's argument was unsound, and he felt constrained to answer Anselm in the interest of intellectual honesty. Gaunilon's criticisms, which reduce essentially to two, are contained in his reply, entitled *In Behalf of the Fool.*

First, Gaunilon denies that the idea of God does in fact exist in his understanding on the grounds that we understand only what is familiar to us. Naturally, Gaunilon employs the word "God" and even the locution "that than which nothing greater can be conceived," though he insists that the meaning or *signification* of these entirely transcend him. Second, Gaunilon argues that even if we did have in our minds the idea of God, or the concept of that than which nothing greater can be conceived, we could not conclude that such a being exists in reality. We might as well argue that

_____

[4]René Descartes, *Meditations*, in *Discourse on Method and Meditations*, tr. Laurence J. Lafleur (New York: Macmillan, 1960), pp. 121f.

because we have in our minds the idea of a lost island, most wonderful, glorious, and perfect, it must actually exist; otherwise, it would not be most perfect inasmuch as we could then conceive of a better one. Gaunilon wonders who would be the bigger fool—the one who submits such an argument or the one who accepts it. Our minds are in fact replete with ideas of wonderful things that have, nonetheless, no counterparts in the real world.[5]

To Gaunilon's first objection Anselm replies (recalling an idea suggested earlier) that if Gaunilon did not have God at least in his mind, that is, if he did not understand the meaning of "God" or "that than which nothing greater can be conceived," then he would not have been able even to follow the argument. Further, is it not a simple matter to formulate an idea of that than which nothing greater can be conceived by ascending from the lesser to the greater? From that which has a beginning to that which has no beginning? From that which has no beginning but an end to that which has neither beginning nor end? From that which changes to that which is immutable? And so on. And is not this procedure quite in accord with the teaching of the Scriptures that God's invisible nature may be grasped through his creation (Rom. 1:20)? Finally, says Anselm, even if it is not possible to entertain an idea of what God is, there is a difference between saying that God is inconceivable and that his inconceivability is inconceivable. An experience may be ineffable, but I can say that it was ineffable; I may not be able to grasp the infinite itself, but I can surely grasp the concept of infinity; and though God may be inconceivable, I can at least know what that means. It's the difference between having a concept of something and comprehending or grasping all that is involved in the concept.

With respect to Guanilon's second (and more familiar) objection, Anselm responds as follows. Concerning the most perfect island, or the most perfect unicorn, or the most perfect man, Gaunilon was right. It is impossible to deduce the real existence of any of these from only an idea, for the idea of none of these involves existence as a defining property. In the dictionary, "island" is not defined as "an area of land completely surrounded by water *and which exists*"; nor does the perfection of a unicorn lie in the addition

---

[5]Gaunilon, *In Behalf of the Fool*, in *St. Anselm: Basic Writings*.

of still another attribute (existence), but rather in the excellence of its proper attributes, namely, the straightness of its ivory horn, the whiteness of its coat, and the like. It is clear, then, that one can just as easily conceive of the nonexistence of such things as of their existence. But there is one thing, Anselm argues, the nonexistence of which is inconceivable. God, unlike an island or a unicorn or a human being, is by his conception the sum of *all* perfections, which must therefore include existence. A lost desert island, however resplendent and glorious, and a unicorn, however elegant, hardly qualify as that than which nothing greater can be conceived. As Descartes might have said, it is one thing to be the most perfect island imaginable but quite another to be the most perfect of all beings; it is one thing to possess certain perfections but quite another to possess all of them. As observed earlier, it does not matter what *name* we give to the greatest possible being, and if Gaunilon's "lost island" turns out to be, in fact, the greatest possible being, then (Anselm dryly remarks) it does exist, it will be found, and it will never again be lost![6]

The Dominican monk St. Thomas Aquinas (1225–1274) also attacked Anselm's argument but on very different grounds. Obviously, Anselm was a rationalist (in the technical sense) who believed, as his argument shows, that we can acquire knowledge of God independently of sense experience. St. Thomas Aquinas, on the other hand, was a classical empiricist whose whole philosophy is built on the epistemological principle *Nihil est in intellectu quod non fuerit prius in sensu*, "Nothing is in the intellect which was not first in the senses." This includes the knowledge of God, which, as will be shown in the next chapter, Thomas reduces ultimately to our knowledge of the world.

For Thomas, the essence of every created thing (*what* it is) is distinct from its existence (*that* it is) just by virtue of the fact that its being is derived; it is easy enough to distinguish the whatness of a table from its whatness plus actual existence or thatness. In God, however, essence and existence are identical, as required by his self-subsistent and indivisible being. God's existence as seen from the standpoint of God himself is therefore self-evident, because his existence is immediately seen to be inseparable from his essence. But

---

[6]St. Anselm, *Apologetic*, in *St. Anselm: Basic Writings*.

from *our* standpoint—the crucial difference—God's existence is not self-evident, because we can know God only indirectly and imperfectly by means of his effects in the created world of nature. Bound as we are to our five senses, we can never ascend to a knowledge of God as he is in himself; we can only know him as he is reflected to us in the empirical world (a fuller explanation of this doctrine is provided in the first section of Chapter 10). Thomas's own analogy may help. It is absolutely self-evident that a whole is greater than any of its parts, though this would not be self-evident to someone who was for some reason incapable of conceiving of wholes or parts. We are in a similar position *vis-à-vis* God. God's existence is self-evident in itself, *though not to us*, who are incapable of grasping the divine being as it is in itself. And if we cannot know what God's essence is, how can we show that his existence follows from it? We might as well try to show that a conclusion follows from its premises without knowing what the premises are.[7]

For our present purpose, it is enough to emphasize that Anselm and Thomas bring to the discussion very different conceptions of knowledge. Anselm (operating in the Platonic tradition) begins with knowledge that is *a priori* and immediately present to the soul. Thomas (in the Aristotelian tradition) believes that we can have knowledge only of what can be imperfectly discerned in sense experience. Further, it is important to realize that this fundamental difference is necessarily reflected at every point in their philosophies, including their judgments concerning our knowledge of God.

The Logic of "Exists"

Of all the criticism of the Ontological Argument, one in particular stands out as especially significant. The German philosopher Immanuel Kant (1724–1804) was the first to emphasize what many regard as the real mistake in this proof. Kant correctly observed that the Ontological Argument, which he knew primarily in its Cartesian and later formulations, treats existence as though it

---

[7]St. Thomas Aquinas, *Summa Contra Gentiles*, I, 10f., tr. Anton C. Pegis (Garden City, N.Y.: Image Books, 1955).

were a predicate; that is, it attributes existence to God in the same manner that it attributes omnipotence, justice, and benevolence to him. Though there is some question of whether this is technically true of Anselm's formulation, there can be no question but that it is true of Descartes':

Here I do not see . . . why [existence] may not be said to be a property as well as omnipotence, taking the word property as equivalent to any attribute or anything which can be predicated of a thing . . . necessary existence in the case of God is also a true property in the strictest sense of the word. . . .[8]

But is existence, in fact, an attribute or a predicate? Can existence be attributed to a thing in the same way as blue or rectangularity? Kant answered, No.

According to Kant, existence adds absolutely nothing to a concept. Take, for example, the concept "unicorn." The idea of a unicorn is not the least bit augmented or otherwise changed by the addition of existence, nor is it in any way diminished by the subtraction of existence. Whether one says "The unicorn exists" or "The unicorn does not exist," the concept "unicorn" remains unaltered: "white, shaped like a horse, and having an ivory horn." Or, to use Kant's own example, 100 actual dollars do not contain the least coin more than 100 possible dollars. Of course, there is a difference between 100 actual dollars and 100 possible dollars, as will become apparent if you try to spend the possible ones. Still, what is involved in the *concept* of 100 dollars is not different. What is different is the relation of the concept to the actual world, but that has nothing to do with the predicates or attributes of the thing, for these have already been exhausted in the concept. Kant summarizes his objection as follows:

By whatever and by however many predicates we may think a thing—even if we completely determine it—we do not make the least addition to the thing when we further declare that this thing *is*. Otherwise, it would not be exactly the same thing that exists, but something more than we had

---

[8]Descartes, *Reply to Objections*, in *The Philosophical Works of Descartes*, II, p. 228.

thought in the concept; and we could not, therefore, say that the exact object of my concept exists.[9]

The question of a thing's existence, then, has nothing to do with the content of a concept but rather with the application of the concept to the real world.

Furthermore, according to the usual interpretation of the Ontological Argument, the existence of God cannot be denied without self-contradiction. The existence of God is thought to be, as we learned from Descartes, an integral part of the very concept of God in the same way that the idea of a triangle necessarily involves the equality of its angles to two right angles. That is, "God exists" is what is called an "analytic" statement (a tautology or redundancy), the predicate simply restating what is contained already in the subject, as in "A triangle is a plane figure having three angles," "All bachelors are unmarried males," and "All barking dogs bark." Now, says Kant,

to posit a triangle, and yet to reject its three angles, is self-contradictory; but there is no self-contradiction in rejecting the triangle together with its three angles. The same holds true of the concept of an absolutely necessary being. If its existence is rejected, we reject the thing itself with all its predicates; and no question of contradiction can then arise.[10]

In other words, the truth of any analytic or tautologous statement is purely conditional or hypothetical. It is analytically certain, for example, that *if* there are any barking dogs, *then* they bark, but from this absolutely nothing can be inferred concerning the actual existence of barking dogs or, for that matter, the existence of anything. Similarly, if we understand "God exists" as an analytic statement, then it is translatable into "If God exists, then he exists"—a true statement, but not very informative.

A more recent variation on this Kantian theme may be found in Bertrand Russell's "theory of descriptions," which has provided a

---

[9]Immanuel Kant, *Critique of Pure Reason*, tr. Norman Kemp Smith (London: Macmillan, 1929), p. 505. Actually, Kant's objection was anticipated by David Hume: "To reflect on anything simply, and to reflect on it as existent, are nothing different from each other. That idea, when conjoin'd with the idea of any object, makes no addition to it" (*A Treatise of Human Nature*, ed. L. A. Selby-Bigge [Oxford, England: Clarendon Press, 1888], pp. 66f.).

[10]Kant, *Critique of Pure Reason*, p. 502.

whole new analysis of the word "exists." According to Russell, the paradox of how such things as unicorns can "be" nonexistent results from the failure to distinguish (echoes of Kant) between the grammatical and logical functions of "exists." In the statement "Sirius exists," the word "exists" is, of course, grammatically a predicate. But its logical function is not to ascribe a certain property (existence) to a subject, but rather to assert that there is an actual something that can be described by the name "Sirius." The real significance of the statement "Sirius exists" becomes more apparent in Russell's translation, "There is an *x* such that '*x* is Sirius' is true." And "Unicorns do not exist" may be better expressed as "There are no *x*'s such that '*x* is a unicorn' is true." In this way, the statement "Unicorns do not exist" is not a statement about the nature of unicorns but rather about the *application* of the concept "unicorn."[11] We saw that for Anselm (maybe) and Descartes' (certainly) existence was conceived as a defining property of God, something that could be predicated of him in the same way as goodness and omnipotence. But if "God exists" means "There is an *x* such that '*x* is God' is true," then in the first statement "exists" says nothing about the nature of God, though it does say something about the universe, namely, that there is an instance of what is described by the word "God." Existence is not a predicate, so the Ontological Argument, as it is usually understood, must be invalid.

But even Russell at one time believed in the Ontological Argument, as he himself relates:

I remember the precise moment, one day in 1894, as I was walking along Trinity Lane, when I saw in a flash (or thought I saw) that the ontological argument is valid. I had gone out to buy a tin of tobacco; on my way back, I suddenly threw it up in the air, and exclaimed as I caught it: "Great Scott, the ontological argument is sound."[12]

---

[11]Bertrand Russell, *A History of Western Philosophy* (New York: Simon & Schuster, 1945), p. 831. For a more extended discussion of Russell's theory of descriptions, see his *Introduction to Mathematical Philosophy* (London: George Allen & Unwin, 1919), Ch. 16. My statement above follows John Hick (*Philosophy of Religion*, 4th ed. [Englewood Cliffs, N.J.: Prentice Hall, 1990], pp. 18f.), whose brief summary is difficult to improve.

[12]Bertrand Russell, "My Mental Development," in *The Philosophy of Bertrand Russell*, Paul Arthur Schilpp (ed.) (New York: Tudor, 1951), p. 10.

Closely related to all of this is the suggestion, often made these days, that only propositions are necessary, not things. Clearly, the statement "A triangle has three angles" is necessarily true because, as we have seen, by "triangle" we *mean* a plane figure having three angles; the statement must be true in view of the rules that govern the symbols of our language; its truth is analytically or *logically* necessary. On the other hand, the statement "Sirius is 8.7 light years away" is contingent—contingent upon whether or not Sirius is, in fact, 8.7 light years away. It is argued further that an existential statement (a statement that either affirms or denies the existence of something) cannot be logically necessary, because its truth depends not upon the conventions of language but, like the statement about Sirius, upon reality, or the way things actually are. If so, the Ontological Argument cannot possibly work; it cannot tell us that God is necessary if only propositions are necessary. If, on the other hand, the Ontological Argument transposes itself into the proposition "The statement 'God exists' is necessarily true," then the necessity it involves is merely a matter of verbal stipulation and the truth of its conclusion is, as we saw earlier, purely hypothetical. In short, the Ontological Argument cannot affirm the real existence of God and at the same time claim the logical certainty thereof.

On this understanding, it has been claimed that any theistic argument that leads to or otherwise involves the idea of God as a logically necessary being involves an absurdity, for that idea is self-contradictory. This position, adopted by many in recent years, received probably its best-known expression in two very influential articles by the British philosophers J. J. C. Smart and J. N. Findlay.

Smart, in his article "The Existence of God," announces that

in asking for a logically necessary first cause we are doing something worse than asking for the moon. It is only *physically* impossible for us to get the moon; if I were a few million times bigger I could reach out for it and give it to you. That is, I know what it would be *like* to give you the moon, though I cannot *in fact* do it. A logically necessary first cause, however, is not impossible in the way that giving you the moon is impossible; no, it is *logically* impossible. "Logically necessary being" is a self-contradictory expression like "round square."[13]

---

[13]J. J. C. Smart, "The Existence of God," in Antony Flew and Alasdair MacIntyre (eds.) *New Essays in Philosophical Theology* (London: SCM Press, 1955), p. 39.

Findlay, in "Can God's Existence Be Disproved?", shrewdly fashions an ontological *disproof* of God's existence on the basis of the same distinction. On the one hand, he says, our conception of God as an adequate object of religious devotion demands that he be conceived as a being who "towers infinitely" above and beyond all other objects, and this conception includes not only the unthinkableness of other things existing without him but also the unthinkableness of his own nonexistence. On the other hand, we modern philosophers know that only propositions—not things—can be necessary, and that the idea of a being whose nonexistence is unthinkable or inconceivable (that is, whose existence is necessary) is therefore unintelligible. Findlay concludes, quite the contrary to St. Anselm, that what follows from an adequate conception of God is that he cannot possibly exist: "It was indeed an ill day for Anselm when he hit upon his famous proof. For on that day he not only laid bare something that is of the essence of an adequate religious object, but also something that entails its necessary nonexistence."[14]

It should be apparent that whether an existential statement can be certain or necessary without being *logically* certain or necessary is still another important possibility, one that we will encounter in the next section and again in the next chapter.

A Recent Reformulation

St. Anselm and Descartes had attempted to derive God's existence from a definition or conception of God. Recent thinkers have proceeded differently, attempting to derive the actual existence of God from its logical possibility. Inasmuch as this form of the Ontological Argument works with the ideas of modal logic (necessity, possibility, and impossibility), it is sometimes called the "modal" Ontological Argument. One of the first—and one of the more easily understood—of these attempts was that of Norman Malcolm, late Professor of Philosophy at Cornell University.

In 1960 Malcolm published an important article entitled "Anselm's Ontological Arguments," in which he argued that Anselm actually (though perhaps unintentionally) presented two different proofs, an invalid one and a valid one. The first (and unsound) of

---

[14]J. N. Findlay, "Can God's Existence Be Disproved?," in *ibid.*

Anselm's proofs is found in *Proslogium*, Chapter 2, and the second (and sound) is found in Chapter 3 and also in Anselm's reply to Gaunilon.

With respect to Anselm's first proof, which was summarized in the first section of this chapter, Malcolm judges that it does indeed presuppose that existence is a predicate, though he agrees with Kant in the rejection of this assumption: "It makes sense and is true to say that my future house will be a better one if it is insulated than if it is not insulated; but what could it mean to say that it will be a better house if it exists than if it does not?"[15] But Malcolm finds a second proof in Anselm that is significantly different from the first. The substance of the second argument is contained in the following passage from *Proslogium*, Chapter 3:

> it is possible to conceive of a being which cannot be conceived not to exist; and this is greater than one which can be conceived not to exist. Hence, if that, than which nothing greater can be conceived, can be conceived not to exist, it is not that, than which nothing greater can be conceived. But this is an irreconcilable contradiction. There is, then, so truly a being than which nothing greater can be conceived to exist, that it cannot even be conceived not to exist; and this being thou art, O Lord, our God.[16]

The difference between the two proofs is the following. The first takes existence as a predicate, inasmuch as it reasons that something is greater if it exists than if it does not exist. The second, on the other hand, takes *necessary existence* as a predicate when it reasons that something the nonexistence of which is logically impossible is greater than something the nonexistence of which is logically possible.

There are some recognized advantages to this second formulation. Though it may be odd to predicate the existence of something that already exists, it would appear to be perfectly possible and meaningful to ask of something existing whether its existence is necessary or not, and if so, to judge it more perfect. In this way, the second formulation bypasses completely the whole problem of

---

[15]Norman Malcolm, "Anselm's Ontological Arguments," *Philosophical Review*, 69 (1960), reprinted with minor changes in *Knowledge and Certainty* (Englewood Cliffs, N.J.: Prentice Hall, 1963), pp. 143f.

[16]St. Anselm, *Proslogium*, Ch. 3, in *St. Anselm: Basic Writings*.

whether existence is a predicate. It also bypasses the problem (if it is a problem) of whether existence is better than nonexistence. At any rate, Malcolm agrees that Anselm's first argument is misguided because existence is not a predicate, but he thinks that the second argument is sound because necessary existence *is* a predicate (he speculates that Descartes' argument too was of this second sort), and he sets out to develop his own version of this argument.

How is it, then, that necessary existence can be legitimately construed as a predicate or defining property of God? Malcolm's argument may be outlined as follows. If God is that than which nothing greater can be conceived, or an unlimited being, then obviously, by his very conception he is not the sort of being whose existence or nonexistence can be caused or can simply happen. In either case, he would be dependent or contingent upon something outside himself and therefore a limited being. It follows that if he does not exist, his existence is logically impossible; and if he does exist, his nonexistence is logically impossible. Now such a being either exists or does not exist. We are, then, driven to a two-fold conclusion: God—the unlimited being—either necessarily does not exist or he necessarily does exist. But the only reason one could possibly have for saying that he necessarily does not exist would be if the concept of such a being were self-contradictory or in some way logically absurd. The concept of that than which no greater can be conceived or of an unlimited being would appear, however, to be a perfectly consistent and meaningful one. We cannot, therefore, say that his existence is impossible, and thus we must say that his existence is necessary.[17]

God is an unlimited being.

The existence of an unlimited being is either impossible or necessary

[17]Malcolm, "Anselm's Ontological Arguments," pp. 149f. Even before Malcolm, Charles Hartshorne had done extensive work along the same lines, formulating versions of the Ontological Argument on the basis of Anselm's second statement. See his *Man's Vision of God* (New York: Harper & Row, 1941) and his more recent *Anselm's Discovery* (La Salle, Ill.: Open Court, 1965).

The concept of an unlimited being is not self-contradictory,
so the existence of such a being is not impossible.

Therefore, God's existence is necessary.

It is important to see—because Malcolm's argument will not
work without this—that nothing prevents the possible truth of an
idea so long as the idea is logically consistent, that is, so long as it is
free from self-contradiction. Thus, however empirically implausible,
it is at least *logically* possible that there are green men inhabiting the
far side of the moon. But it is not even logically possible that there
might exist a square circle for that concept is from the start self-contradictory.

It will be recalled that Kant reduced "God necessarily exists" to
an analytic, tautologous statement, and this Malcolm finds problematic. Kant and others had reasoned that as any analytic statement is translatable into a conditional or hypothetical "If . . . then"
statement, "God necessarily exists" is equivalent to "If God exists,
then he necessarily exists." But according to Kant, this statement
(with its "if") positively implies that far from a being who cannot
not exist, God perhaps may not exist. Malcolm countered this conclusion with the observation that far from asserting anything, the
statement "God necessarily exists" as understood by Kant to be an
analytic statement involves, when translated into its hypothetical
equivalent, a downright contradiction. "*If* God exists . . ." suggests
that maybe he doesn't, and that is clearly incompatible with the
original assertion that he necessarily does! It follows that there is an
important difference (Malcolm calls it a lack of symmetry) between
"A triangle has three angles" and "God necessarily exists": The former may be translated in a meaningful conditional form ("If a triangle exists, then it has three angles"), whereas the latter cannot. The
upshot of this is that whatever else might be said about the statement "God necessarily exists" (or "God is a necessary being"), it is
not equivalent to the hypothetical "If God exists, then he necessarily
exists," and here, at least, is an important exception to what Malcolm calls the "contemporary dogma" that no existential propositions can be necessary.[18]

------

[18]Malcolm, "Anselm's Ontological Argument," pp. 151ff.

Malcolm has hardly had the last word on the subject. As might
be expected, his article produced an avalanche of replies and was
attacked from several directions.[19] One of these objections, something of a historical one, charges that Malcolm's "necessary being"
is probably a far different sort of being from Anselm's original "that
than which nothing greater can be conceived." Malcolm's argument
delivers a being whose existence is logically necessary, or whose
nonexistence is logically impossible, whereas Anselm (so the objection goes) no doubt conceived the greatness of his God not in
terms of logical necessity or impossibility, but in terms of his unity,
immutability, omnipotence, eternity, sovereignty, or aseity (self-exis-
tence). But this is too hard on Malcolm, who did, in fact, emphasize that there are many different conceptions of what a necessary
being might be, depending on the different "language games" (as
Ludwig Wittgenstein expressed it) in which they perform their
duties. As a matter of fact, in defense of one of these legitimate conceptions (and "games"), Malcolm appeals to Psalm 90:2:

> Before the mountains were brought forth,
> or ever you had formed the earth and the world,
> from everlasting to everlasting you are God.

which may be, after all, more akin to how Anselm had conceived
God's greatness long before the necessary/existential distinction was
drawn by the modern mind, a distinction that fails to do justice to
the full breadth of philosophical and linguistic experience. A different kind of challenge to Malcolm is leveled by those who claim to
find fatal flaws in the logic of his position. One example may be
mentioned: the American philosopher Alvin Plantinga. Malcolm
had concluded that (1) if God does not exist, his existence is logically impossible, and (2) if God does exist, his existence is logically
necessary. With respect to (1), it is charged that Malcolm is mistaken in deducing from the observation that God can neither begin
to exist nor cease to exist that if he does not now exist, then his
existence (or "God exists") is logically impossible; what follows,

---

[19]Malcolm himself provides an index to many of these critical responses in
a footnote added in the reprinted version of his article (*ibid.*, p. 162). Special
note should be made of *Philosophical Review*, 70 (1961), containing six different discussions of Malcolm's article.

rather, is that it is logically necessary that if God does not exist, then he simply never will, and that is quite a different idea. Similarly, with respect to (2), from the truth that God can neither come into nor pass out of existence, it does not follow that if God exists, then his existence (or "God exists") is logically necessary; what is logically necessary is that if he exists, then he always exists. In this way, what may be legitimately deduced from the impossibility of God's coming into or passing out of existence is nothing that bears on the contingency or necessity of God's existence or nonexistence, but only on the necessity of his remaining in existence (if he exists) or out of it (if he doesn't).[20] But note well that Plantinga's criticisms of Malcolm did not prevent Plantinga himself from proposing yet another modal version of the argument. And so it goes on.

What to Make of It?

Neither have Malcolm's critics had the last word. Some philosophers believe that it is possible to construct a version of the argument that dispenses entirely with all existence-as-a-predicate talk; some have now claimed to find three and even four arguments in Anselm's statement; others have urged a return to the original one-argument hypothesis; and someone else has turned the proof into an Ontological Argument for the Devil! It is no wonder that the reader by now may be tempted to side with the German philosopher Arthur Schopenhauer, who regarded the Ontological Argument as a "charming joke" and a "piece of scholastic jugglery." To be sure, many important philosophers have dismissed the Ontological Argument as an optical illusion of the philosophical imagination, but those who have embraced some version or other of it as a sound and forceful witness to the reality of God form an impressive list also, including Spinoza, Leibniz, Hegel, and (in their own ways) Barth and Tillich.

This last observation may be taken, I think, as evidence that the contribution of the Ontological Argument (and this applies equally to many of the positions considered in this book) cannot be decided

---

[20]See Alvin Plantinga, "A Valid Ontological Argument?," *Philosophical Review, ibid.*, reprinted with minor changes in *God and Other Minds* (Ithaca, N.Y.: Cornell University Press, 1967), pp. 82ff.

on logical grounds alone. If it were guilty of some simple (or even complicated) logical fallacy, the argument would have been discarded long ago. It has, instead, remained a center of controversy to the present day. The real issue lies much deeper. We have already seen that there are fundamentally different conceptions of knowledge, reality, and language, and it is probably at this level that the success or failure of the Ontological Argument must be decided.

3

The Cosmological Argument

If, in the midst of a street corner conversation, you were to ask your companion why he or she believes in God, the answer might be something like this: "Well, here is the world, and it had to come from *something*." For all its lack of sophistication, this response represents a rudimentary expression of the Cosmological Argument (from the Greek κόσμος: "world" or "universe"), which purports to demonstrate the existence of God from the existence of the world, or some aspect of it. More specifically, this argument reasons from contingent or dependent being to the necessary and independent being of God. The argument states, in effect, that neither the universe, nor any part of it contains within itself its own *raison d'être*, and that God must be posited as the ultimate cause of things. In fact, this argument is often called the "First-Cause Argument."

The "Five Ways" of St. Thomas Aquinas

Of all the philosophical arguments ever propounded for the existence of God, none are more famous than the *Quinque Viae*, or "Five Ways," that St. Thomas Aquinas presents in a few brief paragraphs near the beginning of his *Summa Theologica*. Before considering the substance of Thomas' position, a few preliminary comments are in order.

Briefly, Thomas' first argument begins with the evidence of motion (*motus* might better be rendered as "change") and concludes that God must exist in order for there to be, as is rationally required, an unmoved first mover of all things. The second argument attempts to prove that God must exist as the ultimate efficient cause of things, otherwise the series of causes and effects would have no beginning. The third argues that there must exist a self-subsistent, necessary being, otherwise all things and the universe itself would be merely possible and therefore ultimately nonexistent. The fourth reasons that the gradation in things, such as more and less being, more and less good, more and less true, or more and less noble, implies the existence of an absolute being as the ground of all other, relative being. The fifth is usually regarded as a version of the Teleological Argument, according to which God must exist as the intelligent architect of the orderly cosmos.[1] It will be noted that, wholly unlike the Ontological Argument of St. Anselm or Descartes, Thomas' arguments each begin with some aspect or other of the sensible world, claiming to prove the existence of God in a completely *a posteriori* manner. He sees this procedure as sanctioned by St. Paul's exhortation (Rom. 1:20) that the invisible God may be known, even apart from revelation, through his visible creation. Further, each argument is a causal argument, proceeding by means of the principle *ex nihilo, nihil fit*, "from nothing, nothing comes," that is, for everything that comes into being, there must be an adequate cause. Finally, each argument depends, at some point or other, on the impossibility of an infinite regress of causes and effects—there must be a First.[2]

---

[1]St. Thomas Aquinas, *Summa Theologica*, Part I, Qu. 2, Art. 3, in *Basic Writings of Saint Thomas Aquinas*, ed. Anton C. Pegis (New York: Random House, 1945), I.

[2]The influence of Thomistic natural theology in at least one strain of the Christian tradition is reflected in the decrees of the Vatican Council of 1870: "The same holy mother Church holds and teaches that God, the beginning and end of all things, can certainly be known by the natural light of human reason from created things. . . ." (in Heinrich Denzinger *et al.* [eds.], *Enchiridion Symbolorum*, sec. 1785, 31st ed. [Freiburg/Breisgrau: Herder, 1957]). Thomism was commended by Pope Leo XIII in the 1879 encyclical *Aeterni Patris* as the unofficial philosophy of the Roman Catholic Church, but it is difficult nowadays to find even Jesuit priests who reckon seriously with St. Thomas.

Some further observations may be helpful. First, the precise nature of Thomas' Cosmological Argument and its relation to the Teleological Argument (considered at length in Chapter 4) is not always agreed upon. Some would object, for example, that the imposition of this later distinction on Thomas (a distinction popularized in the eighteenth century by Kant) distorts the essential unity of his fivefold argument, which, after all, he does not call five demonstrations but five "ways." Nevertheless, if we distinguish between reasoning toward God from the existence of some empirical reality or other (usually the world or universe itself) and reasoning toward God from something *about* reality or the world, then only the first three of Thomas' Ways are versions of the Cosmological Argument. Of course, that motion, efficient causality, and contingency are (in Thomas) not facts about the world in the same way that design is would require more explanation, if indeed such could be provided. It is also sometimes thought (the influence of Kant again) that the Fourth Way stands in a somewhat different relation to the first three, being perhaps more of a Moral Argument (Chapter 5). But this distinction too is regarded with suspicion by Thomist scholars. The Five Ways, it would be argued, converge on one ultimate cause of one reality, though arrived at *via* different aspects of that reality: its moved, caused, contingent, graduated, and ordered character.

Second, it is sometimes objected that even though Thomas concludes each of his proofs with some such locution as ". . . and this everyone understands to be God," the God that Thomas proves is actually not much more than an abstract philosophical principle, hardly the object of faith and prayer. In a way this is true, but beside the point. Over the chapters of his main works Thomas believes that he is able to establish (though imperfectly) a knowledge of God's attributes, and in the *Summa Contra Gentiles* it takes him hundreds of pages to move from the First Cause to the God and Father of our Lord Jesus Christ. Nonetheless, in the present passages he is content to establish the foundation of theology, namely, the existence of the First Cause or Necessary Being, though the demonstration of this "philosophical" God is no small task, nor, as Thomas sees it, is it an unimportant one. A philosophical knowledge of God, for Thomas, is a "preamble to faith"; it provides a rational foundation both for the unbeliever in his approach to Christianity and, as for St. Anselm, for the individual who already believes what he does not yet understand.

Finally, it might be noted that none of the Five Ways are entirely original with Thomas. The first two reflect the influence of Aristotle's *Physics* and *Metaphysics*; the third suggests Thomas' indebtedness to the *Guide for the Perplexed*, by the Jewish philosopher Maimonides; the fourth echoes the Platonic *Dialogues*; and the fifth should be considered in light of St. John Damascene's *On the Orthodox Faith*. This is not to say that Thomas' arguments are not his own. Certainly they bear the distinctive imprint of his own reinterpretation and are filled with new significance. Still, this serves to remind us that none of the philosophical and/or theological contributions considered in this book were born in an intellectual vacuum, not even the celebrated proofs of St. Thomas Aquinas.

Of the Five Ways, it will suffice for our purposes to consider the Second and the Third. Thomas' full statement of the Second Way is as follows:

In the world of sensible things we find there is an order of efficient causes. There is no case known (neither is it, indeed, possible) in which a thing is found to be the efficient cause of itself; for so it would be prior to itself, which is impossible. Now in efficient causes it is not possible to go on to infinity, because in all efficient causes following in order, the first is the cause of the intermediate cause, and the intermediate is the cause of the ultimate cause, whether the intermediate cause be several, or one only. Now to take away the cause is to take away the effect. Therefore, if there be no first cause among efficient causes, there will be no ultimate, nor any intermediate, cause. But if in efficient causes it is possible to go on to infinity, there will be no first efficient cause, neither will there be an ultimate effect, nor any intermediate efficient causes; all of which is plainly false. Therefore it is necessary to admit a first efficient cause, to which everyone gives the name of God.[3]

Stated as simply as possible, the argument is:

The universe cannot be the cause of itself.

The universe cannot come from nothing.

The universe cannot be an effect in a chain of causes and effects extending to infinity.

---

[3]St. Thomas, *Summa Theologica*, *loc. cit.*

Therefore, the universe must be caused by a first, uncaused cause.

Any form of the Cosmological Argument will look roughly like this.

In a deductive argument such as this "four-horned dilemma," any uncertainty or ambiguity in the premises is necessarily passed along to the conclusion. We must, then, look carefully at the three premises of this argument. The first presents the least difficulty. As Thomas observes, if the effect is truly dependent upon the cause (and that is the essence of the cause–effect relationship), then the cause must in some sense precede the effect. For something to be the cause of itself, it would have to exist before it exists, and that is absurd. Thomas, like Aristotle, thought that the truth of the Law of Noncontradiction is self-evident: A thing cannot both be and not be at the same time in the same respect. Thus, we may pass over the first premise of the argument. The other two premises, however, may not prove so agreeable, and the major criticisms of the Cosmological Argument have, in fact, focused largely on these premises.

First in the Order of Time

One of the most obvious criticisms of the First-Cause Argument is that a first cause is simply not necessary at all. Why could the universe not have existed from eternity? Why can we not say that the present universe is just one of an infinite number of states extending backward in time without end? Actually, there are two forms of the First-Cause Argument, and it is extremely important to grasp the distinction at this point in our discussion. According to one version, the argument leads to a being who stands at the beginning of the *temporal* series. The other form of the argument interprets God as "first," relative not to the temporal order but to the order of *being*. This last, which is the position of Thomas, is not always easy to comprehend, and we will return to it in a moment.

For the present, we consider the more popular form of the Cosmological Argument, according to which the universe must have had a temporal beginning, and thus there must have been a Beginner way back there at the start of things. I call this the "Popular"

Cosmological Argument because it is what, more often than not, springs to mind when someone speaks of God "causing" the world. This form of the argument was propounded in the Christian tradition by, among others, the Scholastic theologian-philosopher St. Bonaventure, a contemporary of St. Thomas. It was also propounded—and with a vengeance—in the medieval Islamic tradition by several thinkers, such as al-Ghazali (1058–1111). These Islamic thinkers belonged to the *Kalam* movement (the Arabic *kalam* came to mean, loosely, "philosophical knowledge of God") and saw themselves as combating the pagan idea that the world has existed from eternity. After all, the Koran, like the Bible, taught: "In the beginning God created the heavens and the earth." Thus the argument in this form is sometimes also called the "*Kalam* Cosmological Argument."

Almost everyone feels an urge to posit a temporal origin of the universe on the rather instinctive—but not very philosophical—ground, that "Well, there just had to be a beginning of things!" Others believe that it is possible to provide persuasive arguments for this hypothesis. St. Bonaventure argued, perhaps more emphatically than anyone else, at least in the Christian tradition, the impossibility of a *creatio aeterna*, a world that has always existed. Like those Islamic thinkers, he tried to show through a series of *reductio ad absurdum* arguments that the thesis that the world or universe has always existed leads to absurd and impossible conclusions. If, for example, the universe has existed from eternity, then an infinite number of days has already passed by, and every new day is added to the already infinite number of days; yet it is clearly impossible to add to an already infinite number of events. Further, there are twelve lunar revolutions for every one solar revolution; but if the world has always existed, then the moon has gone around the earth an infinite number of times and likewise the sun; but two infinite numbers, one of which is twelve times the other, is absurd.[4]

---

[4]St. Bonaventure, *Commentaria in II Sententiarum*, Dist. I, Part I, Art. 1, Qu, 2, in *St. Thomas Aquinas, Siger of Brabant, St. Bonaventure: On the Eternity of the World*, tr. Cyril Vollert et al. (Milwaukee: Marquette University Press, 1964). For an example of the Islamic counterpart to this reasoning, see al-Ghazali, *Tahafut Al-Falasifah*, tr. Badih Ahmad Kamali (Lahore: Pakistan Philosophical Congress, 1963), esp. Chs. 1 and 2.

Bonaventure's position may more easily be represented by translating it into the following argument: If the world has existed from eternity, then prior to the present moment an infinite number of years has elapsed; but an infinite series can never elapse or be consummated or concluded—that is precisely why it is an *infinite* series. In this way, the suggestion that the universe has always existed is self-contradictory. Or, simplifying the argument still further: If the world has always existed, we would spend forever arriving at the present point in time, in which case we would never have finally arrived at this point. To avoid this absurd conclusion, we must concede that a *finite* number of years, days, or hours has elapsed and that time therefore must have had a beginning. And because something cannot come from nothing or be its own cause, we must posit a transcendent being, God, the first cause of the whole spatiotemporal, cause-and-effect series.

All of this may possess a *prima facie* plausibility, but a warning should be issued against all arguments having anything to do with infinity. The concept of infinity is a most perplexing one. In fact, 2,500 years ago, the Greek philosopher Zeno of Elea posed a series of paradoxes concerning the infinite, some of which continue to baffle philosophers and mathematicians to this day.

We can, however, settle at least two things. First, when Bonaventure speaks of an infinite span of time having gone by, he does not mean an infinity of infinite divisibility. Any finite segment of time contains, of course, an infinite number of moments, just as a segment of a line contains an infinite number of geometrical points. But here we are referring to an infinity of actual and determinate units such as years or minutes, not merely theoretical or ideal points on a geometric line. Second, it is inevitably countered that we should have no more difficulty conceiving of an infinite number of years stretching into the past than we have of an infinite series of negative numbers (0, -1, -2, -3, *ad infinitum*). But there is an important difference between this hypothetical or purely conceptual infinity and an infinity of actually existing spatiotemporal states. It is one thing to entertain the concept of infinite series and quite another to pass through one. I can easily conceive of an infinite number of numbers, but I cannot succeed in counting them, not even if I lived forever. Similarly, I can conceive of an infinite number of years stretching into the past, but it is impossible that they have actually elapsed.

God and Cosmology

Not all of the arguments that the universe had a beginning in time are of a purely logical, philosophical nature. More recently, cosmologists have emerged with scientific empirical evidence for the temporality of the universe. One of the most important of these is the Second Law of Thermodynamics or, as it is also called, the Law of Entropy. According to this principle, often called the best attested of natural laws, the energy in the universe is being progressively and uniformly distributed throughout. Some regions of the universe are hotter than others, and heat is constantly flowing from the hotter to the cooler. The end of this process would be a state of thermal equilibrium, that is, a completely uniform distribution of energy and the stagnation of all physical activity. It should be apparent how all of this may be construed as evidence for a beginning of the universe. If the universe has always existed, then by now such a uniform distribution of energy would have come about, which is obviously not the case. Some rather astute scientists have been willing to affirm a beginning of the cosmos on the evidence of entropy, including the physicist and astronomer Sir Arthur Eddington who claimed that since the universe is running down it must have once been "wound up."[5] Even Bertrand Russell, writing in 1931, concluded, ". . . as arguments of this nature go, it is a good one, and I think we ought provisionally to accept the hypothesis that the world had a beginning at some definite, though unknown, date."[6] Other, and closely related, cosmological evidence for a temporal beginning of the universe is the Lemaître-Gamow concept of the evolutionary cosmos. According to this theory (the "Big Bang Theory"), all of the matter of the universe was originally compressed into something like a huge, superdense "atom" called by George Gamow the primordial *ylem*. More recently, it has been called the "Great Singularity" by Stephen Hawking (*A Brief History of Time*) and others who claim to know what was going on in the universe at 10^{-43} seconds (0.0000000000000000000000000000000000000000001 second)

---

[5]A. S. Eddington, *The Nature of the Physical World* (New York: Macmillan, 1928), p. 83.

[6]Bertrand Russell, *The Scientific Outlook* (London: George Allen & Unwin, 1931), p. 122.

after its origin—about anything earlier, these cosmologists apparently hesitate to speculate! At a definite point in time, calculated at 10 or 15 billion years ago, the primeval atom exploded, flinging energy and creating space. (The actual events are much more difficult to imagine than this; it may help to think of space as the surface, not the inside, of a balloon being inflated.) Our expanding universe, in which galaxies are receding from one another at enormous velocities, is the effect of this colossal nuclear reaction and cosmic explosion.[7] The relevant upshot of all this is that, in Hawking's remarkable statement, "time has a beginning."[8]

The Big Bang Theory appears, indeed, now to have won out over the competing Steady State Theory. According to the Steady State model, hydrogen atoms are continually being created; they then coalesce into clouds that further condense into stellar systems or galaxies, which recede from one another, leaving new emptiness to be filled up by coalescing hydrogen atoms. The evidence of quasars (quasi-stellar objects) detected by radio astronomy now suggests, however, that this is not the case. Furthermore, according to the Big Bang Theory, a remnant of the original thermal radiation should even yet be detectable, and something almost universally recognized to be it (an isotropic microwave radiation of a peak wavelength of 7.2 cm) has been detected. For a time it was hypothesized that the present world order, with its entropic scattering, is but one stage in a cyclic expansion and contraction—Big Bangs and Big Crunches as it were, or, as it has also been called, the "Big Bounce." For various reasons, this view likewise has been generally discarded. For example, there is no conceivable way of determining whether anything physical happened before the last Big Bang, and it is not yet certain that there is enough mass in the universe to cause a Big Crunch at all—appeals to "missing mass" or "dark matter" remain largely speculative. In any event, the Big Bounce Theory has to reckon with the earlier point about the logical impossibility of an

---

[7]George Gamow, *The Creation of the Universe*, rev. ed. (New York: Viking Press, 1961); Stephen W. Hawking, *A Brief History of Time: From the Big Bang to Black Holes* (New York: Bantam Books, 1988). The term "Big Bang" is often mistakenly attributed to Gamow. In fact, it was first used by Gamow's adversary, Fred Hoyle, in a lecture in which Hoyle was poking fun at Gamow's theory.

[8]Hawking, *A Brief History of Time*, p. 136.

infinite part: There could not have been an infinite number of Bangs and Crunches, thus there must have a been first Bang.

Surely it is understandable that universal laws such as the Second Law of Thermodynamics and cosmological theories such as the Big Bang have often caught the theist's eye. Still, one may have the nagging feeling that there remains somehow a great gulf between the deliverances of science and genuine metaphysical claims. Does not such speculation tend to obscure the honored boundaries between physics and metaphysics? Is it really possible to move from considerations about the origin and nature of this particular configuration of matter to conclusions about the absolute beginning of matter? Is not science, by its very nature and limits, barred from making claims about what lies beyond the empirical horizon? It would seem, though, that the theist might appropriately claim that the evidence of physics tends at least to converge, along with the philosophical and perhaps revealed evidence, on the conclusion that the universe was indeed created *ex nihilo* by an omnipotent being at some definite point in the past, or at least that the universe and time began a finite number of years ago, and not out of anything else.

First in the Order of Being

"First cause" is usually understood, as stated earlier, to mean "beginner of the temporal series," and for most people the Cosmological Argument proves, if anything, that there must be a God who created the world once upon a time, or, better, created the original moment. But to return now to our earlier discussion, we have seen that there is another form of the argument, a more classical version, and that this latter is the version of St. Thomas.

If you were to ask someone, "What is the cause of the universe?," and he or she were to answer, "The universe has always existed," you might legitimately respond, "I did not ask for the *age* of the universe but for its *cause*." That is, even if something has always existed, it would still appear quite meaningful to ask why there is that something rather than nothing. Accordingly, Thomas formulated a version of the Cosmological Argument on the supposition of the world's eternity, proving not a first cause in a temporal series at all, but rather a being who is first on the ontological scale, in other words, first in the order of being. As he says in another context, ". . . God is the cause of an everlasting world in the same way as a foot would have been the cause of an imprint if it had been pressed on sand from all eternity."[9] Similarly, Aristotle (whom Thomas reverently called "The Philosopher") did not regard his Unmoved Mover as a first cause in time. He believed that the world has always existed, but that the evident activity and change in the world at every moment derives from the motion of the heavenly spheres (which carry the sun, moon, planets, and the fixed stars in their orbits), which in turn derive their motion from the Unmoved Mover, God.[10] Of course, Thomas believed as an article of faith that the world did have a beginning in time (Gen. 1:1), but he also believed that on purely philosophical grounds, the eternity of the world could be neither affirmed nor denied, and he freely grants it for the sake of the argument.[11]

The first cause to which this form of the argument leads is, in this way, "first" in the sense of *ultimate*: God is the ultimate being. One might represent the temporal cause-and-effect series by a horizontal line and the ontological cause-and-effect series by a vertical line. If the horizontal series were to extend infinitely in both directions, it would, nevertheless, represent a collection (though an infinite collection) of contingent things. And because an infinite number of contingent things can no more be the cause of itself than can a single contingent thing, the infinite series is itself wholly contingent. The horizontal or temporal series, even if infinite, is therefore subject to, conditioned by, and contingent upon a higher and different order of causality. But if there were no first term or ultimate cause in the vertical or ontological series, then the universe as a whole would have no ground, no condition, no cause, no reason for being. There would be, in the final analysis, no final analysis.

This form of the argument, according to which there must be at any moment in the life of the universe an ultimate, necessary being upon which the contingent universe depends, is more clearly seen in Thomas' Third Way:

---

[9]St. Thomas Aquinas, *Summa Contra Gentiles*, I, 43, tr. Anton C. Pegis (Garden City, N.Y.: Image Books, 1955).

[10]Aristotle, *Metaphysics*, XII, 6 (1071b ff.).

[11]St. Thomas (the Angelic Doctor) and St. Bonaventure (the Seraphic Doctor) carried on a running debate on this very question, and their relevant statements have been translated and included in the work mentioned in footnote 3.

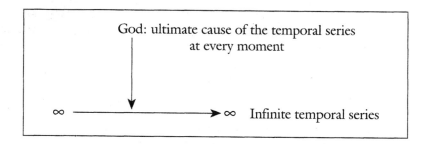

God: ultimate cause of the temporal series
at every moment

∞ ────────────────────────► ∞   Infinite temporal series

The third way is taken from possibility and necessity, and runs thus. We find in nature things that are possible to be and not to be, since they are found to be generated, and to be corrupted, and consequently, it is possible for them to be and not to be. But it is impossible for all things which are, to be of this sort, for that which can not-be at some time is not. Therefore, if everything can not-be, then at one time there was nothing in existence. Now if this were true, even now there would be nothing in existence, because that which does not exist begins to exist only through something already existing. Therefore, if at one time nothing was in existence, it would have been impossible for anything to have begun to exist; and thus even now nothing would be in existence—which is absurd. Therefore, not all beings are merely possible, but there must exist something the existence of which is necessary. But every necessary thing either has its necessity caused by another, or not. Now it is impossible to go on to infinity in nec-essary things which have their necessity caused by another, as has been already proved in regard to efficient causes. Therefore we cannot but admit the existence of some being having of itself its own necessity, and not receiving it from another, but rather causing in others their necessity. This all men speak of as God.[12]

Here it should be clear that Thomas argues for a self-subsisting necessary being, not a first cause in time, and in fact assumes, as he does in all of the Ways, that the universe has always existed. The

[12]St. Thomas, *Summa Theologica, loc. cit.* The translation of the third sen-tence is emended in accordance with the correct textual reading: *Impossibile est autem omnia quae sunt, talia esse.* It is often remarked that Thomas' Third Way best displays the kernel of his theistic proof. In some ways that may be so, but it should be qualified with the observation that in the *Summa Contra Gentiles* (I, 13) he unfolds not summarily but over many ponderous pages a proof for God, and it is not the Third Way but the First Way. Even in the *Summa Theo-logica* the First Way is called the "more manifest" [*manifestior*] way.

argument may be restated as follows. If all things are merely possible or are the sorts of things that come into being and pass away, and if the universe has always been here, then nothing would now exist. For at some time in the infinite past all things would not-be at once (given enough time, everything possible will happen, and it is possible that everything that can not-be will not-be all at the same time). Now out of nothingness, nothing can possibly come. But we exist. It is therefore not the case that all things are merely possible, and there must exist something that is necessary. But this is not the end. By "necessary being" Thomas does not necessarily mean (as Malcolm did in the last chapter) a being who cannot not-exist for all eternity. For Thomas there are, as a matter of fact, *created* necessary beings, beings who might not have existed, though, once created, they cannot cease to exist (for example, angels and human souls). But a series of such necessary beings as these (necessary *ab alio*, "from another") cannot extend *ad infinitum*, so there must exist an ultimate and self-existent necessary being (necessary *a se*, "in itself") upon which all other beings (both necessary and possible) depend for their existence. There you have it.

In the previous chapter, we raised the problem of the concept "necessary existence," and we cannot raise it here all over again in relation to Thomas. But for those who cannot bear the suspense, it may at least be noted that "God exists" is for Thomas (and this *is* similar to Malcolm) a necessary proposition, though one that bears, obviously, on the existence of something. Whether it is a *logically* necessary proposition is another question; it will be recalled that Thomas has already informed us that God's existence is identical to his essence, which would suggest that one cannot deny "God exists" without self-contradiction. Be that as it may, many interpreters view Thomas' proofs as involving not a logical but a sort of factual or metaphysical necessity dictated by the self-subsistent nature of God—*aseity* again—which, in turn, is arrived at through a reflection on the nature of things. We have seen that a whole strain of contemporary philosophers would reject such a proposition as "God necessarily exists" on the grounds that only propositions, not things, can be necessary, but of course, St. Thomas had not heard that. Not that it would have mattered. Thomas, like Malcolm, would have dismissed this as a "dogma of contemporary philosophy" involving a radically different and unjustified conception of philosophical language.

It should be apparent by now that it misses the point entirely to represent the most classical theistic argument (St. Thomas') as reducing the world to antecedent states that originate in a being who stands at the beginning of the spatio-temporal process. The inevitable picture of falling dominoes or bumping billiard balls is wholly out of place here. What the argument leads to is an ultimate being who at this moment (as at every moment) underlies the whole structure of the cosmic process. As someone has expressed it, God is arrived at not by noting what has gone before something, but by looking *into* it. The First Way, then, teaches that if there is now no ultimate mover, then there is now no motion either; the Second teaches that if there is no ultimate efficient cause, then there are no cause-and-effect relations; the Third teaches that if there is no ultimate necessary being, then there are no other beings either; the Fourth teaches that if there is no maximal being, truth, and goodness, then neither is there any relative being, truth, and goodness; the Fifth teaches that if there is no intelligible end of things, then there is even now no purposeful activity. It is all a matter of what must exist right now in order to account for the way the world exists right now.

The Cosmological Argument attempts in various ways to demonstrate the existence of God by beginning with the sensible world and then trying to penetrate to its ultimate cause. But, of course, the argument in none of its forms can prove anything to someone who insists that the world is simply "gratuitous" (Jean-Paul Sartre) or "just there" (Bertrand Russell). On this view, the universe just sits there, a brute fact. Not everyone sees it as crying out for explanation.

Some Common Objections

Surely the most common complaint against the Cosmological Argument (in any of its forms) is that if everything must have a cause, then so must God. But this will not do. When the theist asserts that God caused the world and everything else, what is being claimed is that all things are dependent upon a being who himself necessarily *transcends* space and time, as well as all coming and going. The question "Where did God come from?" can thus be discarded as ill conceived, because it construes God to be, like other things, the sort of being that can come and go. If God himself can come into being, then he cannot possibly be the *cause* of things that come into being and would not therefore be what the theist means by "God." Similarly, St. Augustine (354–430) observes that the question "What was God doing before he created the world?" is nonsensical. What possible meaning can there be in asking what God was doing "then" before the creation, since before the creation there was no time and therefore no "before"? And he castigates those who, enmeshed in the temporal flux of before and after, are incapable of transcending time and grasping the all-is-present and the all-at-once character of eternity in which God exists, impassable and unmoved. (Augustine suggests that his answer is more respectable than the clever but trivial one provided by others: "What was God doing before he created the world? Why, he was preparing Hell for people who pry into mysteries!")[13]

Another common objection alleges that the Cosmological Argument is vitiated by the modern physical concept of the conservation of energy, which encompasses also the older principle of the indestructibility of matter. The reasoning (often directed against Thomas' Third Way) is that whereas particular configurations of matter do indeed come into being and pass away, energy itself abides. But a confusion lurks here. No one who affirms the principle of the conservation of energy has ever denied, at least not on those grounds, that energy is created. If the conservation of energy were incompatible with creation, then no one who is both a scientist and a Christian could believe in the conservation of energy! What the principle actually claims is not that energy can be neither created nor destroyed, but that once it exists, it cannot be destroyed of itself, or that if left to itself in a closed system the total amount of energy remains constant. Moreover, it should be stressed that Thomas himself believes in something similar to the principle when he affirms that the physical world is, along with angels and souls, a necessary (though created) reality, the same kind of necessary being that he explicitly mentions in his Third Way as being dependent for its existence upon some uncreated necessary being.

---

[13]St. Augustine, *The Confessions*, XI, 10ff., tr. R. S. Pine-Coffin (Baltimore, Md.: Penguin Books, 1961).

Perhaps more serious is the charge that the Cosmological Argument (especially in its Thomistic form) is guilty of the fallacy of composition. This is an important point, and we need to slow down here.

We have seen that the Cosmological Argument moves from the contingency of the universe to a cause of the universe. But what is the evidence for the contingency of the universe? Answer: The universe is contingent because everything in it is contingent. It has seemed to some, though, that this is a simple instance of the fallacy of composition, the mistake of attributing to the whole what is true of its parts. As Bertrand Russell once complained, it no more follows from the fact that everything in the universe has a cause that the universe itself has a cause than it follows from the fact that every man has a mother that mankind has a mother! But wait a minute. The fallacy of composition is not a formal but a material fallacy; that is, the fallacy cannot be identified by taking note of the form of a statement, but rather by considering the nature of the ideas involved. It does follow from the fact that every thread in the carpet is green that the carpet itself is green, though it does not follow from the fact that all the books comprising a library have 500 pages that the library has 500 pages, even though both inferences are identical in form: If x is true of each of the members of y, then x is true of y. The problem with the library example is not with the form of the reasoning but with the ideas involved: A library *can't* have pages—and, by the way, mankind can't have a mother. Similarly, the charge that the Cosmological Argument commits the fallacy of composition fails, perhaps, to pay sufficient attention to the kind of causality or contingency involved in the reasoning. If the argument were reasoning from the fact that everything in the universe has a cause in space and time, then it would indeed have to conclude that the universe too has a cause in space and time—which is exactly what the argument denies. In reality, however, the Cosmological Argument reasons from the contingency (or possible nonbeing) of every sensible thing to the contingency of all sensible things (a sound inference, it seems to me), and further reasons that the necessary cause of all sensible things cannot itself be one of those things (another sound inference).

In any event, wouldn't it be possible to sidestep entirely this composition business? Consider an analogy. A watch is, in fact, nothing other than its parts in certain relations to one another; the parts and their relations are contingent, with respect both to the way they are and that they are at all. Thus there is nothing in or about the watch that is noncontingent—the watch is just wall-to-wall contingency. Now, if that reasoning seems forceful, why not the following?

The universe is the sum of all its parts and relations.

All the parts and relations of the universe are contingent.

Therefore, the universe is contingent.

It would be difficult to argue with the first premise, for if there is more to the universe than its parts and relations, then that "more" could hardly be anything empirical and thus part of the *physical* reality that is clearly intended here by "universe." If the second premise is challenged, the answer would be, *à la* Thomas, that all the parts and relations of the universe are, for example, in motion, and anything in motion is, obviously, dependent on something else—its mover.

Now put a twist on this. Take the watch again. Let it begin to enlarge.[14] Now it is as large as the world; now it is as large as the solar system; now it is as large as our galaxy; now it is as large as the *universe*. Is the watch now any less contingent than it was in its original size? Did it at some point in its expansion suddenly and magically become a *necessary* being? Is it now any less the sum of its parts and thus *wholly contingent*?

Hume on Causality

One of the most fundamental philosophical ideas is that for anything that happens, or comes into being, there must be a necessary and sufficient condition. A necessary condition is a condition without which something could not occur (your mother is a necessary condition of your coming into being), and a sufficient condition is a con-

---

[14]The following is suggested by the similar image employed by Richard Taylor, *Metaphysics*, 3rd ed. (Englewood Cliffs, N.J.: Prentice Hall, 1983), p. 93.

dition, or set of conditions, with which something could occur (your mother and father together). As St. Thomas more concisely expresses it, *ex nihilo, nihil fit,* "from nothing, nothing comes," or as a modern might say, "every event must have a cause." Obviously, the Principle of Causality lies at the heart of the Cosmological Argument. Unfortunately, this is not only one of the most fundamental philosophical ideas, it is also one of the most problematic. Causation is, in fact, a central issue in continuing philosophical debate.

The question before us may be narrowed to this: Is the claim that "Every event must have a cause," or "From nothing, nothing comes," universally and absolutely binding? If you find it difficult to resist an *a priori* feeling of certainty with respect to causality, you are in good company. The eighteenth-century Scottish common-sense philosopher Thomas Reid:

That neither existence, nor any mode of existence, can begin without an efficient cause, is a principle that appears very early in the mind of man; and it is so universal, and so firmly rooted in human nature, that the most determined skepticism cannot eradicate it.[15]

Well, maybe. As a metaphysical principle, causality has been attacked by a good many philosophers. One of these was the British empiricist David Hume (1711–1776), who probably did more than anyone else in the history of philosophy to undermine this traditional concept. His treatment of causality is the product of his phenomenalism, the epistemological doctrine that all knowledge reduces to the phenomena or appearances given in sense perception.

According to Hume's analysis, when we observe a causal relation between A and B, all we actually observe is that A is next to B and that A comes before B. These two factors, "contiguity" and "succession," are all that is disclosed to us through sense experience. But clearly, though A may be contiguous with B and precede B, it is not therefore necessarily the cause of B. Hume concludes that a genuine causal relation must involve something more than mere contiguity and succession:

---

[15]Thomas Reid, *Inquiry and Essays,* ed. Ronald E. Beanblossom and Keith Lehrer (Indianapolis: Hackett, 1983), p. 330.

Shall we then rest contented with these two relations of contiguity and succession, as affording a complete idea of causation? By no means. An object
may be contiguous and prior to another, without being consider'd as its
cause. There is a NECESSARY CONNEXION to be taken into consideration;
and that relation is of much greater importance, than any of the other two
above-mention'd.[16]

It is over the nature of this necessary connection that Hume abandons the road followed by most of his predecessors. As traditionally
conceived, causality was viewed as a metaphysical principle, that is,
one of the fundamental laws of reality, a kind of power out there in
the world binding things together with universal and necessary con-
nections. Such an understanding of causal necessity could, of
course, never be admitted by Hume the empiricist who took causality to be not a "relation of ideas" (that is, an analytic statement) but
a "matter of fact" derived ultimately from sense experience, and for
whom causality therefore could never amount to anything more
than the observed "constant conjunction" of one thing with
another. As far as observation and experience go, there is no more
certainty, universality, or necessity in the statement "Every event
must have a cause" than in "All swans are white."

It must be noted, however, that Hume is not denying causal
necessity as such; what he is denying is that causality can be rationally grounded, that it is cognitively or theoretically certain, that it
is knowable:

I never asserted so absurd a Proposition as *that any thing might arise without
a Cause*: I only maintain'd, that our Certainty of the Falsehood of that
Proposition proceeded neither from Intuition nor Demonstration; but
from another Source.[17]

What is this source? Hume answers: a propensity of human nature,
a feeling or sentiment, a habit or custom, a rationally unjustified
belief. In light of Hume's doctrine of "natural belief," the necessity
or power that unites experiences together in a causal relation is now

---

[16]David Hume, *A Treatise of Human Nature*, ed. L. A. Selby-Bigge
(Oxford, England: Clarendon Press, 1896), p. 77 (slightly edited).
    [17]David Hume, "Letter to John Stewart," in Norman Kemp Smith, *The
Philosophy of David Hume* (London: Macmillan, 1941), p. 413 (slightly edited).

understood to lie in the mind's habit of passing from one experience to another, and causal necessity turns out to be a psychological rather than a metaphysical principle, though not for that reason any less important for our thinking about the world, and living:

. . . though the powers and forces by which the course of nature is governed, be wholly unknown to us; yet our thoughts and conceptions have still, we find, gone on in the same train with the other works of nature. Custom is that principle, by which this correspondence has been effected; so necessary to the subsistence of our species, and the regulation of our conduct, in every circumstance and occurrence of human life.[18]

The full significance of Hume's translation of metaphysical necessity into natural belief has sometimes been slighted by his interpreters in favor of his more negative and critical contribution. In this way, the Humeian analysis has contributed more than Hume might have wished to the radical empiricist understanding of causality, which, in its extreme form, dissolves it into an empirical generalization, a mere expression of statistical probabilities, or a methodological postulate. Be that as it may, Hume himself did, in fact, challenge the traditional metaphysical necessities (restricting all necessary truths to the logically necessary relations of ideas), including the metaphysical necessity of causality. And if we cannot be certain that every event must have such a cause, then we cannot be certain that the world did either. Whether the world is an event to start with brings us to Kant.

Kant on Causality

We saw in Chapter 2 that all of us are certain of such truths as "All barking dogs bark" or "All bodies occupy space," because these are analytic statements or tautologies; the predicate repeats what is already given in the subject such that they cannot be denied without self-contradiction; their truth is analytic and *a priori*. But Kant insisted that there is also a universality and necessity about many "synthetic" statements, statements in which the predicate adds something to what is given in the subject. That is, he believed (unlike Hume and a whole string of contemporary philosophers)

---

[18]David Hume, *An Enquiry Concerning Human Understanding*, ed. L. A. Selby-Bigge, 2nd ed. (Oxford, England: Clarendon Press, 1902), pp. 54f.

that there are synthetic *a priori* truths, truths that are both *a priori* certain *and* existentially informative, and he believed that "Every event must have a cause" was one of them. Consider Kant's rejection of Hume's analysis of causality:

> . . . the very concept of a cause so manifestly contains the concept of a necessity of connection with an effect and of the strict universality of the rule, that the concept would be altogether lost if we attempted to derive it, as Hume has done, from a repeated association of that which happens with that which precedes, and from a custom of connecting representations, a custom originating in this repeated association, and constituting therefore a merely subjective necessity.[19]

But how, then, does Kant account for causality as a necessary and universal principle?

According to Kant, the reason every event must have a cause is that the concept of causality is built into the mind itself as one of the ways in which the mind (by its very nature) is disposed to represent reality; or, as someone has represented it, it is "mind-imposed." Causality is one of the *a priori* "categories" of the understanding through which space and time, also contributed by the intellect, are organized into intelligible experience; it is constitutive of experience, a necessary element of experience, part of what we *mean* by experience. Kant thus salvaged the concept of causality as a philosophical principle from Hume's skepticism, as well as explaining how synthetic *a priori* knowledge in general is possible.[20]

But, alas, a high price must be paid for this reinstatement of causality. The *a priori* concepts, such as causality and substance, can now have no application whatever beyond the world of possible experience, inasmuch as they themselves constitute experience—and there goes the Cosmological Argument. In fact, says Kant, when the "theoretical reason" (which operates by means of the spatiotemporal and categorical structure of the understanding) ventures into the metaphysical and transcendent realm, the inevitable result is confusion and contradiction. If causality is a spatiotemporal relation constituting an aspect of experience, and if God transcends space

---

[19]Immanuel Kant, *Critique of Pure Reason*, tr. Norman Kemp Smith (London: Macmillan, 1929), p. 44.
[20]Immanuel Kant, *Prolegomena to any Future Metaphysics*, tr. Lewis W. Beck (New York: Library of Liberal Arts, 1951), pp. 42ff.

and time, then what possible application can the concept of causality have to God? We saw earlier that if God is not the sort of being that can come and go, then surely he cannot be the effect of something. Kant shows that, for the same reason, God cannot be the cause of anything. In a word, the Cosmological Argument is unsound because it tries to apply the concept of causality, which has appropriate application to the sensible world only (what Kant calls the "phenomenal world" or the world of appearance), to the transcendent world (the "noumenal" or real world), where it has no application at all. The gulf between the supreme being and the chain of natural causes is rationally unbridgeable.[21]

Kant provides a series of "antinomies" (two incompatible propositions, both of which are apparently true) as examples of the difficulties that plague the theoretical reason when it trespasses beyond its empirical limits. It so happens that his First Antinomy concerns the beginning of the world in time, a question that is not irrelevant (as we have seen) for one version of the Cosmological Argument. According to Kant, the thesis "The world had a beginning in time" can be demonstrated by a sound argument: If the world did not have a beginning in time, then an infinite number of years has elapsed, but this conclusion is self-contradictory. Unfortunately, the antithesis, "The world did not have a beginning in time," can also be demonstrated: If the world did have a beginning in time, then in that empty period preceding time there could have been no distinguishing condition favoring existence over nonexistence, and thus nothing at all would have been brought into existence.[22] What does this mean? It means that this piece of speculative reasoning is illegitimate. Because the beginning of the world is not an object of possible experience, we cannot discuss it by means of concepts that have to do only with experience. And so it is, for Kant, with all speculative issues; concerning these issues we can expect no help from the theoretical reason—only antinomies.

It should be noted that both Hume and Kant viewed causality as a way of relating objects of experience, Hume psychologizing it, and Kant idealizing it. Kant, for example, thinks that the Cosmological Argument has something to do with "the impossibility of an infinite series of causes, given one after the other, in the sensible

---

[21]Kant, *Critique of Pure Reason*, pp. 511f.
[22]*Ibid.*, pp. 396ff.

world"[23]—like falling dominoes. We have seen, however, that the notion of causality employed by, say, St. Thomas was conceived more richly as an ontological or metaphysical relation, a condition of being itself. The Cosmological Argument defended by the great scholastics was, in fact, unknown to Hume and Kant—not that it would have mattered.

One further observation. Even aside from his delimitation of the theoretical reason to objects of possible experience, Kant judges that the Cosmological Argument would lead us, at best, to the mere idea of an *ens realissimum* ("most real being"). But here we are once again confronted with the difficulty encountered in the Ontological Argument, namely, how to get from the concept of such a being to its objective reality. For Kant, then, the Cosmological Argument rests ultimately upon the Ontological Argument, and the Ontological Argument is fallacious.[24]

We see, then, that an empiricist like Hume presents us with a concept of causality that is taken to be descriptive of the real world but that can never possess any rationally grounded universality or certainty. Kant, on the other hand, presents us with a concept of causality that is universal, necessary, and certain, but applicable only to an idea-istically constituted world of appearances. Many will be unable to suppress the suspicion that neither of these approaches is correct, and, rejecting both of them, they will insist that the principle "Every event must have a cause" is somehow both certain *and* descriptive of the way things really are. But what, then, is the epistemological status of this piece of information? Is it a truth intuited immediately, apart from the intervention of other ideas or sense experience? Is it a fundamental principle of explanation postulated for the sake of other explanations? Is it a metaphysical principle disclosed in the apprehension of any being whatsoever? How to explain the nature and/or derivation of such a concept would be yet another problem, and to pursue it here would be to open an epistemological Pandora's Box that would involve us in issues that range far beyond the scope of these chapters. But they are important issues and sooner or later must be confronted by the serious reader. We have already seen that much can rise or fall with the concept of causality, including the Cosmological Argument.

---

[23]*Ibid.*, p. 511.
[24]*Ibid.*, pp. 509ff.

4

The Teleological Argument

People of all times have been impressed by the apparent order of the cosmos and, not surprisingly, have seized upon it as awesome evidence of an intelligent creator. This almost universal response no doubt inspired the Psalmist's exclamation,

> The heavens are telling the glory of God;
> and the firmament proclaims his handiwork.
>
> (Ps. 19:1)

and the ancient judgment that Wisdom

> reaches mightily from one end of the earth to the other,
> and she orders all things well.
>
> (Wis. 8:1)

It is too much to believe, some have reasoned, that this vast array of orderly and purposive activity is but the product of mere chance, an accidental and fortuitous concurrence of atoms. The universe is rational, and rationality is the product of mind. This argument for the existence of God is called the Teleological Argument (from the Greek τέλος, "end," "purpose," "completeness") or the Design Argument, since it reasons from the apparent design in the universe—sometimes with reference to its patterns and regularities and sometimes its purposiveness—to the existence of a Designer.

Paley and the Watch-Analogy

The Teleological Argument has its roots in Plato and Aristotle, for whom order and purpose were central facts about reality. In a well-known passage from the *Phaedo*, Plato represents Socrates as reflecting upon his earlier despair over the prevailing mechanistic explanations of nature and his subsequent joy upon discovering the philosophy of Anaxagoras, with its doctrine of an all-governing Mind, for therein he found, or at least thought he found, a truly adequate cause of nature's unfolding. This interest in teleology was passed along to later thinkers, most notably to Aristotle and his Christian disciple St. Thomas Aquinas, who employed it most obviously in his Fifth Way:

> We see that things which lack knowledge, such as natural bodies, act for an end, and this is evident from their acting always, or nearly always, in the same way, so as to obtain the best result. Hence it is plain that they achieve their end, not fortuitously, but designedly. Now whatever lacks knowledge cannot move towards an end, unless it be directed by some being endowed with knowledge and intelligence; as the arrow is directed by the archer. Therefore some intelligent being exists by whom all natural things are directed to their end; and this being we call God.[1]

But we have seen already that it probably does violence to the unity of Thomas' theistic proof to separate the Fifth Way as being a different argument from his others. For a statement of the Teleological Argument, in distinction to the Cosmological Argument, we would do well to look elsewhere.

The most famous statement of the Teleological Argument is (for better or for worse) that of the Anglican divine William Paley (1743–1805), who in 1802 published a book entitled *Natural Theology, or Evidences of the Existence and Attributes of the Deity Collected from the Appearances of Nature*. From the opening pages of this book comes Paley's famous analogy of the watch. Let us imagine ourselves, he says, stumbling across a shiny object lying on the ground. A closer examination reveals an intricate mechanism of wheels,

---

[1]St. Thomas Aquinas, *Summa Theologica*, Part I, Qu. 2, Art. 3, in *Basic Writings of Saint Thomas Aquinas*, ed. Anton C. Pegis (New York: Random House, 1945), I.

springs, and levers, precisely constructed and adjusted so as to set it ticking and telling the time of day. We would judge as incredible any suggestion that this watch is the product of mere chance, as if falling snow, rustling leaves, blowing sands, and flaking of minerals just happened to shape the required pieces, bring them together and combine them in just this manner! Rather, our irresistible tendency would be to attribute the watch to an intelligent design. (Someone has suggested an updated scenario: Imagine stepping from a space ship onto an apparently uninhabited planet and finding there a Coke bottle or McDonald's hamburger wrapper!)

There cannot be design without a designer; contrivance without a contriver; order without choice; arrangement without anything capable of arranging; subserviency and relation to a purpose without that which could intend a purpose; means suitable to an end, and executing their office in accomplishing that end, without the end ever having been contemplated or the means accommodated to it. Arrangement, disposition of parts, subserviency of means to an end, relation of instruments to a use imply the presence of intelligence and mind.[2]

The universe displays at every point an infinitely greater order, purpose, and design than that of the watch:

every indication of contrivance, every manifestation of design which existed in the watch, exists in the works of nature, with the difference on the side of nature of being greater and more, and that in a degree which exceeds all computation.[3]

Actually, says Paley, the physiological features of the human body itself present the most compelling evidence of all; he writes at great length documenting the complexities of the human eye and praising its design, claiming that if there were no other instance of design in the whole of experience, the human eye alone would suffice as evidence for the existence of a supreme designer. The fact is, however, that *everything* in the universe and the universe itself manifests "special design." And since, as everyone knows, a cause must be ade-

---

[2]William Paley, *Natural Theology*, ed. Frederick Ferré (Indianapolis, Ind.: Library of Liberal Arts, 1963), pp. 8f.
     [3]*Ibid.*, p. 13.

quate to the effect, any rational person will hold the universe to be ultimately unintelligible apart from the concept of a cause that is commensurate with the overwhelming order and plan of the cosmos. Thus we are compelled by the display of order in the universe, analogous to that of the watch, to draw the inevitable inference to creative intelligence. Such a cause, Paley concludes, is supplied by natural theology, which assures us that "there must be something in the world more than what we see" and that "among the invisible things of nature there must be an intelligent mind concerned in its production, order, and support."[4]

Many versions of the Teleological Argument take, like Paley's, the shape of an argument by analogy, and may be represented more formally as something like this, suggested by my colleague Wes Morriston:

> Watches, houses, ships, machines, and so on all exhibit design, and are planned and produced by intelligent beings.
>
> The universe exhibits design.
>
> ———————
>
> Therefore, the universe was probably planned and produced by an intelligent being.

Hume: The Limits of Experience

David Hume's criticism is rightly considered the classic critique of the Design Argument. In *Dialogues Concerning Natural Religion* (published posthumously in 1779, several years before Paley's *Natural Theology*), Hume attacks the argument from many angles, but these reduce essentially to four, and they all reinforce the Humeian principle that belief must be proportioned to the evidence.

First, Hume argues that if we grant (which we might or might not) that matter and motion have existed from eternity, and that given enough time every possible situation will be actualized, then due to "the eternal revolutions of unguided matter," every possible

———————

[4] *Ibid.*, p. 86.

arrangement and configuration of the elements—even watches—will of necessity come about sooner or later. Further, once a world such as ours is actualized, its displays of contrivance and design should not be surprising. Would not each part stand necessarily in some relation to every other part, and the world itself in some relation to other worlds? Would not the form of something always be adapted to its function? Would not all phenomena take on the appearance of some organization or other and bear the imprint of natural laws and regular processes? The observation that the universe displays "special design" would now appear to be empty.[5] Indeed, one might carry this point even further than Hume did and suggest that a completely chaotic universe is inconceivable: If the constellations of stars were fixed according to some other arrangements, or the planets were shifted from their present orbits, or the parts of animals were adapted differently, what would we have? Not chaos, but simply a different order.

We just saw that the Teleological Argument (at least in its Paleyan form) rests on an analogy when it concludes that there must be something (God) that is to the universe what the watchmaker is to the watch ("like effects prove like causes"). Hume's second and most telling criticism is that this is a dubious analogy, for it assumes that the universe as a whole is the effect of some cause in the same way that a house or watch is the effect of a carpenter or watchmaker. The only reason for judging that a house must be caused by a carpenter, or a watch by a watchmaker, is (as was explained in our discussion of Hume in the previous chapter) that the constant conjunction between house and carpenter, watch and watchmaker is given over and over again in experience. That is, on the basis of past and repeated experiences, we are led to believe that this house too must have have been constructed by a carpenter: "When two *species* of objects have always been observed to be conjoined together, I can *infer*, by custom, the existence of one wherever I *see* the existence of the other; and this I call an argument from experience."[6] The universe as a whole, however, is unique and without parallel, and its creation is certainly not something that is given over and over again in

---

[5]David Hume, *Dialogues Concerning Natural Religion*, ed. Henry D. Aiken (New York: Hafner, 1948), pp. 52ff.
[6]*Ibid.*, p. 23.

experience. There is, therefore, nothing within our experience that can possibly serve as an analogue to the creation of the world, and there is nothing within our experience analogous to a creator. "An intelligent being of such vast powers and capacity as is necessary to produce the universe . . . exceeds all analogy and even comprehension."[7] It might be noticed that this comes very close to the charge (examined in Chapter 10) that claims about God, creation, and the like are, in fact, meaningless.

Third, even if the world as a whole *were* analogous to something in our experience, Hume observes that it would not be most strikingly analogous to human contrivances or machines. For example, the world resembles more an organism than an artifact; it is more like an animal or vegetable than a watch or a loom. And because like effects have like causes, it would appear most reasonable to seek the cause or origin of the world in something analogous to generation and vegetation. On the most likely analogy, then, we should rather say that the world came from something like a seed or an egg than from a watchmaker. It may be answered, of course, that the mechanism of generation itself points to an original and creative reason. But Hume, who admits only experience and observation as our guides, responds in turn that the presence of reason in the world points rather to the primacy of generation, for "reason, in innumerable instances, is observed to arise from the principle of generation, and never to arise from any other principle."[8]

Finally, Hume argues that such reasoning can at best lead only to a disappointing and unsatisfying concept of the divine. If, *per impossibile*, the Teleological Argument were to convince us that nature is the product of an intelligent being, there is little in nature that reflects the infinity, unity, and perfection of God. If significant at all, the analogy requires only a cause that is *adequate* to the effect. God, or the intelligent creator of the cosmos, may be many rather than one, imperfect rather than perfect, limited in power rather than omnipotent, and still be an adequate or sufficient cause of the world. Perhaps a committee of dim-witted gods, without even a chairman, performing experiments in cosmology to amuse them-

---

[7] *Ibid.*, p. 40.
[8] *Ibid.*, p. 51.

selves, botched who knows how many worlds before settling on this one—which, come to think of it, they may have botched also. Is there anything in this alternative analogy that is incompatible with our experience?[9] And, if a further note may be added, how much less able are we, through such reasoning, to ascend to a knowledge, say, of the holy and benevolent God of Christianity, the Father of Jesus Christ, the author of salvation?

All of this rests, of course, on an unrelenting and exclusive empiricism—a refusal to admit into the arena of legitimate ideas anything not entering through the narrow gate of the five senses. Applying this principle to God, Hume concludes:

> Our ideas reach no farther than our experience. We have no experience of divine attributes and operations. I need not conclude my syllogism. You can draw the inference yourself.[10]

Kant: The Limits of Reason

Neither does the Teleological Argument escape the devastating critique of Immanuel Kant. It is almost paradoxical, though, that before destroying the argument (which he calls the "physico-theological" argument), he eulogizes it:

> This world presents to us so immeasurable a stage of variety, order, purposiveness, and beauty, as displayed alike in its infinite extent and in the unlimited divisibility of its parts, that even with such knowledge as our weak understanding can acquire of it, we are brought face to face with so many marvels immeasurably great, that all speech loses its force, all numbers their power to measure, our thoughts themselves all definiteness, and

---

[9]*Ibid.*, Part V. In fairness to Hume, it should be added that though the these criticisms are, in the *Dialogues*, put into the mouth of Philo, to what extent Philo represents Hume is not always clear. Further, Philo, though a skeptic with respect to the traditional arguments, is not an atheist. At the beginning of Part II, he announces that his quarrel is not with the being of God but with the anthropomorphic character of God to which the Teleological Argument leads: "He is infinitely superior to our limited view and comprehension, and is more the object of worship in the temple than of disputations in the schools."

[10]*Ibid.*, pp. 16f.

that our judgment of the whole resolves itself into an amazement which is speechless, and only the more eloquent on that account. . . . This knowledge . . . so strengthens the belief in a supreme Author [of nature] that the belief acquires the force of an irresistible conviction.[11]

Thus, Kant, praises the argument to which he is about to lay waste.

For Kant, two main difficulties are involved in the Teleological Argument. First—and this exactly parallels one of Kant's critiques of the Cosmological Argument—the theoretical concepts and categories with which the mind confronts the world are entirely inappropriate and inadequate to establish a supreme being, a supreme architect, or a supreme anything. Kant believed that the concept of causality is an *a priori* category of the mind, a way in which reality is experienced (recalling our discussion of Kant in the last chapter, one has only to speculate on what experience would be without the relating and unifying contribution of cause-and-effect relations to see that it would not be what is called "experience" at all), and that the concept of causality has therefore no application beyond the domain of possible experience. Now God is obviously not an object of possible experience, he is not a spatio-temporal reality, and thus by his very conception he absolutely transcends the causal relation as Kant conceives it. What efficacy can there possibly be, then, in talking about God (or God's relation to the world) in terms of causality? But the Teleological Argument, no less than the Cosmological Argument, is a *causal* argument; it moves from the observation of the world's order to the *cause* of that order. It follows that the Teleological Argument (at least for Kant) requires an illegitimate extension of the mind's theoretical concepts.[12]

Second, and apart from the preceding criticism, the Teleological Argument in itself would still be powerless to demonstrate the reality of a supreme being. At best, the argument demonstrates the necessity of an architect of the cosmos, a being who, for all we know, merely imposes order on an already existing material. But this is something quite different from an all-sufficient primordial

---

[11]Immanuel Kant, *Critique of Pure Reason*, tr. Norman Kemp Smith (London: Macmillan, 1929), pp. 519f. (translator's bracketing). Kant further honored the Teleological Argument as "the oldest, the clearest, and the most accordant with the common reason of mankind" (p. 520).

[12]*Ibid.*, pp. 518f.

being. It is logically conceivable that though the universe depends for its order upon a higher and more powerful being, this being, in turn, depends for its existence upon a still higher and more powerful being. As Hume has already said, there is clearly a difference between a being who is capable of creating the world and a being who is *omnipotent*. For its full force the Teleological Argument rests, therefore, upon the Cosmological Argument, which does lead to the concept of the necessary and supreme being. But we have already seen that, according to Kant, the Cosmological Argument, in turn, presupposes the truth of the Ontological Argument, and that the Ontological Argument is unsound.[13]

By now it should be apparent that David Hume and Immanuel Kant have played central roles in the history of philosophical theology, and, as it would seem up to this point, decidedly critical and unsympathetic roles. We have seen that in his *Dialogues Concerning Natural Religion* Hume attacks the traditional theistic arguments, and in his famous essay "On Miracles," in the *Enquiry Concerning Human Understanding*, he dealt a blow against belief in the miraculous which is still felt today. Even so, it can be detected that Hume speaks cautiously at a time when the Calvinistic Church of Scotland levied heavy penalties even for an abuse of the Sabbath. His bitterest polemic was the posthumously published *Natural History of Religion* in which he attacks, among other things, the opinion that the "higher religions" such as Judaism, Christianity, and Mohammedanism have produced great benefits for society. On this point Hume judges, to the contrary, that the narrowness, bloodiness, and intolerance of these religions lead rather to the conclusion that they are "sick men's dreams."[14]

---

[10]*Ibid.*, pp. 520ff.

[14]David Hume, *The Natural History of Religion*, ed. H. E. Root (Stanford, Calif.: Stanford University Press, 1956), p. 75. This reminds one of Bertrand Russel's quip: "I regard [religion] as a disease born of fear and as a source of untold misery to the human race. I cannot, however, deny that it has made some contributions to civilization. It helped in early days to fix the calendar, and it caused Egyptian priests to chronicle eclipses with such care that in time they became able to predict them. These two services I am prepared to acknowledge, but I do not know of any others." (*Why I Am Not a Christian, and Other Essays*, ed. Paul Edwards [New York: Simon & Schuster, 1957], p. 24).

With Kant it is very different. Born of pietist parents, Kant was throughout his life sympathetic to religion, though he sought to translate the Biblical faith of his upbringing into rational and philosophically respectable terms. As Kant saw it, his own demarcation of reason made possible a more religiously adequate approach to God: "I have . . . found it necessary to deny *knowledge* [*Erkenntnis*], in order to make room for *faith* [*Glaube*]."[15] This more positive side of his philosophical theology is reflected most notably in his *Religion Within the Bounds of Reason Alone* and the *Critique of Practical Reason*. In the latter work, Kant himself presents a new argument for the existence of God (which we will consider in the next chapter), replacing the ones he destroyed, providing a practical knowledge of God (*Glaube*) in place of theoretical knowledge (*Erkenntnis*).

Scientific Restatements

The traditional Teleological Argument began with the evidence of special design, and from the beauty and adaptability of nature it postulated a special creation. This argument possessed some force as long as one believed that organisms originated in their present forms. In 1859, however, Charles Darwin published *The Origin of Species*, which resulted in the abandonment of this commonsense conviction and, along with it, the whole idea of supernatural creation. It was now possible to account for organic structures in a purely natural way. In place of a special creation by an almighty watchmaker, Darwin, with his principles of "natural selection" and the "survival of the fittest," substituted long sequences of mechanical and proximate causes. What was once thought to be the most obvious example of God's handiwork turned out to be the product of nature alone. And the most forceful evidence for the Teleological Argument turned out to be none.

At least, so it appeared to many. For others, evolution was not at all incompatible with theism, and Darwin himself concluded *The Origin of Species* with a sort of doxology:

---

[15]Kant, *Critique of Pure Reason*, p. 29.

There is grandeur in this view of life, with its several powers, having been originally breathed by the Creator into a few forms or into one; and that, whilst this planet has gone cycling on according to the fixed law of gravity, from so simple a beginning endless forms most beautiful and most wonderful have been, and are being evolved.[16]

Of the many expressions of theistic evolution, one of the most influential was that of F. R. Tennant (1866–1957), a trained chemist, biologist, and physicist. Tennant, who developed his position in full consciousness of the critical contributions of Hume, Kant, and others, believed that though complete proof of God's existence is unattainable, it is possible, proceeding inductively, to amass facts and generalizations that taken collectively may provide a basis for "reasonable belief." God is, for Tennant, a kind of scientific hypothesis, the most rational explanation for a network of empirical facts. (This reminds us of John Stuart Mill, who referred to the Design Argument as "an argument of a really scientific character, which does not shrink from scientific test, but claims to be judged by the established canons of Induction."[17])

In his important work *Philosophical Theology*, Tennant suggested a wider conception of teleology—teleology "on a grander scale"— that is not only compatible with organic evolution but is in fact prompted by it: "The discovery of organic evolution has caused the teleologist to shift his ground from special design in the products to directivity in the process, and plan in the primary collocations."[18] Though evolution may force us to abandon the Paleyan brand of teleology, a broader, richer teleology replaces it, a teleology in which the progressive and purposive evolution of organisms is itself powerful evidence.

---

[16]Charles Darwin, *The Origin of Species*, 6th ed. (New York: Appleton-Century-Crofts, reprint 1923), II, pp. 305f. The explicit reference to the "the Creator" was added subsequently to the first edition in an attempt, no doubt, to placate hostile critics. Note also from his *Life and Letters*: "I cannot think that the world as we see it is the result of chance; and yet I cannot look at each separate thing as the result of design. . . . I am, and shall ever remain, in a hopeless muddle." (*Life and Letters*, ed. Francis Darwin [London: Murray, 1888], II, pp. 353f.)

[17]John Stuart Mill, "Theism," in *Three Essays on Religion*, 3rd ed. (New York: Longmans, Green & Co., reprint 1923), p. 167.

[18]F. R. Tennant, *Philosophical Theology* (Cambridge, England: Cambridge University Press, 1928–30), II, p. 85.

Tennant's more comprehensive teleology focuses not upon particular evidences of design (such as the purposive adaptation of the parts of animals to one another and of the animals to their environments), but rather upon the apparent intelligibility and meaningfulness of nature as a whole:

> The forcibleness of Nature's suggestion that she is the outcome of intelligent design lies not in particular cases of adaptedness in the world, nor even in the multiplicity of them. . . . The forcibleness of the world's appeal consists rather in the conspiration of innumerable causes to produce, by their united and reciprocal action, and to maintain, a general order of Nature.[19]

This universal conspiration manifests itself in six main "fields of fact." In Tennant's words, these are (1) the knowability or intelligibility of the world (or the adaptation of thought to things); (2) the internal adaptedness of organic beings; (3) the fitness of the inorganic to minister to life; (4) the aesthetic value of Nature; (5) the world's instrumentality in the realization of moral ends; and (6) the progressiveness in the evolutionary process culminating in the emergence of man, with his rational and moral status.[20] Though Tennant considers each of these at length, our comments must necessarily be limited.

Consider, for example, the aesthetic value of nature. The beauty and sublimity of nature may certainly fail in themselves as conclusive evidence that the universe is teleological. Strictly speaking, the beauty of nature need not be attributed to artistic production; much that is capable of evoking aesthetic sentiment is not always the result of conscious design. Still, the aesthetic response that nature elicits at every turn is such as to suggest what Tennant called an "alogical probability" that the aesthetic display of nature is grounded in mind. (The concept of alogical probability is a recurring and important one in Tennant's work. The phrase suggests the way in which the mind is often overwhelmed by the weight of evidence, but of a kind that cannot be calculated in terms of statistical or logical probabilities. According to Tennant, many of the fundamental principles upon which we think and act, including the prin-

---

[19]*Ibid.*, p. 79.
[20]*Ibid.*, p. 81.

ciple of scientific induction itself, are grasped and affirmed in just this alogical way.) Thus, the undeniable aesthetic aspect of nature becomes at least a "link in the chain of evidence" presented by the wider teleology.[21]

But nature is more than aesthetic; it is "a theatre for a moral life." The whole of the natural process has come to fruition in man, the moral being:

In the fullness of time Nature found self-utterance in a son possessed of the intelligent and moral status. . . . The world-process is a *praeparatio anthropologica*, whether designedly or not, and man is the culmination, up to the present stage of the knowable history of Nature, of a gradual ascent.[22]

Surely, any account of nature, if it is to be scientifically impartial and philosophically significant, will have to be written in light of the spiritual and moral character of humanity, its ultimate product. Tennant is careful, however, not to commit himself to a naturalistic interpretation of moral value. He emphasizes, in Kantian fashion, that there is an aspect of the human being that belongs properly to the "noumenal" realm and that can never be given a purely naturalistic explanation. This aspect includes the soul and moral constitution. Having observed this important "proviso," as he calls it, we may go on to speak of the human as it is represented in the "phenomenal" realm of nature:

. . . we can affirm that man's body, with all its conditioning of his mentality, his sociality, knowledge and morality, is "of a piece" with Nature; and that, *insofar as he is a phenomenal being*, man is organic to Nature, or a product of the world.[23]

The aesthetic and the moral are but two aspects of nature. There are many others, and they all conspire for the production of unity and intelligibility. Though no one of them, nor all of them together, constitute incontrovertible evidence of a Divine Mind, considered collectively they do support, says Tennant, a reasonable belief.

---

[21] *Ibid.*, pp. 88ff.
[22] *Ibid.*, p. 101.
[23] *Ibid.* (my italics).

In this way, the evolutionary hypothesis undermined the old special teleology, while at the same time providing the foundation for a new one. This wider and more compelling teleological interpretation of nature turns our attention from products to processes; it asks us not to look here or there for a particular evidence of design in nature, but rather to consider the coherence and consummate effect of her well-nigh infinite and diverse strands. As Tennant puts it:

Theism no longer plants its God in the gaps between the explanatory achievements of natural science, which are apt to get scientifically closed up. . . . It is rather when these several fields of fact are no longer considered one by one, but as parts of a whole or terms of a continuous series, and when for their dovetailing and interconnectedness a sufficient ground is sought, such as mechanical and proximate causation no longer seems to supply, that divine design is forcibly suggested.[24]

Tennant believes that we are forced, finally, to explain nature in terms of either wisdom or undesigned coincidence. If we opt for the latter, we are yet confronted with nature's overwhelming complexity and wondrous coherence, and we have provided "not explanation but statement of what calls for explanation."[25]

It remains for Tennant to distinguish his position from the position of those who claim to explain the same unfolding of nature in terms of some "unconscious" will or purpose. Here he has in mind primarily the French thinker Henri Bergson, who taught, in his *Creative Evolution*, that all nature is charged with an *élan vital*, or "life force," carrying it forward into ever higher states of organization. Tennant holds that, aside from the fact that the notion of "unconscious purpose" is a contradiction in terms, it is irreconcilable with the self-corrective course of nature: The simple fact is, as he expresses it in a lively metaphor, that nature seems to keep its head, though the unconscious-purpose theorists claim that it is brainless. Furthermore, nature does not appear to be equally propelled in all of it several kingdoms by blind purpose, contrary to what one would expect on the basis of such a theory. In fact, natural selection moves the species forward only by means of misadapta-

---

[24] *Ibid.*, p. 104.
[25] *Ibid.*, p. 109.

tions and dead ends. In order to explain the facts, what is required is not a force but a Mind. As Tennant puts it rather aphoristically, "If Nature evinces wisdom, the wisdom is Another's."[26]

If any theistic argument could prove persuasive in our empirically minded age, it would undoubtedly be Tennant's or one like it. Say, Swinburne's.

Richard Swinburne, of Oxford University, who speaks of the "explanatory power" and "intrinsic probability" of theism, provides a still more recent version of the Teleological Argument. He distinguishes between regularities of co-presence (think of books on a shelf arranged alphabetically) and regularities of succession (a ball that falls each time it is thrown into the air). He thinks that even Paley's argument, based on the former, or spatial, order has been short-changed and may be given a suitable reconstruction, but it is a Teleological Argument based on the regularities of succession, or temporal order, that he finds most impressive:

The temporal order of the universe has, to the man who bothers to give it a moment's thought, an overwhelmingly striking fact about it. Regularities of succession are all-pervasive. . . . The orderliness of the universe to which I draw attention here is its conformity to formula, to simple, formulable, scientific laws. . . . The universe might so naturally have been chaotic, but it is not—it is very orderly.[27]

Most striking about this temporal order, says Swinburne, is what was suggested by the atomic theory of chemistry and confirmed by the discovery of fundamental particles: Nature throughout its vastness is composed ultimately of a few limited kinds of fundamental particles (electrons, protons, positrons, etc.), each with its peculiar and unvarying properties (charge, spin, etc.). This uniformity and simplicity at the most fundamental level, or physical horizon, are the ultimate basis of the indisputable temporal order in all of nature, the fact that things happen according to natural laws. And *this* science *cannot* account for. This fundamental and universal order is, says, Swinburne, "too big" for a scientific explanation. Even though science may explain particular phenomena by means

[26]*Ibid.*

[27]Richard Swinburne, *The Existence of God* (Oxford, England: Clarendon Press, 1979), p. 136.

of prior phenomena, or specific laws by means of more general laws, it "cannot, from the very nature of science, explain the highest-level laws of all. They are that by which it explains all other phenomena."[28] . Thus the ultimate orderliness of nature (rooted in fundamental particles)

is where all explanation stops, or we must postulate an agent of great power and knowledge who brings about through his continuous action that bodies have the same very general powers and liabilities . . . the simplest such agent to postulate is one of infinite power, knowledge, and freedom, i.e. God.[29]

Of course, one could simply react to all this in a way reminiscient of Bertrand Russell's reaction to the existence of world: "Design in the universe? Yes, it's overwhelming, marvelous, and so on. But it's *just there*, and that's all there is to it." However, it might fairly be responded: It would never occur to us to say "it's just there" when confronted with a more restricted instance of design; how does it occur to one to say "it's just there" when confronted with design on the grandest scale possible? How is it that the *larger* display of design requires *less* explanation?

The Central Problem

Clearly, the Cosmological and Teleological arguments are closely related. They begin with the same reality, they employ many of the same concepts, and they proceed in much the same manner. For this reason, many of the critical issues have already been considered in the previous chapter. With respect to the most obvious objections to the Teleological Argument alone, these too have now been aptly represented in our discussion of Hume and Kant.

It may be appropriate, however, to single out for emphasis the problem that may in fact lie at the bottom of every version of the Teleological Argument, including that of Thomas, Paley, Tennant,

---

[28]*Ibid.*, p. 139.
[29]*Ibid.*, pp. 140f.

and Swinburne: the subjective interpretation of order. We have already observed that both Hume and Kant interpreted (though in very different ways) the teleologist's idea of order or purpose as being a product of the mind itself. Hume and Kant aside, it takes no great imagination to appreciate that the mind does often impose order where there is none, at least none in the sense of deliberate design, and this happens in two ways. Sometimes an otherwise haphazard arrangement assumes an orderly shape, at least in our minds, befitting what our present need or desire calls for. At other times, we uncritically assume that certain features of nature exist for the purpose of producing certain ends, failing to observe that those ends follow rather from the particular character of nature. Thus, someone crossing a stream may optimistically regard the stones so conveniently placed as having been deliberately placed, or view a Rorschach ink blot as fraught with significant configurations, or regard it as a mark of divine prudence that God appropriately situated the nose and ears so as to enable us to hang eyeglasses on them!

Understandably, the question is often raised of whether teleologists have been, on a large scale, guilty of maybe not so flagrant but equally misplaced judgments. It is against this general tendency that Hume poses the following question and warning:

What peculiar privilege has this little agitation of the brain which we call *thought*, that we must thus make it the model of the whole universe? Our partiality in our favour does indeed present it on all occasions, but sound philosophy ought carefully to guard against so natural an illusion.[30]

To this may be added the charge (anticipated earlier) that the teleologist who waxes rhapsodic over nature's abundant order may be simply uttering a truism or tautology. If order involves (as it appears it must) pattern, relation, sequence, and the like, what in the natural world *isn't* possessed of order? This question applies especially to the kind of teleologist who is fond of talking about the just-right distance of the Earth from the sun or about the aesthetics of the heavenly system.

---

[30]Hume, *Dialogues Concerning Natural Religion*, p. 22.

Swinburne, on the other hand, suggests some moves that may be made on behalf of the claim that the order perceived in the universe is, in fact, an objective one. For example, we are justified in believing that the orderliness we perceive in the universe today will be there tomorrow—that the laws of nature will *continue* to hold, and that stones will fall, desks will hold together, and so on. But, of course, we can have no such confidence about the future of nature if this perceived order is a human invention imposed on it. If you really believe that nature has been, is now, and *will be* governed by natural *laws*, then clearly you're talking about something you don't invent but *discover*. "For man cannot make nature conform subsequently to an order which he has invented."[31]

Likewise, Swinburne responds to the "Anthropic Principle" (though he does not label it such). The Anthropic Principle (so called from the Greek ἄνθρωπος, "man"), in its most interesting form, asserts that it is inevitable and unsurprising that people perceive an ordered universe, since if the universe were otherwise, they would not be here to perceive it, inasmuch as its order has made their own presence possible. To say it another way: It is not possible that we could perceive an unordered universe, because an ordered universe is required for our very existence. But, with Swinburne, one may wonder why such a principle has ever been deemed relevant for the Teleological Argument. Doesn't it confuse the necessity (if that's what it is) of our perceiving order in the universe with the objective order itself? And, whether our perception of order is inevitable or not, the order itself is nonetheless mind-boggling—is it not?

Be that as it may, the further burden of the teleologist is to show how his or her teleological view implies *purpose*, which, in turn, involves (1) consideration of a goal and (2) the intention of actualizing it. Presumably this would be shown either in Paleyan fashion, by piling up as many specific instances as the skeptic requires (it will be recalled that even though Paley called his a "cumulative argument," he himself required only the eye), or, with Tennant, by conducting broad surveys of whole spheres of continuities and convergences in nature. Even so, such evidence is in the end wholly empirical and finite, and whether teleologists such as we

---

[31]Swinburne, *The Existence of God*, p. 137.

have considered are able to succeed depends inevitably on an interpretation of the evidence they present.

Argument or Point of View?

It must not be taken lightly that reflective people of all ages have found in teleology cogent grounds for belief in God. To the list of thinkers already mentioned many others might be added. The "beautiful system" revealed by astronomy led Newton, in his *Principles of Nature* (1687), to reject blind necessity in favor of divine will. More recently, the English physicist Sir James Jeans, in *The Mysterious Universe* (1930), concluded from the new influx of scientific knowledge that the universe must have been constructed by a mathematician. Lecomte du Nuöy reasons in his well-known *Human Destiny* (1947) to the presence of divine intelligence from the staggering improbability of chance organization of the atoms of even a single protein molecule. The late Catholic theologian-biologist Teilhard de Chardin, in *The Phenomenon of Man* (1955), was compelled to posit a divine "Omega point" as the end and explanation of nature's unfolding. The catalogue of those who argue in these ways for the existence of God could be extended seemingly without end.

But a similar catalogue could be constructed on the other side. Hume, for example, expresses a quite different sentiment:

The whole presents nothing but the idea of a blind nature, impregnated by a great vivifying principle, and pouring forth from her lap, without discernment or parental care, her maimed and abortive children![32]

Another writes,

If we are to be intellectually honest, we must frankly admit that we can detect no purpose or meaning in the vast distances and wild eruptions of the universe—and certainly no purpose centered on the welfare of man.[33]

---

[32]Hume, *Dialogues Concerning Natural Religion*, p. 79.
[33]H. J. Paton, *The Modern Predicament* (London: George Allen & Unwin, 1955), p. 218.

So, the question becomes this: If the universe thus abounds with an overwhelming display of order and purpose, why do so many fail to see it or interpret it aright? The answer is probably very simple and has little to do with scientific hypotheses, or analyses of "purpose," or issues in probability theory. At the beginning of this chapter, St. Thomas told us:

We see that things which lack knowledge, such as natural bodies act for an end, and this is evident from their acting always, or nearly always, in the same way, so as to obtain the best result.

It has been said that anyone who sees that much is no doubt prepared to see God also. That is, the Teleological Argument, like many important arguments, begins with a feeling about things rather than ending with one.

5

The Moral Argument

Many remain unswayed by the icy logic of the Ontological Argument, as well as by the more tangible evidence adduced by the Cosmological and Teleological arguments. There is, however, another argument for God's existence. This argument, turning our attention from the world of sense experience to the world of moral experience, seizes moral consciousness as its evidence for God, and hence it is called the "Moral Argument."

Kant and the Moral Law

As was mentioned earlier, even though Immanuel Kant rejected the Ontological, Cosmological, and Teleological arguments, thereby undermining traditional philosophical knowledge of God, he himself proposed a new and very different one. And now there begins to emerge the positive side of Kant's contribution.

Kant's argument for the existence of God begins with a kind of fundamental sense or apprehension of moral meaningfulness. If you do not share the conviction that there is moral rhyme or reason to the world and human experience, then this argument is, for you, doomed to failure from the very start. Kant, however, believed that most of us find ourselves inescapably confronted with moral experience. There is no better expression of this confrontation than Kant's own lines, which occur near the conclusion of his *Critique of Practical Reason*:

89

> Two things fill the mind with ever new and increasing admiration and awe, the oftener and the more steadily we reflect on them: the starry heavens above me and the moral law within me.[1]

At the very least, this suggests that for Kant the reality of moral experience can no more be doubted than the reality of sensible experience. In the same way that I find myself in a sensible world, conditioned by objects outside me and to which I can only respond passively, so do I find myself in a moral world, conditioned by an objective moral law existing independently of my own opinions or inclinations. If we ask someone to survey the starry heavens above and he or she responds, "What starry heavens?", we judge that person to be blind, irrational, or otherwise lacking in a certain faculty present in normal people. Similarly, we would certainly entertain serious doubts about someone who appears utterly oblivious to moral duty and responsibility. Like the starry heavens above, moral law is *just there*; it is given.

It is extremely important to realize that when we speak here of the givenness of moral law, we are not talking about any *particular* moral law such as "Thou shalt *x*" or "Thou shalt not *y*." There is an important difference between moral consciousness and moral code.

Some people do think that a more or less specific moral code can be detected in virtually all societies and in every period of human history. The cultural relativists and anthropologists have, in fact, probably exaggerated the moral diversity among societies, and C. S. Lewis, the late Oxford scholar and Christian writer, invites us to consider rather the essential unity of the moral doctrines of different civilizations and cultures:

> If anyone will take the trouble to compare the moral teaching of, say, the ancient Egyptians, Babylonians, Hindus, Chinese, Greeks and Romans, what will really strike him will be how very like they are to each other and to our own. . . . Men have differed as regards what people you ought to be unselfish to—whether it was only your own family, or your fellow countrymen, or everyone. But they have always agreed that you ought not to put yourself first. Selfishness has never been admired. Men have differed as to

---

[1]Immanuel Kant, *Critique of Practical Reason*, tr. Lewis White Beck (New York: Macmillan, 1956), p. 166.

whether you should have one wife or four. But they have always agreed that you must not simply have any woman you liked.[2]

Furthermore, some believe that the Bible, too, supports the belief in a universally apprehended moral order, as in St. Paul's statement (something of a counterpart to his earlier statement about the invisible God who is evidenced in nature) that

when Gentiles, who do not possess the [Mosaic] Law know instinctively what the law requires, these, though not having the law, are a law to themselves. They show that what the law requires is written on their hearts, to which their own conscience also bears witness. . . . (Rom. 2:14–15).

Not surprisingly, there is a version of the Moral Argument based on just the sorts of empirical observations that Lewis indicates, and he himself speaks of "a Somebody or Something behind the Moral Law."[3]

Though the question whether there are universally recognized moral laws (in the plural) may be an interesting one, and it certainly is a debated one, it has nothing whatever to do with Kant's *a priori* concept of moral law (in the singular), and it has nothing to do with his formulation of the Moral Argument. (The difference between moral laws and moral law is important both here and in the following discussion. By moral law, in the singular, I mean morality as it is in itself; by moral laws, in the plural, I mean morality as it is variously and imperfectly interpreted, codified, expressed, and perhaps legislated, in the form of prohibitions and the like.) It is essential to note that Kant does not claim that there is a universal sense as to *what* is right, though he does claim that there is a universal sense that *something* is right. Duties may vary, but duty itself does not. And it is this feeling of "ought," this feeling of being morally conditioned, this sense of duty that points to an objective moral order and moral law. If there were no objective basis for

---

[2]C. S. Lewis, *Mere Christianity*, rev. ed. (New York: Macmillan, 1952), p. 5.

[3]*Ibid.*, p. 23. Concerning the relation of the moral law to Christianity, Lewis says: "It is after you have realized that there is a real Moral Law, and a Power behind the law, and that you have broken that law and put yourself wrong with that Power—it is after all this, and not a moment sooner, that Christianity begins to talk" (p. 24).

morality, then all moral experience and moral judgments would be ultimately unfounded and unintelligible.

What has all this to do with God? Kant answers that the basis for moral law and the source of moral consciousness can be nothing other than a supreme being of intelligence. His reasoning is this: Moral law or duty requires for its fulfillment nothing less than the *summum bonum*, the highest good, which is perfect happiness. The attainment of the highest good must therefore be possible if the idea of moral duty is not to be completely vacuous. That is, there must be some proportion or agreement between our acting in accordance with moral duty and our achievement of the highest good. And this requires God as a kind of guarantor that the moral agent will receive the just consequence of his act. Kant concludes that

it [is] our duty to promote the highest good; and it is not merely our privilege but a necessity connected with duty as a requisite to presuppose the possibility of this highest good. This presupposition is made only under the condition of the existence of God, and this condition inseparably connects this supposition with duty. Therefore, it is morally necessary to assume the existence of God.[4]

Kant thus builds his argument for the existence of God on the very evidence that is so often used to disprove God's existence, namely, the observed disparity between moral worthiness and the possession of happiness. If the universe is a truly moral place, then God must exist as an omnipotent being capable of ensuring a just relation (if not in this world, then in the next) between moral worthiness and the attainment of its reward.

For Kant, then, we can have absolutely no knowledge of God through "theoretical reason," though we can ascend to a knowledge of God (and, as we shall see in Chapter 9, to a knowledge of immortality and freedom as well) through "practical reason." Theoretical reason begins and ends with sense experience, whereas practical reason begins with the moral law within, or moral consciousness, through which it is enabled to penetrate the reality (the noumenal world) that lies behind appearance (the phenome-

---

[4]Kant, *Critique of Practical Reason*, p. 130.

nal world). Kant's Moral Argument is not, in fact, a proof in the sense that the other traditional arguments are. In the Moral Argument, the existence of God is not, strictly, deduced from premises or in any way inferred from empirical evidence. He is seen, rather, to be *practically* required in the sense that he must exist as a "postulate" or necessary condition of an objectively valid morality. Kant makes clear what such knowledge isn't and what it is: "By a postulate of pure practical reason, I understand a theoretical proposition which is not as such demonstrable, but which is an inseparable corollary of an *a priori* unconditionally valid practical law."[5]

Kant's Moral Argument for God has, by and large, hardly proven persuasive, though many thinkers after him have formulated other versions. One of the most influential was Hastings Rashdall (1858–1924), an English theologian and idealist philosopher. In the second volume of his *The Theory of Good and Evil*, Rashdall conceded that if God does not exist, it does not follow necessarily that there can be no morality at all. The materialist, for example, can devise a purely naturalistic and relative morality by which to order the practical life. But if God does not exist, it does follow that there can be no such thing as *objective* morality:

The belief in God, though not . . . a postulate of there being any such thing as Morality at all, is the logical presupposition of an "objective" or absolute Morality. A moral ideal can exist nowhere and nohow but in a mind; an absolute moral ideal can exist only in a Mind from which all Reality is derived. Our moral ideal can only claim objective validity in so far as it can rationally be regarded as the revelation of a moral ideal eternally existing in the mind of God.[6]

If one affirms the reality of moral ideals, it might be asked, not unfairly, where they exist. Obviously, they do not exist in tables or in chairs or other such brute things. It is the nature of an ideal to subsist in a mind. But whose mind? Surely not in any human, finite mind, for these are constantly changing. We must therefore believe

---

[5]*Ibid.*, p. 127
[6]Hastings Rashdall, *The Theory of Good and Evil* (Oxford, England: Clarendon Press, 1907), II, p. 212.

in an eternal and unchanging Mind as the only adequate *locus* of eternal and unchanging ideals.

> If there is an absolute morality, then there must exist an Absolute Mind as its source.

> There is absolute morality.

> ---

> Therefore, there must exist an Absolute Mind.

It will be observed that Rashdall uses the words "objective" and "absolute" interchangeably. But inasmuch as these words are often the source of much confusion, a distinction may be in order. Whereas an *objective* moral principle derives its validity and authority outside of and independently of human beings (for example, from God), an *absolute* moral principle is often regarded as claiming in addition to be universally binding on everyone in all circumstances. In the matter of going to war, for example, an objectivist would insist that there is involved here a genuine moral truth and an objective good to be realized through going or not going, and presumably he or she would attempt to consider all facets of the situation in order to arrive, as best as possible, at a moral decision. The absolutist, on the other hand, may insist that war is wrong in any way, shape, or form, and that no possible circumstances can ever justify participation in it. Clearly, moral absolutism implies moral objectivism, though the converse does not hold; and both are incompatible with subjectivism or relativism, the doctrine that there is no moral value outside of individual or collective opinion. What is important for our present discussion is that it would appear that a Moral Argument such as Kant's or Rashdall's (in spite of Rashdall's terminology) requires only belief in moral objectivism.

In any event, all Moral Arguments teach that ideals and duties are unintelligible until viewed in light of their divine origin, understood in some sense or other. Like the Teleological Argument, the Moral Argument begins with a confrontation with order, though now understood, of course, as an order or teleology of moral experience rather than of sense experience, which it judges as inexplicable apart from God. As yet another proponent expresses it, "Either our moral values tell us something about the nature and purpose of reality . . .

or they are subjective and therefore meaningless."[7] That they are meaningless is, for many of us, too much to accept—you might as easily deny the starry heavens above!

(Before moving on, it may be useful to note that there are, by a happy coincidence, two different forms of each of the theistic arguments we have considered. In the case of the Ontological Argument, it will be recalled that Malcolm and others found two different arguments in St. Anselm, one construing existence as a divine attribute and the other construing necessary existence as a divine attribute. In our discussion of the Cosmological Argument, we distinguished between the popular version that leads to a first cause in the order of time and the more classical version that involves a first cause in the order of being. The Teleological Argument has been developed both on the grounds of narrow and direct teleology, as well as in terms of a broader and evolutionary teleology. And now we have seen that there are also two different Moral Arguments, one taking evidence from the empirical fact of universal moral convictions and the other beginning with the *a priori* givenness of the general moral consciousness.)

The Rejection of Objective Morality

Many do, nevertheless, reject the idea of a universal moral consciousness and the belief in an objective moral order. And inasmuch as the Moral Argument rises or falls with just this idea—we have seen that it is a necessary premise—we must consider it a bit further.

One of the most popular objections to the belief in objective moral values is that we achieve moral consciousness through learning or conditioning, and far from its being universally and objectively binding, it is therefore purely subjective and relative. At least two responses may be made to this charge. First, that something is learned is hardly evidence against its objective truth and validity. We learn that 2 plus 2 equals 4 and that murder is bad, and we learn all kinds of things that we believe to be nonetheless true. Is there, in

---

[7]D. M. Baillie, *Faith in God and Its Christian Consummation* (Edinburgh: T. & T. Clark, 1927), p. 173.

fact, anything that we claim to know that we have not learned in one way or another? And though people may disagree on their interpretation of "good," it does not follow from this that there *is* no objective good. We may just as easily conclude from the fact that people often disagree in their interpretation of the world that there is no world, or from the fact that some people can't see that murder is wrong that perhaps it isn't.

Second, this objection is usually directed to specific moral codes like "Thou shalt not commit adultery." Admittedly, these codes or laws (in the plural) are usually learned or acquired through conditioning and are therefore in many instances relative to a given culture—no one cares to deny that. But, as we have already empha- sized, this is not what Kant and others mean by our consciousness of moral law (in the singular). They are referring, rather, to our fun- damental feeling of "ought" or duty. The knowledge of what I ought to do may be something that I learn through culture and upbringing, but the awareness that I ought to do *something* is part of my very humanity. If someone is found to be completely devoid of any such moral consciousness, we may simply judge that that person lacks the faculty of moral sensitivity in the same way that we would judge that someone denying the reality of red obviously lacks a certain sense faculty. We may, in fact, judge that a completely amoral person is, in some sense, not a real person at all.

More important is the rejection of objective value on philo- sophical grounds. Of these arguments we will briefly consider two examples: the reductionistic naturalist and the atheistic existential- ist. Naturalism is the doctrine that nature is the ultimate reality, but there are many different naturalisms, just as there are many interpre- tations of "nature." When it is said, then, that the naturalist believes that the criterion of what is good, along with everything else, is nature, it matters very much just what brand of nature is being entertained. Clearly, some form of ethical naturalism is exemplified by the ancient Greek philosopher Epicurus, who reasoned from the fact that men seek pleasure above all else to the conclusion that pleasure must be the highest good. Similarly, John Stuart Mill (in his *Utilitarianism*) provides a naturalistic justification for the utili- tarian principle that one ought to seek the greatest happiness for the greatest number: There is only one proof that a sound is audible, namely, that people hear it; likewise, the only evidence that some- thing is desirable is that people do desire it; it follows, for Mill, that only one proof that happiness is desirable can be given, namely, that each person does in fact desire happiness.

One extreme version of naturalism takes "nature" to mean physics and chemistry, and reduces statements of value to statements about the empirical world and psychology. This crude reductionism holds that the ultimate basis of value commitments is an individual's own desires or feelings about things. The judgment "Stealing is wrong" simply expresses one's subjective feelings or emotions concerning something in the same way as "Cherry pie is good." This interpretation of moral judgments finds support in Bertrand Russell, who (at least in one place) suggests that our varying opinions on moral questions, just like our varying perceptions of colors, can no doubt be explained by the physicist.[8] The criterion for condemning immoral conduct is, on this view, no more objective than that for condemning color blindness, with the result that morality is simply the way a majority of people feel. Moral claims are just expressions of subjective empirical or psychological states—you might call it the "Hurrah!"/"Boo!" theory of ethics.

Whereas the reductionistic naturalist bases morality somehow or other in empirical or psychological states, others appear to deny any justification whatsoever for moral ideals and choices. One good example of this is the French existentialist Jean-Paul Sartre (1905–1980). Sartre's point of departure is God's demise, especially as eternal law giver and justifier of morality. For Sartre, God is unbelievable, dead, and gone, and gone with him is all possibility of any objective and binding moral principles:

The existentialist . . . thinks it very distressing that God does not exist, because all possibility of finding values in a heaven of ideas disappears along with Him; there can no longer be an *a priori* Good, since there is no infinite and perfect consciousness to think it . . . and as a result man is forlorn, because neither within him nor without does he find anything to cling to. . . . if God does not exist, we find no values or commands to turn to which legitimize our conduct. So, in the bright realm of values, we have no

---

[8]Bertrand Russell (with Frederick Copleston), "The Existence of God: A Debate," reprinted (with deletions) in Ed. L. Miller (ed.), *Believing in God: Statements on Faith and Reason* (Englewood Cliffs, N.J.: Prentice Hall, 1996). For a statement of the similar and influential position known as "emotivism," see Alfred Jules Ayer, *Language, Truth and Logic*, 2nd ed. (London: Gollanz, 1946), Ch. 6.

excuse behind us, nor justification before us. We are alone, with no excuses.[9]

A recurring theme of Dostoevsky's classic *The Brothers Karamazov* is that if there were no God, everything would be possible, at least in the sense of being morally legitimate. For the atheistic Sartre, there is no God and everything is, indeed, possible. In the world of choices and moral commitments, "we are condemned to be free"— free to do what we want and thus free to be what we want.

Sartre is not, however, a complete nihilist, that is, someone who utterly rejects all value and meaning. Sartre simply shifts the *locus* of value from the absent God to human beings. Because we can no longer believe in God or some transcendent world of preestablished essences in terms of which humanity and meaning can be defined, we believe, says Sartre, that "existence *precedes* essence": The individual first exists and then, through choices and commitments, defines his or her own nature. In this "ethics of involvement," choices do matter. What we decide, we decide for humanity; what we do, we make of humanity, for we are all involved in humanity, and each of us is, therefore, responsible for humanity. Like the artist, we on the ethical plane are in a "creative situation," and the finished product, whatever it may be, will have to be judged in terms of the values evolved along the way. (More of this in Chapter 9.)

Rejection of the Rejection

The impression may have been given that the believer in the Moral Argument rests the case with an (unpersuasive?) appeal to some intuitive grasp of objective value. Some defenders of the argument may indeed be happy with such an appeal, and, after all, every argument must begin somewhere. Others, however, feel that the objective nature of moral value can be demonstrated by showing that alternatives such as those just suggested are ultimately impossible.

It may be argued, for example, that any moral judgment, such as "*x* is right" or "*y* is wrong," is ultimately empty unless it is

---

[9]Jean-Paul Sartre, "Existentialism," tr. Bernard Frechtman, in *Existentialism and Human Emotions* (New York: Citadel Press, 1957), pp. 22f.

believed that there is somewhere, somehow, something *in terms of which* the rightness or wrongness of *x* or *y* may be adjudged. We may not always be very articulate as to the nature of the objective source of moral value, and may indeed change our minds from time to time as to what is right or wrong; but each time we make such judgments, not only in reference to ourselves but in reference to others, or otherwise express (in our actions and choices) our moral commitments, we give evidence that we do, in fact, take such judgments as counting for something and as being ultimately and objectively significant. In this way, it may be argued, it is self-contradictory (practically speaking) to make moral judgments and to deny at the same time that there is any objective basis for morality. What is more absurd than someone who spends the day fanatically and passionately crusading for the eradication of certain evils and in the evening delivers cool lectures on the relativity of all ideals!

In *The Abolition of Man*, C. S. Lewis has written as forcefully as anyone on the follies of subjectivism. For Lewis, too, the rejection of objective value renders impossible any meaningful judgment about the most important issues. Adopting from Chinese wisdom the term *Tao*, or "Way," as a designation of the universally recognized though differently represented Absolute Reality and Value, he announces, quite rightly:

An open mind, in questions that are not ultimate, is useful. But an open mind about the ultimate foundations of either Theoretical or of Practical Reason is idiocy. If a man's mind is open on these things, let his mouth at least be shut. He can say nothing to the purpose. Outside the *Tao* there is no ground for criticizing either the *Tao* or anything else.[10]

Gabriel Marcel, the late Catholic existentialist, who disliked being called an existentialist, applies this reasoning specifically to Sartre's concept of freedom as the "baseless basis of value":

Sartre has announced that the third volume of his *Les Chemins de la Liberté* is to be devoted to the praise of the heroes of the Resistance. Now I ask you in the name of what principle, having first denied the existence of values or at least of their objective basis, can he establish any appreciable difference between those utterly misguided but undoubtedly courageous men

---

[10]C. S. Lewis, *The Abolition of Man* (New York: Macmillan, 1947), p. 60.

who joined voluntarily the Anti-Bolshevik Legion, on the one hand, and the heroes of the Resistance movement, on the other? I can see no way of establishing this difference without admitting that causes have their intrinsic value and, consequently, that values are real. . . . he quite often uses the words "good" and "bad," but what can these words possibly mean in the context of his philosophy?[11]

If there is no objective human essence—something outside that defines the individual—then there can be no real justification for any conception of the human being whatever, not even the one that Sartre urges us to actualize through our choices and commitments. The ideal of the Resistance fighter can claim no more legitimacy than that of the anti-Bolshevik.

It should be noted, incidentally, that Sartre himself accepts the Moral Argument in a kind of left-handed way. When he says that God does not exist, and therefore that all possibility of finding objective values disappears, he is conceding that if there were an objective moral order, then God *would* have to exist as its basis. Sartre accepts, then, the inference from an objective morality to its necessary source in absolute being; what he rejects is that any such morality is given to start with.

Still, what of the naturalistic interpretation of value? One of the most telling criticisms of ethical naturalism in general was leveled by G. E. Moore, whose *Principia Ethica* (1903) set in motion a debate that has not yet completely subsided. According to Moore, every attempt to ground morality in the properties and states of nature is guilty of the "naturalistic fallacy." This mistake comes of trying to derive *ought* from *is*, or concluding, as Epicurus and Mill did, that because we do in fact desire something, we ought to desire it. It was Kant himself who first exposed this error (if it is an error) and insisted on a wholly nonempirical origin of moral concepts:

Is it not of the utmost necessity to construct a pure moral philosophy which is completely freed from everything which may be only empirical and thus belong to anthropology? That there must be such a philosophy is self-evident from the common idea of duty and moral laws. . . . the ground

---

[11]Gabriel Marcel, *The Philosophy of Existentialism*, tr. Manya Harari (New York: Citadel Press, 1962), p. 87.

of obligation here must not be sought in the nature of man or in the circumstances in which he is placed, but sought a priori solely in the concepts of pure reason. . . . [12]

Notwithstanding the naturalistic fallacy, the reductionistic (or materialistic) version of ethical naturalism must at least face up to its implications for moral reasoning. Where is the contribution of reason more necessary than in relation to Kant's question, "What must I do?" It is in regard to questions of value and moral decision that we expect the most from critical reflection. But if moral judgments themselves reduce finally to statements of feeling and fact, then they can hardly be judgments *about* feeling and fact, so that here, where it is most needed, no contribution is forth-coming from reason. More specifically, if the statement "*x* is good" amounts to no more than my subjective feelings about *x* at the moment, then these absurd consequences would follow: First, it would be impossible for me ever to be mistaken in my value judgments; second, because my feelings constantly change, my value judgments could never mean the same thing twice; and third, no two people could ever, even in theory, intend the same thing in their value judgments. It would appear patently impossible to reconcile these conclusions with any meaningful concept of morality and ethical discourse. As for the attempt to ground morality in a communal state of mind, do we have to be reminded that in our time a whole nation ran amok and created a society in which the murder of 6 million Jews was considered by many to be morally justified?

It may be objected, understandably, that false alternatives have been posed here, that it is not a matter of either a Kantian-type grounding of morality in a wholly nonempirical or transcendental source *or* a reductionistic interpretation of moral awareness in purely physiological and psychological terms. The naturalist with a broader conception of nature will charge that here neither transcendence language nor physics-and-chemistry language have special priority over other ways of speaking. Human nature is a multifaceted affair, the intersection of differing dimensions of reality, and there are, consequently, differing ways of picturing him, many kinds

---

[12]Immanuel Kant, *Foundations of the Metaphysics of Morals*, tr. Lewis White Beck (New York: Macmillan, 1959), p. 5.

of language in which he may be represented: physical, moral, religious, axiological, aesthetic, and so on. Dostoevsky's literary picture is very different from B. F. Skinner's behavioristic one, and both of these are different from John Milton's or Immanuel Kant's; each, however, portrays something true and important about what it means to be human. There is a form of naturalism, then, that would concur in the rejection of a purely physical or reductionistic theory of human nature and moral response.

Our discussion has given way largely to the question of objective morality, but that is because this is the *crux* of the Moral Argument. Obviously, many (including myself) are convinced that we cannot at any cost give up the idea of objective value, and that this, in turn, provides for the possibility of a Moral Argument for God. It might be added, though, that with respect to the real ethical problem, the objectivists and absolutists can claim no monopoly on moral understanding. Those most enamored of reason and objective truth are often the first to sanction irrational and intolerant measures against their opponents. In a passage from St. Thomas' *Summa Theologica* (not frequently reproduced, understandably), the Angelic Doctor defends the Catholic Church's Inquisition, arguing that heretics must be "shut off from the world by death." It is one thing to appeal to absolute truths and values; but, when that fails, to hand over the unbelieving soul to the executioner tends not to reflect too well on the first thing.

God's Will and the Good

Another question inevitably arises in relation to talk about God as the source of value. According to some, any attempt to make God the basis of value and morality presents us with this problem: Is x good because God wills it, or does God will x because it is good? Either alternative leaves much to be desired. If right and wrong, good and bad, are the result of God's unconditional fiat, then it would appear that all value is ultimately arbitrary. On the other hand, if goodness is something that exists outside of God, then it turns out that there is something anterior even to God and to which he himself is subject. This problem, an old and vexing one, received perhaps its earliest statement in Plato: "Do the gods love piety because it is pious, or is it pious because they love it?"[13]

A scholastic like St. Thomas Aquinas or Duns Scotus would no doubt answer along the following lines. Of course, the moral law proceeds from God's will; the divine will is the cause of all good, and anything is good from the mere fact that God wills it. But this answer does not, as it may seem, make the moral law or the good arbitrary because God, the supreme and perfect being, wills the greatest good necessarily. If in God there is no difference between his existence (that he is) and essence (what he is), then God's goodness (what he is) is, like his existence, underived and infinite. Furthermore, there can be no contradiction between what he is and what he wills; he can will neither more nor less than the greatest good (his own nature) without, in either case, ceasing to be God. The moral law, then, far from being arbitrary or capricious, is based upon the nature of things, indeed upon the highest nature.[14] On the other hand, it is not difficult to see how such reasoning has been passed off as merely a theological version of the naturalistic fallacy insofar as it identifies the good with what Is, though now with a capital "I."

Also related to this general problem is Mill's objection that a duty that derives from the command of a lawgiver does not qualify as *moral* obligation at all. Genuinely moral obligation "supposes something that the internal conscience bears witness to as binding in its own nature; and which God, in superadding his command, conforms to and perhaps declares, but does not create."[15] But at least two counterobservations may be proposed here. First, whereas moral obligation may not be enjoined upon me through the command of just any lawgiver, it may be different in the case of a lawgiver that can be shown to be wholly good and, in fact, the foundation of all value. That is, my obligation to obey the law would seem to be a moral obligation if, for some reason, I am persuaded that the law originates in the will of a being who can only will what is

---

[13]Plato, *Euthyphro*, 10A, in *Euthyphro, Apology, Crito*, tr. F. J. Church, rev. Robert D. Cumming (New York: Macmillan, 1956).

[14]See St. Thomas Aquinas, *Summa Theologica*, Part One, Qu. 19, Arts, 2–4.

[15]John Stuart Mill, "Theism," in *Three Essays on Religion*, 3rd ed. (London: Longmans, Green & Co., 1875), pp. 164f.

good. Second, the shift from external commands to the data of "internal conscience" (or whatever) is irrelevant inasmuch as the most powerful version of the Moral Argument does not, as we have seen, proceed on the basis of particular rights and wrongs anyway, but rather on the basis of the general moral consciousness that necessarily points beyond itself to an adequate source.

Scholastic distinctions and other scruples aside, surely there would be something strange about asking someone to abandon belief in an objective moral order because of a difficulty in explaining adequately the precise nature of its divine origin. It would be as absurd as informing someone that because he or she can't give an articulate account of how the starry heavens came into being, the belief in them ought to be given up!

The Existence of God and Proof

As we have now completed our survey of the traditional theistic arguments, perhaps it is appropriate at this point to raise realistically the question of whether God's existence can be proved.

The answer depends on what one means by "prove." In one sense, proof has to do only with formal validity. In this sense, an argument constitutes proof if it conforms to the rules of logical inference—in other words, if the conclusion follows logically from the premises. For example, any argument of the form

If p, then q

p

_____

Therefore, q

constitutes a formally valid proof no matter what may be substituted for p and q. There is a big difference, however, between validity and truth. The argument

All Presidents have beards.

Hermes is a president.

_____

Therefore, Hermes has a beard.

is a perfectly valid piece of reasoning (and in that sense a proof), though not one of its propositions is true. In fact, any proposition whatsoever can be proved in this sense, so long as one is willing to supply the appropriate premises. Although the notion of formal validity is obviously very important—where would any argument be without it?—what we are after at the moment is clearly something more.

Presumably, when we ask if God's existence can be proved, we are taking proof to be a presentation of evidence that gives rise to conviction. But now, proof in this sense is "person relative," as it is called. This means that whether or not a proof is successful depends on—we might say—"where you're is coming from." And this relativity, which conditions any theistic proof, is evident in two critical respects. First, such a proof is impossible for someone who does not share the same *philosophical* frame of reference. For example, the Moral Argument cannot compel assent from someone who does not accept the starting point of an objective moral order. Similarly, the Cosmological Argument can hold no force for someone who denies the Principle of Causality. All of the theistic arguments come to rest ultimately on certain givens. But this fact is hardly anything against these arguments, inasmuch as it is equally true of every other argument. All reasoning and demonstration involves at some point a fundamental, undemonstrable affirmation of something, and the parties involved will have to agree on those basic assumptions or presuppositions concerning knowledge, language, and reality if the argument is to avoid a vicious regress and deliver any conviction. With this in mind, Aristotle comments that it is the mark of an uneducated person not to know that some things cannot be demonstrated.

Second, proof in this sense is impossible for someone who does not share the same *psychological* frame of reference. Clearly, people have been known to accept the premises of an argument, agree that the premises imply the conclusion, and then reject the conclusion nonetheless. In such cases, the principle at work is: Whatever the evidence and however cogent the reasoning, you can't believe it if you don't *feel* it. Here, too, the evidence does not elicit conviction, and therefore no proof has been provided. Thus, it is not possible to prove the existence of God (or anything else, for that matter) to someone who does not share the necessary epistemological and metaphysical assumptions and who does not approach the evidence with a certain openness.

A related matter. An objection frequently raised against the theist, especially the religious theist, is that he or she believes in God by virtue of having been born into a certain society, raised in a religious home, sent to parochial schools, and so forth. But this is a flagrant instance of the "genetic fallacy," the mistake of thinking that the truth of a person's position is somehow undermined by identifying its origins. Though the origins or causes of belief may be of some interest to psychologists or sociologists, they are completely irrelevant from a philosophical standpoint. The philosopher is concerned not with the geographical, biological, or environmental *causes* of a person's belief (all of them purely accidental) but with the *reasons* for it. What the skeptic must do is expose the inadequacy of a person's argument or reasoning. And, for that matter, the skeptic's causal explanation works both ways—it itself may be explained and discarded on the same grounds.

The psychoanalytic critique of religion, such as Sigmund Freud presents in his *The Future of an Illusion*, commits somewhat this same mistake, though on a much larger scale. As Freud himself had to acknowledge, even if religious beliefs, and religion itself, could be explained psychoanalytically in terms of sublimated desires, projected father images, and Oedipus complexes, the question of the *truth* of religion would still remain. And that is a philosophical question. Besides, someone has turned the tables on the psychoanalytic critique by observing that the hackneyed "Religion is a crutch" itself may spring from a neurotic refusal to admit that one is lame.

As for the general question before us—namely, what if anything may be accomplished by the traditional arguments for God?—probably no better conclusion can be suggested than is provided in Job 26:14:

> These are indeed but the outskirts of his ways;
> and how small a whisper do we hear
> of him!

A whisper that must no doubt be given full voice by revelation, but a whisper at least.

6

Religious Experience

We have concluded our survey of the four most important traditional arguments for the existence of God. As we indicated at the beginning, however, the rational approach to God is not the only one. There is an altogether different approach that some consider superior precisely because it transcends reason. Such is the position of the late theologian John Baillie:

We are rejecting logical argument of any kind as the first chapter of our theology or as representing the process by which God comes to be known. We are holding that our knowledge of God rests rather on the revelation of His personal Presence as Father, Son, and Holy Spirit. . . . Of such a Presence it must be true that to those who have never been confronted with it argument is useless, while to those who have it is superfluous.[1]

There is a tradition that even St. Thomas Aquinas enjoyed near the end of his life a religious experience that made all the discursive treatises that he had previously written seem like straw. St. Anselm was not so fortunate. It is reported that he cried out in anguish because he had not experienced what he had proved. This approach claims an immediate, direct, and personal confrontation with the divine.

---

[1]John Baillie, *Our Knowledge of God*, 2nd ed. (New York: Scribner, 1959), p. 132.

Christian Experience

If someone perceives a fire burning in the fireplace, the most persuasive arguments and evidence to the contrary might not sway
that person an inch from the emphatic conviction that there is a fire
burning in the fireplace. Indeed, if everyone in the world were to
insist that there was no fire in the fireplace, that person might
judge that they were somehow deluded rather than give up the
truth of such clear and emphatic a testimony as his or her own
immediate experience. Similarly, it is often futile to argue with
someone who rests a case for theism on the self-authenticating evidence of religious experience.

There is a great variety of religious experience, but for our purposes we can distinguish broadly three types: the experience rooted
in revealed religion, the universal sense of a supernatural presence,
and mystic experience. Strictly speaking, the first of these belongs
properly to the sphere of revealed theology; it is conceived to be
largely (if not from beginning to end) the work of God himself,
with humans on the receiving end. But as this experience has played
an important and sometimes central role in theological thinking, it
seems wise not to pass over it in silence even in a discussion concerned primarily with philosophical or natural theology. And while it
could be considered in terms of any one of a number of religious
contexts, say, Islamic, Jewish, or Christian, it is the last that is most
familiar to most readers.

The experience of grace and faith, at least as it is understood
broadly among Christians, begins with a special revelation in which,
it is believed, God has revealed himself along with the human need
for salvation. The believer recognizes himself or herself as fallen,
estranged from God, and spiritually lifeless. But also recognized is
God's gracious work in Christ his Son. In his humiliating death,
Jesus Christ (on the traditional, orthodox view) made atonement
for sin; on the other hand, his righteousness is "imputed," or attributed vicariously, to the believer as God's gift of forgiveness, and justification is appropriated through faith. The believer now stands
before God freed from guilt, redeemed, justified, righteous: "For if
while we were enemies, we were reconciled to God through the
death of his Son, much more surely, having been reconciled, will we
be saved by his life" (Rom. 5:10); again, "For our sake he made
him to be sin who knew no sin, so that in him we might become

the righteousness of God" (2 Cor. 5:21). This understanding of God's work on behalf of the sinner was given classic expression in Martin Luther's brief essay, "Two Kinds of Righteousness," in which he distinguished the righteousness of Christ, which has been freely bestowed upon us, making us worthy of salvation before God, and the subsequent righteousness, wrought in our practical lives by the Holy Spirit, that we practice always imperfectly before one another.

According to this interpretation, it is through the atoning and mediating work of the God-Man that the Christian believer enjoys, by faith, the divine mercy and grace. Through the regenerating work of the Holy Spirit one becomes—to use Pauline expressions— a "new creation in Christ" and, by "adoption," a child of God.

For the Christian, all of this involves considerably more than simply reading a book and following the instructions and considerably more than a mere theological doctrine. It may, in fact, take the form of a conversion experience, with its overpowering sense of release and personal transformation. St. Paul seems to have in mind just this sort of decisive experience when he writes, ". . . if anyone is in Christ, there is a new creation: everything old has passed away; see, everything has become new! All this is from God, who reconciled us to himself through Christ. . . ." (2 Cor. 5:17–18). For others, especially those born into a community of faith, this experience may reveal itself more quietly through participation in the sacramental life of the church and the buttressing fellowship of believers. Certainly for those in the Roman Catholic, Anglican, and Eastern Orthodox traditions, participation in the Holy Eucharist is central, for here, it is believed, the very body and blood of Christ are supernaturally ingested for spiritual strength. Whatever form it may take, the Christian is one who has experienced not only contrition over sin, but also a personal renewal and the joy of God's salvation; one who has experienced a divine operation in his or her own being; one who exclaims with St. Paul, "I have been crucified with Christ; and it is no longer I who live, but it is Christ who lives in me. And the life I now live in the flesh I live by faith in the Son of God, who loved me and gave himself for me" (Gal. 2:20).

This whole way of talking must surely seem strange—perhaps even bizarre—to some readers. On the other hand, a multitude of others (who can deny it?) in every period of the Christian tradition have claimed such an experience of the indwelling Christ, the forgiveness of sins, and the love of God shed abroad in their hearts. And for the certification of this they claim nothing more—or less— than the *testimonium internum Spiritus Sancti*.

The "Numinous" and the "Thou"

We turn now to types of religious experience that are not tied exclusively to a particular religion. Rudolf Otto (1869–1937), a German theologian and student of world religions, did much to explain and interpret those rare but widespread and real moments when the soul is rapt and swayed by an ineffable Something. Such an experience is almost universal; virtually everyone is introduced to it at some point in one's life. Moreover, Otto asks us to consider whether this experience is not the innermost core of all religions worthy of the name.

To be sure, Otto was fully aware of reason's necessary contribution to religion. This awareness is clearly reflected in the full title of his influential book *The Idea of the Holy: An Inquiry into the Non-rational Factor in the Idea of the Divine and Its Relation to the Rational*, and in his frequent reference to the rational and the non-rational as the "warp and woof" of religion. But he believed that the nonrational contribution had become lost in the shuffle of a prevailing intellectualist and rationalist interpretation of religion, so he set out to emphasize and analyze "the *feeling* which remains where the concept fails" and to postulate a nonrational, *a priori* "faculty of divination" to be distinguished "from both the pure theoretical and the pure practical reason of Kant, as something yet higher and deeper than they."[2] Like the beauty of a musical composition, Otto says, this feeling defies complete analysis. At one point he quotes Tersteegen's line, *Ein begriffener Gott ist kein Gott*, "A God comprehended is no God." Nevertheless, he felt that an analysis was called for, and his 1917 publication *Das Heilige* (translated as *The Idea of the Holy*) was soon hailed as a classic of religious psychology.

What, then, is the nature and content of this experience? The expression "the sense of the holy" comes closest to capturing its essence. But the word "holy" has become so burdened with ethical

---

[2]Rudolf Otto, *The Idea of the Holy*, tr. J. W. Harvey, 2nd ed. (New York: Oxford University Press, 1950), p. 114.

overtones that it is not quite appropriate for the experience or sense that Otto seeks to describe: "It is true that all this moral significance is contained in the word 'holy', but it includes in addition—as even we cannot but feel—a clear overplus of meaning, and this it is now our task to isolate."[3] In his attempt to identify this additional element in the meaning of "holy," Otto employs the word "numinous" (from the Latin *numen*: "divine will," "power," "presence") and speaks of a unique numinous category of value, the numinous state of mind, and the numinous feeling. We must not be misled by the latter and somewhat ambiguous locution. By "the numinous feeling" (*das numinose Gefühl*) Otto does not intend a subjective feeling (as in emotion) but rather a certain awareness of an object, a nonrational or suprarational apprehension of something "out there." This experience of the numinous Otto describes as a feeling that

may at times come sweeping like a gentle tide, pervading the mind with a tranquil mood of deepest worship. It may pass over into a more set and lasting attitude of the soul, continuing, as it were, thrillingly vibrant and resonant, until at last it dies away and the soul resumes its "profane," nonreligious mood of everyday experience. It may burst in sudden eruption up from the depths of the soul with spasms and convulsions, or lead to the strangest excitements, to intoxicated frenzy, to transport, and to ecstasy. It has its wild and demonic forms and can sink to an almost grisly horror and shuddering. It has its crude, barbaric antecedents and early manifestations, and again it may be developed into something beautiful and pure and glorious. It may become the hushed, trembling, and speechless humility of the creature in the presence of—whom or what?[4]

For the object of this wondrous experience, Otto says, there is only one appropriate name: *mysterium tremendum*. He then analyzes the *mysterium tremendum* into five aspects. The adjective *tremendum* involves at once the elements of Awfulness, Overpoweringness, and Urgency; the noun *mysterium* suggests a confrontation with the Wholly Other and the consequent captivation or Fascination.[5] All of this suggests the image of the soul, conscious of its creatureliness, shuddering and yet longing in the awe-inspiring and uncanny presence of the supernatural.

---

[3]*Ibid.*, p. 5.
[4]*Ibid.*, pp. 12f.
[5]*Ibid.*, pp. 12ff.

Some readers may recognize Otto's debt to the German theologian Friedrich Schleiermacher, who, in the first parts of his *The Christian Faith* (1830), had developed a theory of religious consciousness based on the feeling of absolute dependence. But this debt does not detract from the originality of Otto's analysis, which he himself regarded as more penetrating than Schleiermacher's in two important respects. Schleiermacher's "feeling of dependence" relativizes religious consciousness into a merely heightened form of a feeling (of dependence) that is experienced more or less in many contexts, whereas Otto's "creature feeling" suggests an experience without parallel, explicable only through itself. Second, in the feeling of dependence, the "feeler" is required to move inferentially from consciousness about himself to God as the cause of his feeling, whereas Otto insists that his creature feeling is inseparably bound up with and is cast like a shadow by an immediate consciousness of an Object. In these ways Otto is persuaded that his analysis has illuminated a more fundamental consciousness and has displayed the source of authentic religion.

Otto believed, it may be added, that his analysis explains, among other things, certain elements and motifs in artistic activity: The megaliths of Stonehenge, the Sphinx of Gizeh, the Chinese art of the T'ang and Sung dynasties, Gothic architecture, the liturgies of the church, Bach's B minor Mass—all of these are human artistic expressions of the numinous.[6] However, he finds the most striking witnesses to the numinous in the Bible, as when Abraham addressed God: "Let me take it upon myself to speak to the LORD, I who am but dust and ashes" (Gen. 18:27); and especially Isaiah's vision of the Lord:

In the year that King Uzziah died, I saw the Lord sitting on a throne, high and lofty; and the hem of his robe filled the temple. Seraphs were in attendance above him; each had six wings: with two they covered their faces, and with two they covered their feet, and with two they flew. And one called to another and said:

"Holy, holy, holy is the LORD of hosts;
the whole earth is full of his glory."

---

[6]*Ibid.*, pp. 65ff. Or at least they bear a numinous imprint.

The pivots on the thresholds shook at the voices of those who called, and the house filled with smoke. And I said: "Woe is me! I am lost for I am a man of unclean lips, and I live among a people of unclean lips; yet my eyes have seen the King, the LORD of hosts." . . . (Isa. 6:1–5).

The Jewish philosopher Martin Buber (1878–1965) has provided still another account of our experience of the divine in his celebrated and oracular work *I and Thou*. For Buber it makes no sense to seek God, because there is nothing in which he is not present. To turn aside from this life in the pursuit of God is necessarily to miss him. But where, more specifically, is God to be found in this life? Certainly not in the world of space and time where mechanistic causality reigns unlimited, where things as mere objects are experienced, manipulated, observed, and used. This is what Buber calls the realm of the *It*. Rather, God is disclosed as *I* transcend the world of *It*, as *I* confront the spiritual dimension in something, as *I* meet, encounter, and enter into relation with it, as *I* address it as *Thou*. In every authentic and spiritual relation with a being (not an *It*), "its *Thou* is freed, steps forth, is single, and confronts you."[7] And every particular *Thou* is a glimpse through to the eternal *Thou*, the Spirit, the absolute, illimitable Person, the *Thou* that can never become an *It*, the Being that is neither inferred nor expressed but addressed. Hence, the sanctity of the *I–Thou* relationship must be contrasted with the stultifying, stagnant, and oppressive character of the *I–It* relationship. Buber believes that his position represents an advance upon Otto:

Of course God is the "wholly Other"; but He is also the wholly Same, the wholly Present. Of course He is the *Mysterium Tremendum* that appears and overthrows; but He is also the mystery of the self-evident, nearer to me than my *I*.

If you explore the life of things and of conditioned being you come to the unfathomable, if you deny the life of things and of conditioned being you stand before nothingness, if you hallow this life you meet the living God.[8]

---

[7]Martin Buber, *I and Thou*, tr. R. G. Smith, 2nd ed. (New York: Scribner, 1958), p. 78.
[8]*Ibid.*, p. 79.

Both Otto and Buber have, however, at least this much in common: They do not, strictly speaking, argue for anything; rather, they call attention to a kind of experience, revelatory and *sui generis*. Their contribution lies in their statements and analyses of the experienced *presence* of something.

Mystic Experience

In the history of both Oriental and Occidental thought, one of the most dominant and persistent witnesses to the existence of a divine reality is the mystic tradition.

Unfortunately, the words "mysticism" and "mystic" are among the slipperiest of our intellectual vocabulary and can suggest all sorts of things, including astrology, Ouija boards, fortune telling, and other occult and murky interest. What I mean by "mysticism" is something rather specific, and if we are to appreciate what it is, we must appreciate what it is not, and it most certainly is not any of these things.

We should also distinguish it from the experiences of those who see visions and hear voices, and no doubt also from the "instant mysticism" of LSD, mescaline, and other hallucinogenic or mind-expanding drugs. We need not doubt that the latter type of experience does produce, on occasion, insight into something or other; one could hardly draw any other conclusion from, say, Aldous Huxley's accounts of his experiments with mescaline as he relates them in *The Doors of Perception*—a book that sold well in the 1960s and 1970s. But such experiences titillate and heighten the sensations of consciousness (Huxley speaks recurringly of dazzling sights, brilliant colors, and the like),[9] and this too is wide of the mark of the kind of experience we're interested in. As for visions and voices, it should be enough that many of the great mystics themselves have cautioned us not to mistake those phenomena for the mystical state

---

[9]Huxley's *The Doors of Perception* (New York: Harper & Row, 1954) represents only one approach to the question of artificially induced "mystical" states. One would do well to compare the Huxley-type approach with the alternative understanding of, say, R. C. Zaehner as he presents it in the first two chapters of his *Mysticism: Sacred and Profane* (Oxford, England: Clarendon Press, 1957).

and have, in fact, generally regarded them as impediments to the achievement of genuine mystical consciousness.

Well, what is this consciousness? It is a transcendent consciousness in which the soul achieves oneness with God, or the Divine, or the One, the Absolute, the Void, or whatever you choose to call it. This, for all its inadequacy, is what I would call the essence of *classic* mysticism, in an attempt to distinguish it from all that other stuff. One key word, of course, is "transcendent," and more will be said about it in the next section. For the moment, though, consider some other angles.

Though all mystics claim a union with the divine, there are striking differences in their accounts of their experiences. For some it is the consummation of a prolonged and tortuous preparation; others seem to be grasped by it in a spontaneous and rapturous flash. Some mystics claim to apprehend an impersonal "ultimate"; to others the experience discloses the three Persons of the Holy Trinity. Nevertheless, certain overlapping features are more or less common to all mystical experiences. First, the mystic experience is, as was just emphasized, completely *transcendent*, freed from all consciousness of space and time. Second, it is *ineffable*, an inexpressible experience that transcends even the concepts and categories of language; it defies expression or description. Third, it is characterized by an element of *passivity*. It is true that the mystic may make certain preparations and actively set upon the quest, but once in the grip of the mystical experience itself (at least in its highest stages), the mystic is oblivious to all else and can only respond passively to the divine revelation. Fourth, the experience is attended by an *ecstatic* quality ("ecstasy" means, literally, a standing outside oneself) in which the soul is buoyed up to God in a state of joyous and blissful exaltation. Finally, there is a *noetic* aspect to the experience. The mystic claims to know something otherwise unknowable; to behold and love a Truth that lies beyond all sense experience and reasoning.[10]

---

[10]This list is somewhat of a variation of William James' "four marks" of the mystic experience in his influential *The Varieties of Religious Experience* (New York: Modern Library, reprint 1929), pp. 371f., which, in turn, should be compared with Evelyn Underhill's four criteria in the classic study *Mysticism* (London: Methuen, 1911), pp. 80ff.

The distinction is sometimes drawn between introverted and extroverted mysticism. The goal of the mystic is to penetrate to the underlying Unity of all things and to become one with it. The extroverted mystic claims to apprehend the essential Unity as it is radiated through the external world of sensible things, transfigured by the mystic consciousness. The introverted mystic discovers the Divine, or the One, or the Absolute, by turning *away* from sense experience to the world of one's own consciousness and self. Insofar as the distinction between these two types of mystical experience is legitimate at all, it is clearly introverted and introspective mysticism that has been the more dominant and influential.

The Ascent of the Soul

In the Christian tradition, this form of mysticism is exemplified in the writings of St. Augustine, Pseudo-Dionysius, St. Francis of Assisi, St. Bonaventure, Julian of Norwich, Nicolas Cusanus, Meister Eckhart, St. Teresa, St. John of the Cross, St. Catherine of Siena, and others. These mystics inherited (more or less) the Platonic idea that only that which is absolutely One and Immutable is wholly real and true. God is to be apprehended only by turning away from multiplicity and change, and by turning toward unity and immutability.

The world of sense experience must therefore be abandoned as a distraction from our highest pursuit. But withdrawing into ourselves and closing out all sense experiences, we find ourselves yet in possession of what is often called the "sensory consciousness," pervaded by impressions and images drawn from sense perception. So we must move beyond the sensory consciousness, with its distracting multiplicity and change. Withdrawing even further into ourselves, we discover that even the "intellectual consciousness" is characterized by multiplicity and change; the pure *a priori* operations of the intellect ("If A, then B; A, therefore B") involve a plurality of concepts and movement of the mind. We must, then, transcend even our own thoughts. Having stripped away all sensations, passions, desires, and ideas, and having abandoned all our faculties, we confront finally the ego or self, the very principle of our being. And the soul, thus withdrawn into its own unity, is prepared for union with the Absolute, the One, or God.

The following passage from Pseudo-Dionysius (c. 500) is an excellent statement of the introverted and transcendent nature of the mystic experience:

Thou then, my friend, if thou desirest mystic visions, with strengthened feet abandon thy senses and intellectual operations, and both all non-being and being; and unknowingly restore thyself to unity as far as possible, unity of Him Who is above all essence and knowledge. And when thou hast transcended thyself and all things in immeasurable and absolute purity of mind, thou shalt ascend to the superessential rays of divine shadows, leaving all behind and freed from ties of all.[11]

There transcending all distinction, all plurality, all movement, the mystic enjoys ecstatic union with the Divine. This pilgrimage of the self from its involvement in the world of sense experience to beatific union with the One (a progress often requiring extraordinary discipline) has been called, appropriately, the "mystical ascent of the soul."

One of the most gifted Christian mystics was St. John of the Cross (1542–1591), whose poetry is regarded as among the most accurate and eloquent expressions of the mystical life. Employing one of the favorite motifs of mystic writers, he developed the concept of the "dark night of the soul," the title of his most important poem and attending commentary. In this state all sensations, images, and ideas have been blotted out, all desires eclipsed and extinguished, and the soul thus darkened is prepared to pass from the purgative stage of the mystical ascent to the dazzling and resplendent light of the illuminative stage, and finally to the ecstatic and utterly transcendent unitive stage in which the soul is at last rendered completely transparent to the divine will.

---

[11]Pseudo-Dionysius, quoted in St. Bonaventure, *The Mind's Road to God*, tr. George Boas (New York: Macmillan, 1953), p. 45. St. Bonaventure's work is itself an instructive account of the several stages leading to the mystical union with God from the standpoint of a scholastic mystic of the thirteenth century.

John's poem *Verses Written After an Ecstasy of High Exaltation*[12] emphasizes the "darkness" as well as other features of the mystic experience as conceived in terms of Christian theology:

> I entered in, I know not where,
> And I remained, though knowing naught,
> Transcending knowledge with my thought.

> Of when I entered I know naught,
> But when I saw that I was there
> (Though where it was I did not care)
> Strange things I learned, with greatness fraught.

> Yet what I heard I'll not declare.
> But there I stayed, though knowing naught,
> Transcending knowledge with my thought.

> Of peace and piety interwound
> This perfect science had been wrought,
> Within the solitude profound
> A straight and narrow path it taught,
> Such secret wisdom there I found
> That there I stammered, saying naught,
> But topped all knowledge with my thought.

> So borne aloft, so drunken-reeling,
> So rapt was I, so swept away,
> Within the scope of sense or feeling
> My sense of feeling could not stay.
> And in my soul I felt, revealing,
> A sense that, though its sense was naught,
> Transcended knowledge with my thought.

> The man who truly there has come
> Of his own self must shed the guise;
> Of all he knew before the sum
> Seems far beneath that wondrous prize:
> And in this lore he grows so wise
> That he remains, though knowing naught,
> Transcending knowledge with his thought.

> The farther that I climbed the height
> The less I seemed to understand

---

[12]St. John of the Cross, *Poems*, tr. Roy Campbell (Baltimore: Penguin Books, 1960), pp. 46ff.

The cloud so tenebrous and grand
That there illuminates the night.
For he who understands that sight
Remains for aye, though knowing naught,
Transcending knowledge with his thought.

This wisdom without understanding
Is of so absolute a force
No wise man of whatever standing
Can ever stand against its course,
Unless they tap its wondrous source,
To know so much, though knowing naught,
They pass all knowledge with their thought.

This summit all so steeply towers
And is of excellence so high
No human faculties or powers
Can ever to the top come nigh.
Whoever with its steep could vie,
Though knowing nothing, would transcend
All thought, forever, without end.

If you would ask, what is its essence—
This summit of all sense and knowing:
It comes from the Divinest Presence—
The sudden sense of Him outflowing,
In His great clemency bestowing
The gift that leaves men knowing naught,
Yet passing knowledge with their thought.

Every line in this poem suggests something important about the mystic experience. For example, when John says, "I know not where" and "I know not when," he is emphasizing that this experience cannot be localized in space or time inasmuch as the soul has been purged of all sensible perception. "The solitude profound" suggests that state in which, transcending both external and internal multiplicity, the soul has completely withdrawn into its own unity in anticipation of the divine and gracious infilling. The picture of the mystic "stammering" in the presence of the "secret wisdom" expresses the ineffability of the experience. The fourth stanza attempts to describe the indescribable ecstasy, a rapture unlike any other that the soul can know. The line "The farther that I climbed the height" is an image of the soul's struggling progress from darkness and estrangement to illumination and union with the divine.

And the recurring "knowing naught" signifies the soul's withdrawal from all images and ideas; this is actually, therefore, a claim to know All, an All that lies beyond the grasp of experience and reason and thus beyond all knowledge in the ordinary sense.

As a whole, the poem is an example of the way in which the mystic seeks through indirect, poetic, and often paradoxical expression to point the reader in the direction of something that cannot, in fact, be argued or even expressed. It is, as it were, an invitation to the reader to come and see for himself, or, as the Psalmist says, "O taste and see that the LORD is good" (Ps. 34:8).

Mysticism East and West

It is sometimes claimed that Western thought is characteristically academic and rational, whereas Eastern thought is essentially mystical and religious. But one should not exaggerate this point, and certainly it is false that there is no such thing as Eastern "theology." Eastern literature, as well as Western, includes vast tomes of discursive treatises, and even a counterpart to St. Thomas' Five Ways can be found. Still, it is true that Eastern philosophical and theological investigations are usually to be viewed in the context of a larger setting wherein the highest truth is revealed in a nondiscursive, mystical way.

In light of what has been said concerning Christian mysticism, one might compare two representative passages from the literature of Hinduism. The first, from the *Bhagavad-Gita* (often called the Gospel of Hinduism), is suggestive of the universal mystic interest in the subjugation of the senses and the elimination of all sensible distractions. Krishna (an incarnation of the god Vishnu, and one of whose epithets is "subduer of the senses") is instructing Arjuna (Everyman) in Sankhya-Yoga (the Way of Knowledge):

> The wind turns a ship
> From its course upon the waters:
> The wandering winds of the senses
> Cast man's mind adrift
> And turn his better judgment from its course.
> When a man can still the senses

I call him illumined.
The recollected mind is awake
In the knowledge of the Atman
Which is dark night to the ignorant:
The ignorant are awake in their sense-life
Which they think is daylight:
To the seer it is darkness.[13]

The second passage, from the *Mandukya Upanishad* (part of the oldest extant mystical literature), is an exhaustive summary of the unity of the mystic experience:

The Fourth [and highest aspect of the Self], says the wise, is not subjective experience, nor objective experience, nor experience intermediate between these two, nor is it a negative condition which is neither consciousness nor unconsciousness. It is not the knowledge of the senses, nor is it relative knowledge, nor yet inferential knowledge. Beyond the senses, beyond the understanding, beyond all expression, is the Fourth. It is pure unitary consciousness, wherein awareness of the world and of multiplicity is completely obliterated. It is ineffable peace. It is the supreme good. It is One without a second. It is the Self. Know it alone![14]

There is, however, one especially fundamental difference between the Christian and Eastern (at least the Upanishadic Hindu) conceptions of mystic union: the difference between a monistic and a theistic conception. According to Upanishadic Hinduism, for example, all reality, unconscious and conscious, is an appearance or manifestation of the absolute Reality called Brahman, the primordial ground and essential unity of all things. The mystic seeks through the various *yogas* ("yokings" or "Ways" of enlightenment) to rise above *maya* (the present illusory world) and achieve *moksha* (liberation from the cycle of change) and *nirvana*, that blissful state in which the soul is completely reabsorbed into the impersonal unity of Brahman. Actu-

---

[13]*The Bhagavad-Gita*, tr. Swami Prabhavananda and Christopher Isherwood (New York: New American Library, 1951). Otto cites also the eleventh chapter of the *Gita* (where Krishna reveals himself in all of his glory to Arjuna) as yet another remarkable expression of the feeling of the numinous; in fact, he calls this "one of the perfectly classical passages for the theory of Religion" (*The Idea of the Holy*, p. 62, n. 1).
[14]*The Upanishads*, tr. Swami Prabhavananda and Frederick Manchester (New York: New American Library, 1957), p. 51.

ally, the being of Brahman and the being of the mystic (as well as of all other things) is believed to be one and the same, and enlightenment is the realization that one *is* Brahman, a matter of overcoming an illusory cleavage or estrangement within a self-identical reality.

In the Western tradition, mystic union is conceived very differently, operating as that tradition does with a very different theology—more specifically, a very different conception of the relation between the world and God. Jewish, Christian, and Islamic theologies all teach as one of their central doctrines that the being of God is essentially different from the being of creatures. All created being, and thus the human being, is necessarily unlike God's since God did not make things out of himself (either through a Platonic emanation or any other means) but *ex nihilo*, "out of nothing." Union with God can never mean, therefore, union with the One-In-the-All, but rather with the One-Above-the-All. It can never mean a unity of being or substance, but rather a complete conformity of the mystic's will to the divine will, a complete infilling of the divine love. To use a metaphor from St. John of the Cross, it means a complete cleansing of the mirror of the self so that the divine being and light and love may be wholly reflected without distortion or blemish.

The preceding discussion serves to emphasize that there are important differences in the ways in which mystics interpret and represent their experiences, and that these differences are the products of divergent philosophical and theological positions, to say nothing of differences of a more cultural nature—language, symbols, customs, moral sensibilities, and so on. A Christian's representation of the mystic experience might naturally involve Jesus, the church, the Holy Spirit, and the like, whereas a Hindu's naturally wouldn't. But the important point concerns the common nucleus that seems to underlie the differing representations. Any mystical tradition (Protestant, Catholic, Jewish, Islamic, Hindu) would appear, from a cosmopolitan point of view, to be a particular expression of a universal and persistent phenomenon.

Satori Experience

In addition to the Hindu, there are other strains of Eastern religion that are relevant to a discussion of religious experience—Zen Buddhism, for example. As it turns out, Zen has to do neither with

God nor with reason, but it should be mentioned in view of its great popularity in the West, where, indeed, it thrives. Any form of Buddhism has its roots in the teaching of the Buddha, born about 560 B.C. in what is today Nepal. At the center of this teaching is the exhortation to Enlightenment, and life in accordance with it, as expressed in the traditional Four Noble Truths and the Eightfold Noble Path:

The Four Noble Truths

1. Life is permeated by suffering.
2. The origin of suffering lies with desire.
3. The cessation of suffering is possible through the cessation of desire.
4. The way to the latter is the Eightfold Noble Path.

The Eightfold Noble Path

1. Right views.
2. Right aspiration.
3. Right speech.
4. Right conduct.
5. Right effort.
6. Right mindfulness.
7. Right contemplation.
8. Right livelihood.

Over the centuries Buddhism has taken innumerable shapes, advocating different ways of achieving the state of Enlightenment, but they all claim that it consists in the indescribable experience of Emptiness. Of course, since it's indescribable, there's not much one can say about it. But the idea is not, as with the mystics we have considered, to move from relative reality to the Ultimate Reality as the cause, but rather to cultivate an appreciation of the ephemeral, superficial, and transparent character of things, and simply to allow them *to be that and nothing more.* The personal payoff of this enlightened state is a healthy attunement of the self to its transparent environment, or better—since the self likewise is not a permanent reality—a complete transparency of the *self.*

In the West, by far the most familiar of the Buddhist ways to enlightenment is the way of Zen, a Japanese word meaning "meditation" (*ch'an* in Chinese). Zen grows out of one of the main branches of Buddhism, namely, Mahayana, though in its most developed form it shares the completely nontheistic perspective of Theravada Buddhism. There is certainly no talk here about anything remotely resembling God, in any usual sense of the word, or even talk about knowledge or experience of some Ultimate Reality, or about a gracious infilling from Beyond. At the heart of Zen is the experience of *satori*, cultivated by various exercises including, foremostly, meditation but also tea ceremony, archery, gardening, and other practices intended to induce a sense of the utter simplicity, unity, and naturalness of things. *Satori* (Japanese for "enlightenment") is a sudden illumination, but the content of which cannot be described. We're used to this by now, but here the point is made even more emphatically. We have seen that Western mystics, such as St. John of the Cross, resort to a sort of indirect communication to describe their ineffable experience. The Zen Buddhist is, we might say, more honest, refraining from any attempted description whatsoever. The most that may be expected are parables and *koans* (intellectual puzzles) that jar and jolt one into the experience of *satori* for oneself. D. T. Suzuki, a leading exponent and interpreter of Zen Buddhism (1870–1966), makes some points about *satori*:

. . . there is no Zen without satori, which is indeed the Alpha and Omega of Zen Buddhism. Zen devoid of satori is like a sun without its light and heat. . . .

Satori may be defined as an intuitive looking into the nature of things in contradistinction to the analytical or logical understanding of it. Practically, it means the unfolding of a new world hitherto unperceived in the confusion of a dualistically-trained mind. . . .

Without the attainment of satori no one can enter into the mystery of Zen. It is the sudden flashing of a new truth hitherto altogether undreamed of. . . . Satori comes upon you unawares when you feel you have exhausted your whole being. Religiously this is a new birth, and, morally, the revaluation of one's relationship to the world. . . .

Satori is the most intimate individual experience and therefore cannot be expressed in words or described in any manner. All that one can do in the way of communicating the experience to others is to suggest or indicate, and this only tentatively.[15]

---

[15]Daisetz Teitaro Suzuki, *Essays in Zen Buddhism* (First Series) (London: Rider, 1926), pp. 227ff.

We have already seen that the aim here is not to uncover some Ultimate Reality. Nor is it the bliss of some ecstatic consciousness. Nor is it the achievement of transcendence. Nor does it have anything to do with God. Is this, then, a *religious* experience? Might it be claimed, rather, that *satori* is an awakening to the purest possible form of *naturalism*? That may be on the right track, provided that naturalism here is not understood—as it usually is in the West—to mean a developed philosophical perspective on reality. If Zen is a form of naturalism, it must be naturalism in the sense of the living of life in the simplest, most harmonious way. Zen is, after all, a spiritual path.

Evidence for God?

But back to the issue.

What good is religious experience as evidence for God? You may be tempted to answer, "None." That people do have such experiences is undeniable. The question, rather, is whether their experiences have anything to do with God. Many have argued that such experiences may be explained quite simply through purely natural causes such as sublimated sexual desires or even physiological disorders! William James contemptuously attacks the latter sort of explanation, which he calls "medical materialism," as one that

finishes up Saint Paul by calling his vision on the road to Damascus a discharging lesion of the occipital cortex, he being an epileptic. It snuffs out Saint Teresa as an hysteric, Saint Francis of Assisi as an hereditary degenerate. George Fox's discontent with the shams of his age, and his pining for spiritual veracity, it treats as a symptom of a disordered colon. Carlyle's organ-tones of misery it accounts for by a gastro-duodenal catarrh.[16]

The relevance of such explanations may be left for the reader to decide. As for those who relegate mysticism to the study of abnormal psychology, the fact is that the classic mystics appear no less sane than most of us. But even so, it is sometimes observed that perhaps those who are slightly cracked are those in whom the light shows through more easily—an observation that just may be as

---

[16]James, *The Varieties of Religious Experience*, p. 14.

insightful as it is clever. St. Teresa herself suggested something of this sort when she complained of a "great noise" in her head, as of "rushing rivers . . . and many little birds and whistling sounds," and concluded: "I wouldn't be surprised if the Lord gave me this headache so that I could understand these things better."[17]

Philosophically, a yet more important matter must be raised. If someone says "There is a fire burning in the fireplace," it would not normally occur to me to doubt that he or she really does *perceive* a fire in the fireplace. On the other hand, I might at that very moment observe that there is, in fact, no fire in the fireplace. But there is a big difference between saying "There is a fire burning in the fireplace," and saying "I have had an experience with the divine." The difference is, of course, that we can all gather around and see for ourselves whether there is a fire in the fireplace, whereas the religious-experience claim is by its nature subjective and private. On the other hand, it may be a mistake to conclude from this that all notions of verification or falsification are wholly inappropriate to such a claim or to say with one philosopher that "in describing his vision the mystic does not give us any information about the external world; he merely gives us indirect information about the condition of his own mind."[18] This, of course, may be true in a way, but it must be admitted that the mystic's is a most extraordinary and interesting state of mind—so interesting as to constrain us to reflect seriously upon it.

William Alston has reflected seriously on it and has published the results in *Perceiving God*, a book with which future discussions will have to reckon. Alston's effort is not directed toward proving God by means of religious experience, but rather toward clarifying the epistemic status of claims made by those who have allegedly perceived or experienced him. And the outcome is positive.

The thesis defended here is not that the existence of God provides the best explanation for facts about religious experience or that it is possible to *argue* in any way from the latter to the former. It is rather that people

---

[17]St. Teresa of Avila, *The Interior Castle*, in *Collected Works of St. Teresa of Avila*, tr. Kieran Kavanaugh and Otilio Rodriguez (Washington, D.C.: ICS Publications, 1980), II, pp. 320f.

[18]Alfred Jules Ayer, *Language, Truth and Logic*, 2nd ed. (London: Gollancz, 1946), p. 119.

sometimes do perceive God and thereby acquire justified beliefs about God. In the same way, if one is a direct realist about sense perception, as I am, one will be inclined to hold not that internal facts about sense experience provide one with premises for an effective argument to the existence of external physical objects, but rather that in enjoying sense experience one thereby perceives external physical objects and comes to have various justified beliefs about them, without the necessity of exhibiting those beliefs (or their propositional contents) as the conclusion of any sort of argument.[19]

Alston grants that the alleged knowledge delivered through religious experience is direct or noninferential. This, however, does not relegate it somehow to a dark, epistemological realm populated by self-insulating and uninvestigable claims—at least, no more so than with ordinary perception claims. Indeed, the comparison and relation of religious-perception claims and sense-perception claims is fundamental to Alston's treatment. His central thesis, surely startling to some, is that religious perception is in all important respects analogous to sense perception, and that the claim of the religious perceiver might therefore well survive the same tests of veridicalness that we ordinarily impose on the claim of the sense perceiver. Both are, as it were, innocent until proven guilty, and both are subject to possible defeat or vindication by elements in our "general background knowledge," the sum total of input that constitutes at any moment the coherent system of ideas that defines our perspective. For Alston, it turns out that the religious-experiencer's state of mind is not that extraordinary after all. And he thus calls for an end to the double standard employed in evaluating sense experience and religious experience. In the end, we must honestly accord religious-perception claims the same status, rights, and privileges that we accord sense-perception claims.

A final point. Even if it were not possible to weigh the veracity of specific religious-experience claims, it is not difficult to verify at least the fact of, say, the mystic tradition itself, and that this tradition continues to be a dominant, forceful, historical reality. Perhaps, then, the mystics, considered collectively, constitute a universal and

---

[19]William P. Alston, *Perceiving God: The Epistemology of Religious Experience* (Ithaca, N.Y.: Cornell University Press, 1991), p. 3.

historical witness that skeptics have never quite explained and probably never will. Of course, none of this kind of talk is of much
interest to the *mystic*, for he or she does not claim to provide evidence for God or anything else. The appeal is to a private certainty
that carries its own guarantee. As for everybody else, the one who
sees, sees, and the one who doesn't, doesn't. As St. Teresa said, "I
do not think that anyone could believe it or understand it who has
not already experienced it."[20] Or as it may be otherwise said,
"There's no substitute for being there."

---

[20]St. Teresa, *The Life of St. Teresa of Avila by Herself*, 20, tr. J. M. Cohen
(London: Penguin Books, 1957).

7

Faith and Reason

The question of God's existence, as we have already emphasized, occupies a central position among the concerns of philosophical theology. There is, nevertheless, a multitude of related issues that must also be considered if our survey is to be complete. One of the most important and obvious of these is the problem of faith and reason. In fact, a case could be made that this is the most fundamental issue of all, having a sort of logical priority over the rest. It has to do, as it were, with the rules of the game—and the rules have to be understood at the start.

Rational and Nonrational

The word "faith" is usually associated with religion and the Bible, and the problem of faith and reason immediately suggests a theological or religious issue. The issue involved in faith and reason, though, is actually a general epistemological problem, a problem concerning knowledge, and a real problem for every thinking individual, not only the theologian or the religious person.

If we use the word "reason" to denote the mind's logical, rational, discursive activity, then many would insist that there is more to knowledge than what is contributed by reason alone. For example, someone might appeal to creative imagination as playing an essential role in our intellectual life. Another might suggest the necessity for intuition, a direct apprehension of truth, unmediated either by sense experience or logical deduction. There are those who appeal to feeling, claiming that certain kinds of truth can just be "felt." We have already seen that various religious experiences are alleged to have cognitive significance. The religious person, further, may distinguish what is known through natural reason from the knowledge attained through sacred writings. In one way or another, we thus tend to analyze our knowledge into two elements: the *rational* and the *nonrational*. I suggest that the problem of faith and reason, when reduced to the real issue, represents just this distinction between the rational and the nonrational elements of our understanding and the difficulty of estimating, weighing, and relating their respective contributions. (It should be apparent that we are presently regarding faith as a cognitive activity, that is, as a way of knowing something. Admittedly, this would be disagreeable to those who take faith as having to do not so much with our knowledge of something as with our trust in something. This latter opinion may be, in fact, a richer understanding of faith, at least from a religious point of view.)

Though the problem of faith and reason can be construed in this way as a general philosophical problem, it is no accident that it has been treated by and large as a theological or religious one. "Faith" is not necessarily a religious word; certainly the Greek πίστις ("belief," "faith") suggested nothing particularly religious or theological in antiquity, and even we speak of our faith in scientific laws or our belief that tables and chairs are still there even though no one is observing them. For those in the Western tradition of Judaism, Christianity, and Islam, however, "faith" is in fact heavily weighted with religious overtones. In the case of Christianity, this is primarily because of the New Testament emphasis on "believing" and, more specifically, the Pauline doctrine of justification by faith. Moreover, for nearly 2,000 years theology has been juxtaposing revealed and natural knowledge, and the believer has been insisting on the centrality of revelation and religious experience. Clearly, the religious expressions of faith have been sifted out from the other expressions as the most consequential; witness, for example, the ragings in past years over the supposed conflicts between science and the Bible. The religious problem of faith and reason is, then, only one version of the larger philosophical problem concerning the relation of the rational to the nonrational aspects of our knowledge, but it is, at the same time, the most obvious and most important version.

Athens or Jerusalem?

All believers in divine revelation agree, obviously, that we have, in one way or another, supernatural knowledge revealed by God, but they do not necessarily agree (as we saw in Chapter 2) about the contribution of natural knowledge. The problem of faith and reason (in its religious version) has therefore amounted to this question: Inasmuch as God has revealed himself in a supernatural self-disclosure, to what status shall we assign natural reason in the theological sphere? In the case of the Christian tradition, two ancient Church Fathers, Tertullian of Antioch (c. 160–230) and Clement of Alexandria (c. 150–215), reflect that from the beginning of Christian theology there existed two radically different answers to this question. Of course, something important is already betrayed by the fact that Antioch was an early stronghold for the literalist interpretation of the Bible, whereas in cosmopolitan, intellectualist Alexandria the Old Testament had been translated into Greek, Philo Judaeus had synthesized Platonic and Jewish thought, and Christian theologians were pursuing the allegorical method of Biblical interpretation. It should not be surprising that very different approaches to the question of faith and reason should arise from these two centers of early theology.

Tertullian took as his point of departure St. Paul's declaration that

Jews demand signs and Greeks seek wisdom, but we preach Christ crucified, a stumbling block to Jews and folly to Gentiles, but to those who are called, both Jews and Greeks, Christ the power of God and the wisdom of God. For the foolishness of God is wiser than men, and the weakness of God is stronger than men (I Cor. 1:22–25).

Armed with this, as well as with Paul's warning, "See to it that no one makes a prey of you by philosophy. . . ." (Col. 2:8), Tertullian set out to vindicate the divine foolishness of Christianity while denouncing philosophy as the demon-inspired mother of heresies. No better evidence is found for Tertullian's contempt for philosophy and vain reason than his rhetorical challenge, "What has Jerusalem to do with Athens, the Church with the Academy?", and his famous outburst concerning the death and resurrection of Christ, "I believe because it is absurd; it is certain because it is impossible!"[1] For Tertullian, it is sufficient that God himself has spoken. The Scriptures must be our only guide and standard in all matters pertaining to faith and doctrine, and we must be on constant guard against those who seek to ensnare us with sophistical reasonings and to corrupt the pure and simple Christian teachings. After all, does not St. Paul warn us that "Satan disguises himself as an angel of light" (2 Cor. 11:14)? Tertullian concludes that the Christian knows through revelation all that he needs to know; beyond that, it would be better to remain ignorant than to risk falling into the evil clutches of philosophy and heresy.

Clement of Alexandria, on the other hand, was an early representative of those who saw in pagan philosophy a direct benefit for Christian faith. According to Clement, Christ is the *Logos* ("Reason"),[2] the Instructor of all humanity. We should therefore expect that even the pagans have apprehended something of God's truth. More specifically, Clement taught that philosophy was perhaps even a divine gift directly bestowed upon the Greeks, just as St. Paul taught (Gal. 3:24) concerning the Law given to the Jews, as a preparation for Christianity. Philosophy lifted and turned the Hellenic mind toward Christ and helped to set the stage, historically and culturally, for the advent of the Gospel. Indeed, Clement documents his own writings profusely from Greek culture, in which he sees many anticipations of Christian ideas. Further, God's will is that the believer should, as much as possible, *know*, and philosophical activity equips him in his progress from faith to understanding or genuine *gnosis*.[3] Thus, Clement calls philosophy the "handmaid of theology," one of the ways in which God has made the world responsive to the Gospel and a useful tool through which Christian understanding is cultivated and established.

---

[1]Tertullian, *Prescription Against Heretics*, 7; *On the Flesh of Christ*, 5. Actually, Tertullian never said, *Credo quia absurdum*; what he said was, *Credible est, quia ineptum est.*

[2]*Logos*: a Greek word (λόγος) applied to Christ by the writer of the Fourth Gospel (John 1:1,14) with the meaning of "(redemptive) Word." Clement's application reflects a common meaning of the word in Greek philosophy, especially Stoicism.

[3]*Gnosis*: a Greek word (γνῶσις) meaning "knowledge" that Clement borrowed from the heretical Gnostics who professed a kind of secret wisdom concerning things divine.

Clement supports his position, too, with numerous passages from the Scriptures (often allegorized to his advantage), drawing especially upon the Wisdom literature of the Old Testament. For example:

"Now," says Solomon, "defend wisdom, and it will exalt thee, and it will shield thee with a crown of pleasure" (Prov. 4:8–9). For when thou hast strengthened wisdom with a cope by philosophy, and with right expenditure, thou wilt preserve it unassailable by sophists. The way of truth is therefore one. But into it, as into a perennial river, streams flow from all sides. It has been therefore said by inspiration: "Hear, my son, and receive my words; that thine may be the many ways of life. For I teach thee the ways of wisdom; that the fountains fail thee not. . . ." (Prov. 4:10–11).[4]

And concerning St. Paul's warning against philosophy (Col. 2:8), Clement explains that the full statement reveals Paul's true intent: "See to it that no one makes a prey of you by philosophy and empty deceit, according to human tradition, according to the elemental spirits of the universe, and not according to Christ." That is, according to Clement's exegesis, Paul is not denouncing philosophy as such, but rather the return to philosophy by one who has already passed through its elemental, rudimentary, and preparatory counsels; once having served its preparatory function in the life of the believer, human philosophy should be left behind for the higher knowledge (Paul often uses the word ἐπίγνωσις: "super-knowledge," or "full knowledge") that is given by God. As for the wisdom of this world that is foolishness with God (I Cor. 1:18ff.), Clement assures us that Paul had in mind only the materialistic Epicurean philosophy. Not even Clement claimed that all philosophy is divinely inspired.[5]

Tertullian and Clement represent, in this way, extreme positions on the question of faith and reason. Nevertheless, many, if not most, Christian thinkers also incline to one or the other of these poles, so there arises the distinction between fideism (from the Latin *fides*: "faith"), which affirms the sufficiency of faith to the well-nigh exclusion of reason, and rationalism or intellectualism,

---

[4]Clement of Alexandria, *Stromata*, I, 5, tr. William Wilson, in *Ante-Nicene Christian Library*, IV (Edinburgh: T. & T. Clark, 1884).

[5]*Ibid.*, I, 2ff.; VI, 5ff.; and *passim*.

which, though not denying the priority of faith, stresses also the contribution of reason.

Faith in Search of Understanding

It would clearly be a mistake to think of St. Thomas Aquinas, and even more of a mistake of St. Augustine, as Clement types or extreme rationalists in theology. Nevertheless, they do represent a strain of thinkers within the Christian tradition who, though acknowledging the final authority of revelation, theologize with a distinctly intellectualist bent. Their theologies are classic examples of *fides quaerens intellectum*, "faith in search of understanding." Of course, we have already seen this principle at work in the birth of St. Anselm's Ontological Argument.

St. Thomas inherited from Greek philosophy an interest in the human being as a rational being. According to that tradition, and especially Plato and Aristotle, there is implanted in all human beings a natural appetite for knowledge, and it is by virtue of their reason that human beings are elevated above all other creatures. Everything has its proper good or end, and the human's proper end is rational activity. Contemplation and the pursuit of knowledge actualizes, enhances, and perfects the essential nature and happiness of the human being. It is clear that Thomas adopts this understanding of man when he says, "Among all human pursuits, the pursuit of wisdom is more perfect, more noble, more useful, and more full of joy."[6] More specifically, he derived his doctrine from the Aristotelian conception of reality that came finally to exert so much influence over the entire Thomistic system. God, the highest reality, is pure form or actuality; in him there is no matter or unrealized potency. This means, in a word, that God is pure intelligence. Now insofar as human beings are possessed of intelligence, they partake, says Aristotle, in the life of the gods. Thomas agrees with Aristotle that the ancient poets were simply wrong when they insisted,

> It ill befits a mortal
> To think immortal thoughts.

---

[6]St. Thomas Aquinas, *Summa Contra Gentiles*, I, 2, tr. Anton C. Pegis (Garden City, N.Y.: Image Books, 1955).

It behooves us, rather, to soar as high as our intellect can take us, thereby realizing and exercising as much as possible the divine element within us.

With respect to Christian truth specifically, we have seen earlier that Thomas insisted on the necessity of a special revelation. Even the knowledge about God that lies within reach of natural, unaided reason would, due to the difficulty of the subject and the weaknesses of human nature, be grasped by only a few, and after a long time, and with the admixture of many errors. Indeed, "if the only way open to us for the knowledge of God were solely that of the reason, the human race would remain in the blackest shadows of ignorance."[7] And if revelation is required for an adequate knowledge of the truths that reason can know, how much more is it required for a knowledge of those truths that would otherwise lie forever beyond the reach of all human understanding? Still, though many divine truths utterly exceed our ability to understand (such as the truth of the Trinity), some knowledge of God is yet attainable, however imperfectly, through the natural light of reason (such as knowledge of his existence and many of his attributes). Thus we have the Thomistic concept of the "twofold mode of truth": (1) those truths about God that lie beyond the reach of natural reason and (2) those truths about God that lie within the reach of natural reason.

Now the Christian ought, as much as possible, to pursue philosophical knowledge concerning the divine since he or she, being a human, possesses a natural desire and proper inclination to understand what is already accepted on faith. Reason, moreover, is necessary for the clarification and explanation of revealed doctrines, the refutation of opposing and erroneous teachings, and the apologetic purpose of reasoning with those who do not accept the authority of the Scriptures. With respect to the last motivation, Thomas reminds us that St. Paul himself (as is recorded in Acts 17:28) documented one of his sermons from a Stoic philosopher, showing that he was willing to meet the pagan thinkers on their own ground.[8]

---

[7] *Ibid.*, I, 4.

[8] *Ibid.*, I, 2ff.; St. Thomas Aquinas, *Summa Theologica*, Part I, Qu. 1, Art. 8. in *Basic Writings of Saint Thomas Aquinas*, ed. Anton C. Pegis (New York: Random House, 1945), I.

St. Augustine (who antedated Thomas by nearly nine centuries) also follows this approach, though with an important difference. Both Thomas and Augustine recognized as their foes certain intellectualists whose positions excluded Christian faith and revelation. Thomas, preoccupied with the possibilities of reason, was inspired to show against the Averroists (followers of Averroës, a twelfth-century Islamic thinker) that the truths of revelation could be harmonized with the truths of philosophy. Augustine, on the other hand, who was more interested in the interior life of the soul and who composed no systematic *Summas*, sought to vindicate the necessity of faith before understanding, and wrote an instructive little book entitled *The Advantage of Believing* directed at the Manichaean teaching (from Mani, a third-century Persian thinker) that a saving knowledge should be attained through reason apart from revelation.

Augustine's position on the role of faith pervades his entire philosophy, though he draws together his central reasoning for it in the previously mentioned work. His argument is that no understanding is possible to a person who willfully persists in skepticism and unbelief. It is easy to support this position from ordinary experience. Friendship, for example, would be impossible apart from a willingness to entrust oneself to another. What would become of parental discipline if the child is not required to believe what he or she does not yet understand? In fact, what would be left of society if we refuse to act save on knowledge and certainty, and if the fool refuses to trust the wise? The principle applies *a fortiori* in the context of religion, where the distance between the fool and the wise is often much greater than in everyday affairs and where the consequence of mistakes and disobedience is infinitely greater. Let us therefore begin, says Augustine, by believing the religious authorities and God himself; the Gospel then purifies the natural intellect, disposes it toward God, and leads it into full wisdom and understanding. Augustine's position is aptly summarized in his famous exhortation, ". . . understanding is the reward of faith. Therefore do not seek to understand in order to believe, but believe that thou mayest understand."[9] It is important to note, however, that Augustine under-

---

[9] St. Augustine, *Homilies on the Gospel of St. John*, XXIX, 6, tr. John Gibb and James Innes, in *Nicene and Post-Nicene Fathers*, VII (Edinburgh: Clark, 1888).

stood faith to consist not only in *assensus* ("intellectual assent") but also in *fiducia* ("trust").

Augustine was not in any way an anti-intellectualist. The emphasis of the famous dictum *Credo ut intelligam* is that "I believe *in order that* I may understand." Faith is not the termination of reason but the prerequisite and beginning of reason. We know, furthermore, that God is the author of all truth and illumination and that the Logos is "the true light that enlightens every person" (John 1:9). Augustine was, in this way, much interested in the potential contribution of philosophy to faith: ". . . I have broken and cast away from me the odious bonds by which I was kept back from the nourishing breasts of philosophy through despair of attaining that truth which is the food of the soul."[10] He did, in fact, draw heavily upon Platonic philosophy (as we saw earlier and will see again), with its conception of a transcendent and spiritual realm, insisting that the Christian understanding of reality was to be found there even if the doctrine of the Incarnation was not.

The Leap of Faith

Very different from either St. Thomas or St. Augustine are those who believe that in the presence of divine revelation the natural intellect should be abandoned, at least in the sphere of theological and spiritual wisdom, because it contributes little or nothing, or may even be a downright obstacle to the truth. This attitude, which recalls Tertullian, recurs throughout the Christian tradition, especially in Protestantism. The sixteenth-century Protestant reformer Martin Luther insisted that God is a *Deus Absconditus*, a "hidden God," unknown except through his supernatural self-disclosure in Christ. John Calvin, another reformer, emphasized that the effects of original sin extend even to the natural intellect, blinding and distorting it such that it cannot, by itself, make an adequate approach to divine truth. As we saw in Chapter 2, the late Karl Barth, stressing in his earlier writings the wholly otherness of God, announced a resounding "Nein!" to natural theology and philosophy: The loss of

---

[10]St. Augustine, *Letters*, I, 3, tr. J. G. Cunningham, in *Nicene and Post-Nicene Fathers*, I (Edinburgh: T. & T. Clark, 1886).

the *imago Dei* resulted in a great gulf fixed between God and man, bridgeable only through acceptance of God's gracious act in Christ. For Thomas and Augustine, it is possible to move from prerational faith to genuine (if incomplete) understanding; but for these other thinkers, spiritual truth by its very nature cannot be attained through the categories and concepts of reason—ever.

An example *par excellence* of this fideist approach is the Danish philosopher and writer Sören Kierkegaard (1813–1855). Kierkegaard is usually regarded as the founder of modern existentialism, a philosophy that (among other things) tends to repudiate rationalism and speculative philosophy as academic, superficial, and irrelevant. Kierkegaard himself regarded intellectual approaches to the highest truth as ludicrous. He rejected virtually a whole tradition of speculative philosophy with its abstractions, proofs, and eternal verities. And he was especially annoyed by the prevailing concept of truth, propounded by the German philosopher G. W. F. Hegel and his followers, according to which ultimate truth and reality is identified with, as it were, the Grand Idea of the Whole. All of this, says Kierkegaard, has contributed to a gross misunderstanding of the nature of Christian truth and faith. And in his determination to set the matter straight, he produced some of the most provocative, challenging, and enigmatic writings ever conceived. His mammoth literary production included religious discourses, journal entries, and pseudonymous works, and his use of parables, irony, and humor makes him one of the greatest stylists of all time.

According to Kierkegaard, most people blunder into thinking that Christianity is some sort of philosophical system and that faith is a rational assent to it, a kind of signing intellectually on the dotted line. This misunderstanding, in turn, produces the weekly comedy of vast numbers of people rising from their pews like machines to recite the Apostles' Creed and thinking that they therefore have faith. In fact, "every misunderstanding of Christianity may at once be recognized by its transforming it into a doctrine, transferring it to the sphere of the intellectual."[11] This distorted view of Christianity, says Kierkegaard, is the product of the long succession of philosophers and thinkers for whom truth means *objectivity*. For

---

[11]Sören Kierkegaard, *Concluding Unscientific Postscript*, tr. David F. Swenson and Walter Lowrie (Princeton, N.J.: Princeton University Press, 1941), p. 291.

them, truth—even Christian truth—is something "out there," like tables and chairs, common to all of us, such that with enough intellectual effort and the right methodology we should be able to grasp it, systematize it, and demonstrate it.

For Kierkegaard, the objective approach may be appropriate for scientific, mathematical, or other trivial and inconsequential truths, though it is most certainly not the appropriate approach to existential truths, that is, those truths that bear immediately on one's own existence and meaning. In the case of the objective inquirer, thought is turned away from the thinking subject and is directed to an object outside the self; this person is not, as Kierkegaard says, "infinitely and personally and passionately interested on behalf of his own eternal happiness for his relationship to this truth."[12] Truth, at least the kind that ought to concern us most, is not a matter of objectivity but *subjectivity*. This truth cannot be grasped through philosophical, scientific, or historical methods, but only when through the passion of infinite concern the existing individual abandons the self to the Teacher in a "leap of faith." This leap occurs in the decisive Moment in which the individual surmounts the infinite, qualitative difference between time and eternity and grasps (or is grasped by) God. There is, then, a kind of inverse proportion between the existential urgency of a truth and the mind's ability to come to terms with it. As for Christian truth, which concerns us most, human reason finds itself at a complete loss, and Christian apologetics—the rational defense of Christian claims—is, thus, utterly misguided:

There is only one proof of the truth of Christianity and that, quite rightly, is from the emotions, when the dread of sin and a heavy conscience torture a man into crossing the narrow line between despair bordering upon madness—and Christianity.[13]

One is not rationally persuaded, but existentially *driven* to an either/or decision about Christianity.

(Some writers speak of Kierkegaard's "subjectivism," but this invites a great misunderstanding. By "subjectivity" Kierkegaard

---

[12]*Ibid.*, p. 23.

[13]Sören Kierkegaard, *The Journals*, sec. 926, ed. and tr. Alexander Dru (London: Oxford University Press, 1938).

does not mean that the individual subject becomes the source or standard of truth, but that the highest truth, which yet remains objective in some sense, can be discovered only in inwardness or subjective consciousness. His doctrine is not a variation of Protagoras' relativistic principle, "A man is the measure of all things," but of Socrates' introspective "Know thyself." It would be best to avoid altogether any reference to subjectivism and to speak instead of Kierkegaardian subjectivity.)

It may be claimed that the central and controlling idea of the whole Kierkegaardian philosophy is the idea of *faith*. For Kierkegaard faith lies at the opposite end from intellectual assent to propositions—it is not a *what* but a *how*. It is passion, inwardness, infinite concern, and personal assimilation. All this issues in the famous definition of faith as *"an objective uncertainty held fast in an appropriation-process of the most passionate inwardness"*[14] and in an emphasis on the risk that faith involves:

> Without risk there is no faith. Faith is precisely the contradiction between the infinite passion of the individual's inwardness and the objective uncertainty. If I am capable of grasping God objectively, I do not believe, but precisely because I cannot do this I must believe. If I wish to preserve myself in faith I must constantly be intent upon holding fast the objective uncertainty, so as to remain out upon the deep, over seventy thousand fathoms of water, still preserving my faith.[15]

It should be noted, however, that the emphasis here is on "objective uncertainty" and "God." This concerns what Kierkegaard calls "Religiousness A" and the kind of faith that approaches God on the basis of what is given within the individual. It may be thought that an impassioned leap to God amid objective uncertainty is bad enough, but in the case of "Religiousness B," or *Christian* faith, the situation is even worse. Here, our sinful nature blocks any natural approach to God, rendering us entirely dependent on a *revelation* from without; and faith is directed to *Christ* and the intrinsically paradoxical idea of the God-Man. Thus, instead of a mere objective uncertainty, we are confronted with the *certainty of an objective absurdity*. Kierkegaard draws the contrast:

---

[14]Kierkegaard, *Concluding Unscientific Postscript*, p. 182.
[15]*Ibid.*

Instead of the objective uncertainty, there is here a certainty, namely, that objectively it is absurd; and this absurdity, held fast in the passion of inwardness, is faith.[16]

Whether Kierkegaard here uses "absurdity" in the strict sense of a logical contradiction or in the loose sense of what is completely contrary to our experience, expectations, and so on is debated. I favor the latter interpretation. I don't see how, even on the strictest fideist view, it can be demanded of the Christian or anyone else to believe that something happened that can't happen! Nonetheless, at best, Kierkegaard calls upon the Christian to believe "in opposition to reason," and he is, thus, in some important sense, an irrationalist.

Thus, as Kierkegaard expresses it, Christianity *for Kierkegaard* is not a doctrine, and faith is not a refuge for numbskulls or the feeble-minded. Christianity is a Person: Jesus Christ, the God-Man, a Paradox to reason (I Cor. 1:18ff.); and faith is a relation to that person. Further, faith is not something exercised once and for all. The existential individual lives continually in dread of the meaningless, dread that can be assuaged only by a continued and renewed commitment to Christ. In this sense one never *is* a Christian but is always *becoming* one.

Finally, faith is an acutely personal matter. It is a decision, born of an individual's pain and crisis, in which he or she chooses to stand in fear and trembling alone before God: "Christianity proposes to endow the individual with an eternal happiness, a good which is not distributed wholesale, but only to one individual at a time."[17] (Kierkegaard suggested, for his epitaph, "That Individual.")

The faith that springs from despair and rests continually on the intensity of personal commitment is not the superficial faith of institutional "Christendom." Toward the end of his brief career, Kierkegaard (who had resolved early to raise trouble everywhere) vented a fiery outburst against Christian society like that of his native Denmark, with its official state church. In such a society it is not required that one be contemporary with Christ and suffer with him. Indeed, in such a society, to be a Christian is the acceptable

---

[16]*Ibid.*, p. 188
[17]*Ibid,.* p. 116

thing. It is easy to be a Christian and everyone is a Christian. *But in such a society no one is a Christian.* There is no existential concern, no real appropriation of grace, no anguish, no suffering, no passion, no faith. An example of Kierkegaard's stinging indictment of the pseudochurch is his sarcastic comment:

In the magnificent cathedral the Honorable and Right Reverend Geheime-General-Ober-Hof-Prädikant, the elect favorite of the fashionable world, appears before an elect company and preaches *with emotion* upon the text he himself elected: "God hath elected the base things of the world, and the things that are despised"—and nobody laughs.[18]

The *crux* of Kierkegaard's conception of existential truth is this: The mainstream of traditional, speculative philosophy rendered the world rational or intelligible by subordinating particulars to universal concepts and general laws. This culminated, in Kierkegaard's day, in the philosophy of Hegel, already mentioned. On the Hegelian view—to tell a very long story in a very short time—ultimate truth and reality is the Universal Idea that nature and history are actualizing by means of the continual and higher synthesis of opposite states. In this "dialectical" process, existing individuals are increasingly dissolved, so to speak, in the evolving Universe, the Great Abstraction. Such talk repelled Kierkegaard, who located the highest truth, and genuine faith, not in uninteresting universal ideas ("All men are mortal") but in the passion of individual existence ("I too must die!"). In this state of subjectivity the existential person is enabled to transcend both the aesthetic level with its interest in immediate enjoyment, as well as the ethical level with its interest in conformity to general principles, and approach God on a truly religious plane where ethical principles are suspended and the individual stands before God in a unique relation.

The Kierkegaardian categories of individuality and particularity (the opposite of universality) resist, of course, precisely the sort of rational manipulation that traditional philosophers glorified and shift our attention from the domain of objective, intellectual observation to the sphere of subjective, passionate assimilation, from the

---

[18]Sören Kierkegaard, *The Instant, No. 6,* "Short and Sharp," 2, in *Attack Upon "Christendom,"* tr. Walter Lowrie (Princeton, N.J.: Princeton University Press, 1944).

approximation-process to the appropriation-process. In Christianity, the supreme object of this appropriation is the event of the God-Man, an event characterized by its utter uniqueness and particularity, incapable of being subsumed under any general principle and for that reason a scandal to the intellect. As was suggested above the greater the existential import of a truth, the less does that truth fall within the grasp of the objectivizing intellect. But what is lost to the objective way is precisely what is recovered and preserved in the subjective way—the existing Individual.

In all of this may be seen a Christian expression of what Jean-Paul Sartre called the common ground of all existentialism, the principle that "existence precedes essence," and it is difficult to miss the Kierkegaardian sound of Sartre's charge that philosophy's waywardness lies with its power to drain people of their lifeblood and turn them into pale abstractions.

Though Kierkegaard has been criticized from many directions, the most famous charge is that he was insane. One writer castigates Kierkegaard for a rejection of reason that borders on perversion, maintaining that his obsessions, self-centeredness, and other neuroses qualify him as a dubious guide for training in Christianity. This writer concludes that the less we have of this kind of faith the better.[19] No doubt, Kierkegaard's relation to his father and his ill-fated love affair with Regina Olsen left their imprint on his works; it is true that he was in fact a deeply subjective person; and it was not for nothing that he was called the "melancholy Dane." But to judge that he was really sick may be a bit much. And in any case, one might prefer that kind of sickness to the spurious life of the detached and dispassionate spirit who turns aside from the crisis of concrete and conscious existence. Kierkegaard proclaims, rightly, that authentic philosophy is not a fantasy speculation concerning fantasy people; the philosopher addresses *human beings*.

The Will to Believe

Another variation on the subordination-of-reason-to-faith theme is William James' concept of "the will to believe," a concept that must

---

[19]H. J. Paton, *The Modern Predicament* (London: George Allen & Unwin, 1955), pp. 75, 120.

be understood against the backdrop of the American philosophy known as Pragmatism, to which James (1842–1910) was a chief contributor. For this philosophy, workability or the satisfaction of needs is the criterion of truth: A proposition is true if it works, that is, if it is profitable or expedient (either intellectually or practically) to believe it. As James emphasizes, with italics, Pragmatism is

the attitude of looking away from first things, principles, "categories," supposed necessities; and of looking towards last things, fruits, consequences, facts. . . . The true is the name of whatever proves itself to be good in the way of belief, and good, too, for definite assignable reasons.[20]

It is no wonder that James himself called Pragmatism the philosophy of "cash value."

James' pragmatic point of view is given specific shape in his well-known essay "The Will to Believe," directed against William K. Clifford, an English mathematician and thoroughgoing rationalist. Clifford himself had written an essay entitled "The Ethics of Belief," in which he argued that it is immoral and harmful, both for the individual and for society, to affirm the truth of something that lacks complete intellectual justification: ". . . it is wrong always, everywhere, and for anyone, to believe anything upon insufficient evidence."[21] According to James, however, it often turns out that an important decision may have to be made even though the rational evidence for the decision is insufficient on either side. In such a situation, the only intelligent thing to do is to make a decision or judgment in light of its practical consequences—in other words, *to will* something to be true. James called himself a radical empiricist, and he believed that at best God lay on the "fringe" of experience, hardly an object of scientific knowledge. On the other hand, he believed also that there may be just such a practical value, a pragmatic truth, in the theist position. He summarizes his thesis against Clifford:

[20]William James, *Pragmatism* (New York: Longmans, Green & Co., 1907), pp. 54f., 57.
[21]William Kingdon Clifford, *Lectures and Essays*, ed. Leslie Stephen and Frederick Pollock (London: Macmillan, 1886), p. 346.

Our passional nature not only lawfully may, but must, decide an option between propositions, whenever it is a genuine option that cannot by its nature be decided on intellectual grounds. . . .[22]

It is important to emphasize that James in no way seeks to skirt the possible contribution of reason; of course, we must be as reasonable and as evidenced in our positions as possible. But in those situations where no dictate is forthcoming, then James offers his principle as both applicable and necessary. Further, his principle does not work for just any dilemma but only for those involving a "genuine option," that is, an option that is living, forced, and momentous. Whether the choice between believing or not believing in God cannot be made on rational grounds is, of course, an individual matter, and only the reader knows whether reason is successful in tipping the scale one way or the other. Be that as it may, for most readers the decision does constitute at least a genuine option—living (not dead), forced (not avoidable), and momentous (not trivial).

It is a *living* option inasmuch as both theism and atheism (or agnosticism) commend themselves to us as real possibilities. A decision between, say, Jesus as the Son of God or Krishna as an incarnation of Vishnu would be for most Westerners a dead option since belief in Krishna simply does not fit and cohere with our general view of things. We must, after all, begin where we find ourselves, with whatever frame of reference we happen to enjoy and with whatever tools happen to be at hand. To believe or not believe in God is, further, a *forced* option. Of course, many decisions may be avoided by refusing to choose at all; the decision to prepare my Greek lesson or read a novel may be avoided by simply going to a movie. But in the present case, like many others, it is quite different. It is not possible not to choose; the issue demands from us a decision one way or the other; the option is a forced one:

We cannot escape the issue by remaining skeptical and waiting for more light, because, although we do avoid error in that way *if religion be untrue,* we lose the good, *if it be true,* just as certainly as if we positively chose to disbelieve.[23]

---

[22]William James, *The Will to Believe and Other Essays* (New York: Longmans, Green & Co., 1905), p. 11.

[23]*Ibid.,* p. 26.

Finally, the issue is a *momentous* one. Many questions, such as whether Sirius is 8.7 light years away, may strike us as fairly inconsequential, leaving us completely indifferent and unmoved; they make no intellectual or practical demand on us. There are, however, other issues that make a difference, perhaps a great difference. For many of us, the existence of God and the truth of Christianity are two such issues. They press themselves upon us as urgent questions, and we recognize that we stand possibly to lose something if we judge wrongly.

There may be, therefore a *prima facie* attractiveness about the rationalist ideal of objectivity and suspension of judgment in the face of inadequate evidence, but it quickly goes bankrupt in the face of the concrete and practical decision situations portrayed by James. After all, what kind of a principle is it that would prevent me from believing in the truth if the truth were actually there? And if the point of it all is to be, as James says, "on the winning side," why is dupery through fear of being wrong to be preferred to dupery through hope of being right? "In truths dependent on our personal action, then, faith based on desire is certainly a lawful and possibly an indispensable thing."[24] Just a few years before, John Stuart Mill had, in fact, predicted that more attention would be given to the imaginative and pragmatic consideration of the theist position:

. . . the indulgence of hope with regard to the government of the universe and the destiny of man after death, while we recognize as a clear truth that we have no ground for more than a hope, is legitimate and philosophically defensible. The beneficial effect of such a hope is far from trifling.[25]

James' voluntarism (so called because of the primary of volition or will) has, understandably, been severely criticized by those who see in it only an egotistical concern for saving one's skin at any cost. But it may be doubted whether such critics have always appreciated the full force of this reasoning. If there were *no* other reason to believe, what could possibly be a better reason than to save one's

---

[24]*Ibid.*, p. 25.
[25]John Stuart Mill, "Theism," in *Three Essays on Religion*, 3rd ed. (New York: Longmans, Green & Co., 1875), p. 249.

skin? In fact, what could be more intelligent than to want to be right, to attain the good, to be saved, to escape evil, and to act accordingly? And as for the suggestion that God could hardly honor any faith thus motivated, it might be countered that presumably God honors also the prudent man over the fool. Furthermore, can it be believed that God esteems faith only in proportion as it is evidenced, rationalized, and certified? If so, many believers will be found sadly wanting. A better criticism, perhaps, is the following: Is such a belief in God as James proposes really a *belief*? A child can really believe in Santa Claus, but an adult cannot, not even if he or she recognized some advantage in really believing. Likewise, there is a difference between believing in God and believing that there is a pragmatic advantage in believing in God. Still, one must not be too hasty, even in this indictment. James himself stresses that it is a misapprehension to regard faith as did the schoolboy who defined it as "believing what you know ain't true." Neither the hypothesis of Santa Claus nor any other can be an object even of pragmatic belief unless it is a *live* hypothesis.

All of this reminds one, of course, of the famous Wager of the French thinker Blaise Pascal (1623–1662), upon whom James draws more than once in his own argument. Pascal urged the unbeliever to believe, for consider: Would you not wager without hesitation against high stakes if you stood to lose nothing?

Let us weigh the gain and the loss in wagering that God is. Let us estimate these two chances. If you gain, you gain all; if you lose, you lose nothing. Wager, then, without hesitation that He is.[26]

Obviously, this reasoning gains even more force when it is realized that if we fail to wager, or if we wager that God does not exist and it turns out that He does, then we lose everything! Actually, Pascal's voluntarism goes further than James' for he taught that in this matter one ought to wager *no matter what the rational evidence may be.* If there is but one chance in an infinite number that reason may be mistaken and that God may exist, we may still have something to gain and certainly nothing to lose by betting on God. Thus reason

---

[26]Blaise Pascal, *Pensées,* no. 233, in *Pensées and the Provincial Letters,* tr. W. F. Trotter and Thomas M'Crie (New York: Modern Library, 1941).

must be renounced if it may mean the preservation of our souls. Pascal goes further than James in another respect. He believes that just as seeing comes through looking, so for many it is only by participating in Christianity that they may come to recognize its truth. For James it was a matter of making a decision in view of its practical value and then hoping for the best. For Pascal there is a sense in which the truth discloses itself through and in the willing of it. Thus he urges the skeptic to act as if he believed, to take holy water and have masses said: "Even this will naturally make you believe and deaden your acuteness."[27]

A further note. Pascal is often considered an eloquent spokesman for the nonrational approach to religious truth, and rightly so. Strewn throughout his celebrated *Pensées* ("Thoughts") are warnings against overintellectualizing the faith. For example, he distinguishes the God of the philosophers from the God of Abraham, Isaac, and Jacob; and he correctly emphasizes that the writers of the Bible never attempted to prove the existence of God. Pascal's best statement on this subject is his well-known comment,

The heart has its reasons, which reason does not know. . . . It is the heart which experiences God, and not the reason. This, then, is faith: God felt by the heart, not by the reason.[28]

(For Pascal "heart" does not mean anything akin to emotional feeling; reason is *above* sense and feeling, and "the order of charity," where the heart operates, is above reason.) But though he sees clearly that there is a decidedly nonrational aspect to Christian faith, and even appears to be preoccupied with it, he does not deny that reason has also a necessary role to play. In one remarkable passage, Pascal emphasizes the necessity of *both* the rational *and* the nonrational contributions to religious truth:

If we submit everything to reason, our religion will have no mysterious and supernatural element. If we offend the principles of reason, our religion will be absurd and ridiculous.[29]

---

[27]*Ibid.*
[28]*Ibid.*, nos. 277–278.
[29]*Ibid.*, no. 273.

Belief in God as "Properly Basic"

Closely related to all of this is the recent claim, and one that has created a considerable stir, that belief in God, like many other beliefs, may be embraced as a *properly basic* one. The argument here is against *evidentialism*. As the name suggests, evidentialism insists that important beliefs, such as belief in God, should be based on evidence: You consider the factors that support the belief, you consider the factors that weigh against the belief, and then you cast your vote in accordance with the strongest evidence—or, if the evidence for and against balances out, then you suspend judgment. In the previous section, we encountered an example of a strict evidentialist, William K. Clifford, and we saw how William James sought to refute him, at least with respect to those instances when the evidence balances out. The view we consider in this section also rejects evidentialism but argues, more broadly, that it is legitimate to believe in God apart from any rational evidence—which is, of course, how most people believe in God anyway.

Evidentialism has gone hand in hand with foundationalism, an epistemological doctrine that has dominated our philosophical tradition. Foundationalism is the belief that any proposition is accepted as true either on the basis of some other proposition that is accepted as true or because it is just seen to be true immediately. If the latter, then the proposition is part of the foundational propositions that underlie and uphold our "noetic structures" or belief systems.

So far, so good. Most foundationalists, however, have operated with a stronger and more restrictive principle ("strong foundationalism"): No proposition can be properly basic unless it is either (1) self-evident, that is, true on the face of it, as with "2 + 2 = 4;" (2) incorrigible, that is, expresses an immediate state of consciousness, as with "I have a pain in my chest;" or (3) expresses an immediate deliverance of sense experience, as with, "There is a fire in the fireplace." This has proven problematic to many nowadays, and especially to a group of thinkers spearheading what is called "reformed epistemology." This label reflects a similarity between these thinkers and the sixteenth-century Protestant reformer John Calvin; it was originally used as a joke, but it stuck. The reformed epistemologists include Alvin Plantinga, William Alston, Nicholas Wolterstorff, and others. According to Plantinga, in an important piece called "Reason and Belief in God,"[30] the strong version of foundationalism is rejected because, first, it fails utterly to account for a vast number of things we surely know but, nonetheless, fall short of the criterion of strong foundationalism; such knowledge would include, for example, my knowledge that you are in pain, that I had breakfast this morning, and that the world has existed for more than five minutes. Second, it is "self-referentially incoherent" (a fancy way of saying that it refutes itself) inasmuch as it fails to measure up to its own criteria: The thesis of strong foundationalism is itself neither self-evident, nor incorrigible, nor an immediate deliverance of the senses! This leaves the door open for many more beliefs than we thought to qualify as properly basic. And why not belief in God? If I can legitimately start with knowledge of other minds, breakfast, and a world that has existed longer than five minutes, why can't I just start with God? Everyone starts with certain slants, presuppositions, and prephilosophic commitments. Why can't the theist? Thus, even though these thinkers discard strong foundationalism, they do not discard foundationalism itself. They keep the distinction between properly basic beliefs and those beliefs that are derived from them. They just broaden the pool of what qualifies as properly basic beliefs, those that are legitimate foundations of our noetic structures.

Still, this doesn't quite bring us to what is distinctive in the approach of the reformed epistemologists. Others before them have observed that belief in God may be no more or less legitimate than belief in other things, say, the continued existence of objects outside of our minds. What is distinctive is their specific appeal to Calvin for an explanation of the ground of this belief. God has, in fact, so constituted us that we have a natural inclination to believe in him:

There is within the human mind, and indeed by natural instinct, an awareness of divinity. . . . God himself has implanted in all men a certain understanding of his divine majesty . . . men one and all perceive that there is a God and that he is their maker.[31]

---

[30]Alvin Plantinga, "Reason and Belief in God," in, Alvin Plantinga and Nicholas Wolterstorff (eds.), *Faith and Rationality: Reason and Belief in God*, (Notre Dame, Ind.: University of Notre Dame Press, 1983).

[31]John Calvin, *Institutes of the Christian Religion*, I, 3, 1, tr. Ford Lewis Battles, in *Library of Christian Classics*, XX (Philadelphia: Westminster Press, 1960), I.

Plantinga amplifies the idea:

> When the Reformers claim that this belief is properly basic, they do not mean to say, of course, that there are no justifying circumstances for it, or that it is in that sense groundless or gratuitous. Quite the contrary. Calvin holds that God "reveals and daily discloses himself in the whole workmanship of the universe," and the divine art "reveals itself in the innumerable and yet distinct and well ordered variety of the heavenly host." God has so created us that we have a tendency or disposition to see his hand in the world about us.[32]

Other "justifying circumstances" include situations involving the individual's experience of guilt, gratitude, danger, God's presence, and the like. The goal is to have a noetic structure that is functioning properly as God intends it.

Calvin aside, the point is that the believer is perfectly within his or her "epistemic" rights to believe in God apart from any *rational* grounds. Does this mean, first, that belief in God (or any other belief, however crazy) may be arbitrarily declared "properly basic"? This is the point of the Great Pumpkin Objection: You might as well say that Linus, in the Peanuts comic strip, has a perfectly rational belief as he sits in the pumpkin patch on Halloween waiting for the promised arrival of the Great Pumpkin. The reformed epistemologist's answer is something like this: Nobody can affirm at all, much less as properly basic, a belief that is not—to use an expression from the last section—a living option, and if belief in the Great Pumpkin, or whatever, *is* for someone a pressing truth, well, we sometimes differ, don't we, with respect to fundamental convictions. Surely we are free to say: "I think you're wrong—your noetic structure is out of sync with reality." Nor does it mean, second, that the believer affirms his or her truth in a manner that is insulated from any scrutiny or criticism. There is nothing to prevent one from reflecting critically on what is already held as a properly basic belief—with the possibility, in fact, that the belief may be abandoned.

---

[32]Plantinga, *Reason and Belief in God,* p. 80.

Importance of the Problem

It can hardly be denied, on the one hand, that the nonrational (whether understood as a transcending religious experience, feeling of the numinous, acceptance of divine authority, willing appropriation, basic belief, or whatever) is a central and distinctive ingredient of religion, if not, as Otto insisted, its very core. On the other hand, it is apparent that it cannot be a matter of faith to the *utter* and *absolute* exclusion of reason. For one thing, the statement "In matters pertaining to faith, the reason makes no contribution whatsoever" is self-refuting: It itself pertains to faith and yet commends itself to reason! And if the *imago Dei* is so warped, bent, or obliterated that we cannot in our own power say anything true about God, then how can we even say *that*? Further, what about the inevitable role of reason in critical Biblical scholarship? And what about the grounds for accepting revelation in the first place, or the truth of Christianity as opposed to competing religions, and so on and so forth? More generally, must not any religious or theological position that is represented to the world by means of concepts and language (and what position isn't?) at some point or other be rendered at least intelligible, if not credible? Even Kierkegaard, who believed that the first thing we must understand is that there are some things we cannot understand, and that Christian faith is about something that offends the reason, and that the God relationship can at best be expressed only indirectly, displayed a mind-boggling erudition and, in his own way, *made a case*. It is evident that any adequate position on religious truth will have to do justice both to its rational and to its nonrational dimensions.

We emphasized at the beginning of this chapter that the problem of faith and reason is not, after all, merely a religious or theological problem. Everyone, including the nonreligious person, must decide if he or she is going to acknowledge at all the presence of the nonrational in his or her understanding of the world, and if so, what its source and authority are. The problem of faith and reason is, therefore, a general philosophical problem, one that must be confronted by anyone who attempts to interpret human knowledge.

But there is something further. Though it was suggested in Chapter 1 how the problem of God is, in a way, foundational to all the questions of philosophical theology, it is now apparent that in another way the problem of faith and reason is the most basic. The British philosopher John Locke judged that the failure to settle first the "measures and boundaries" of faith and reason has certainly led to disputes and perhaps to grave errors as well. He concludes:

> . . . till it be resolved how far we are to be guided by reason and how far by faith, we shall in vain dispute, and endeavour to convince one another in matters of religion. . . . This ought to be the first point established in all questions where faith has anything to do.[33]

As was said at the beginning of this chapter, we are not allowed to make up the rules after the game has gotten underway. Similarly, we cannot properly begin to theologize until we have made it clear to ourselves whether theoretical knowledge is even possible, and have established the role of special revelation, reason, sense experience, the "heart," and so forth. Whether or not that is strictly true (not everyone would agree that theology rises or falls with epistemology), it does appear that at least in some sense the problem of faith and reason is fundamental to all the others. And that is why in both of St. Thomas Aquinas' massive works, the *Summa Theologica* and the *Summa Contra Gentiles*, the *first* question he considers is the question of faith and reason.

---

[33]John Locke, *An Essay Concerning Human Understanding*, ed. Alexander Campbell Fraser (Oxford, England: Clarendon Press, 1894), II, pp. 415f.

8

The Problem of Evil

Refuting an argument in favor of God is not the same as giving an argument against God. Even if one could effectively refute all the arguments for God, it would not follow that God doesn't exist, but merely that those arguments fail to demonstrate it. What is called for, if one would defend atheism, is a positive *dis*proof of the existence of God. By and large, only one main argument has been raised against God, but it is a lulu. It is the argument from the existence of evil, both innocent suffering and moral perversity—what someone has called the "Undesign Argument." The issues addressed in this book may seem at times to be academic and out of touch with the real world, but evil sooner or later touches everyone, and sometimes in appalling ways and proportions. It has been said that the Psalmist who announced (Ps. 37:25),

> I have been young, and now am old,
>> yet I have not seen the righteous forsaken
>> or their children begging bread.

must have been either very lucky or very blind. And who of us living today in the shadow of the mind-numbing horrors of the Jewish Holocaust needs any further prompting: "Where was God?!"

Statements of the Problem

Obviously, the problem of evil (also called the problem of "theodicy," meaning literally "justification of God") is not a concern of religious people alone. Any sensitive person, whether religious or not, is sure to be troubled by the presence of evil and pain in the world. At the same time, it should be evident why it is in a religious or theological context that this problem receives its most forceful expression. The religious person or the theologian is always talking about how good God is. But how is the hideous reality of evil—both the *natural* evil that is produced by nature's calamities and the *moral* evil that springs from human free will—to be reconciled with the theologian's omnipotent and omnibenevolent God? John Stuart Mill delivers the challenge in this way:

. . . every kind of moral depravity is entailed upon multitudes by the fatality of their birth, through the fault of their parents, of society, or of uncontrollable circumstances, certainly through no fault of their own. Not even on the most distorted and contracted theory of good which ever was framed by religious or philosophical fanaticism can the government of nature be made to resemble the work of a being at once good and omnipotent.[1]

Goethe puts the matter more passionately:

Who never ate his bread with tears,
Who never the sorrowful nights
Sat weeping on his bed,
Knows you not, you heavenly powers!

You lead us off into life,
You let the wretch incur guilt
Then abandon him to his torture:
For all guilt is avenged on earth.[2]

The simplest and most famous statement of the problem of evil is probably that of David Hume, who, rephrasing an ancient question, asked: "Is he willing to prevent evil, but not able? then is he

---

[1]John Stuart Mill, *Utility of Religion*, in *Nature and Utility of Religion*, ed. George Nakhnikian (New York: Macmillan, 1958), pp. 26f.

[2]Johann Wolfgang von Goethe, *Harfenspieler* (my translation).

impotent. Is he able, but not willing? then is he malevolent. Is he both able and willing? whence then is evil?"[3] The theologian's inability to supply the skeptic with a straightforward and satisfying answer to this challenge has made evil no doubt the biggest single stumbling block to belief in a God. It must be noted, though, that it is not just any old idea of God that is involved here; it is the God of classical theism, who is the sum of all perfections and who therefore must be omnipotent (all-powerful) and omnibenevolent (all-loving).

A Question of Logic or Evidence?

Almost anyone can feel the tension or see some sort of incompatibility involved in the two claims,

> There is an all-powerful, all-loving God.

> There is evil.

But what sort of incompatibility is it? It is important to distinguish two different senses of "incompatibility" and, correspondingly, two ways in which the theist has been at this point attacked.

It is sometimes claimed, first, that the two propositions above involve a problem at the purely intellectual level, that is, a *logical* incompatibility: Both claims cannot be true; when put together a self-contradiction results. Now if this is so, then the game is over and the theist has lost. For if one of the two propositions has to go, it will surely not be the evil-proposition. What could be more counterintuitive (Christian Scientists to the contrary) than the denial of the awful reality of evil? But *is* it a logical incompatibility that is involved here? Someone has said that "since the critic alleges that it is logically impossible that both God and evil exist, the theistic defender must show that it is logically possible."[4] Really? I would have though that the burden lies with the critic to reveal the alleged logical contradiction. This is an important point because it would

---

[3] David Hume, *Dialogues Concerning Natural Religion*, ed. Henry D. Aiken (New York: Hafner, 1948), p. 66.

[4] Michael Peterson *et al.*, *Reason and Religious Belief: An Introduction to the Philosophy of Religion* (New York: Oxford University Press, 1991), p. 95.

seem impossible to show such a contradiction, with the result that the *worst* position the defender is in is that of pleading ignorance as to *how* both propositions could be true.

As a matter of fact, however, some claim to be able to prove that the two propositions are *logically consistent*, that is, free from self-contradiction. The principle is this: Two propositions may be shown to be logically consistent if a third is introduced that, when taken with one of the two, and is logically consistent with it, implies the other of the two. (It should be noted that inasmuch as this is a test for logical consistency, not truth, it doesn't matter if any of the propositions are actually true.) A possible application:

*There is a wholly good God.

God has morally compelling reasons for creating a world in which he knows there will be evil.

----

*Therefore, there is evil in the world.

It would appear that the two original propositions (the starred ones) are at least logically consistent and that both, therefore, may be true.

But are they? This brings us to a second meaning of "incompatible." Even if the two propositions are logically compatible, most of us feel a tension nonetheless. It's an incompatibility we "feel in our bones," an *existential* incompatibility. And this gives rise to what is called the "evidential" (as opposed to "logical") problem of evil. The problem here concerns not the formal relation of propositions, but our actual experience of evil, and, more emphatically, our confrontation with such a *profusion* and *variety* of evil. And *gratuitous* evil.

But, again, the theist is not without some moves. First, concerning the amount of evil: Wouldn't it be meaningless to speculate on the "right amount" of evil in the world and draw a line? For once you've gotten rid of Hitler, you've reduced the amount of evil in the world, but then you've got to get rid of Himmler too. And then, wouldn't you have to get rid of Mussolini, then Stalin, and then finally *yourself*, inasmuch as a world without you would be somewhat freer of evil? At what point would it suddenly appear that the right balance of good and evil has been achieved? Would not *any* amount of evil have to be judged as too much? It's like the

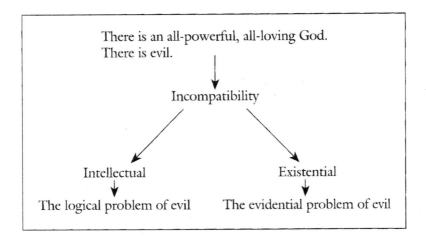

There is an all-powerful, all-loving God.
There is evil.

Incompatibility

Intellectual   Existential

The logical problem of evil   The evidential problem of evil

concept of the shortest person possible. It's meaningless—it has no real content—because there's always possibly somebody shorter.

As for gratuitous evil: It has been answered that gratuitous moral evil, for example, is the product not of God but of human free will; one may blame God, of course, for endowing some of his creatures with free will, but that's another question. Similarly, the meaningful exercise of free will presupposes an ordered and predictable natural world, but such a natural world, if it is to be an authentic one, must be allowed to run its course, at least generally, and this inevitably will mean migraine headaches and much worse. This is to say nothing of the claim that "pointless" suffering actually has an uplifting and ennobling effect, often for the individual and always for humanity. But we are now anticipating some discussions that follow, and which continue to address, in one way or another, the evidential problem of evil.

The Goodness of the Whole

Many thinkers, persuaded of the ultimate intelligibility of things and of reason's ability to grasp it, have made important attempts to come to grips philosophically with evil in the hope of reconciling it with belief in an omnipotent and benevolent deity, or at least a rational universe, or both.

A striking example of this confidence is found in the seven-teenth-century German philosopher G. W. Leibniz, who, in his tightly reasoned *Theodicy*, deduced that this is the "best of all possible worlds" on the grounds that it would be impossible for God, infinitely wise and good, to have chosen any other. His vindication of the presence of evil in the world proceeds along several lines, all of which have been suggested, in one form or another, both before and after him.

One of these arguments asserts that it is logically impossible to have a world devoid of evil. Leibniz, who had formulated his own version of the Cosmological Argument, reasoned that God, who is absolutely perfect, cannot create a second God, for the second, just by virtue of having been created, would possess contingent exis-tence and for this reason would lack something of the perfection and goodness of the first. It is *logically* required, therefore, that cre-ation manifest some degree of imperfection or evil. Another of Leibniz's arguments, otherwise known as the *ad maiorem gloriam Dei* ("to the greater glory of God") solution, portrays God as using sin and evil as a kind of foil by which he magnifies and enhances his own grace and glory. The reasoning is that if God had not permit-ted sin, then he would have been prevented from displaying his benevolent mercy, thus frustrating the manifestation of the divine glory, as well as the greater good for humanity attained through divine grace. Another of Leibniz's views, sometimes called the "therapy theory of evil," finds people emotionally matured and strengthened in character through the experience of suffering: Evil often turns out to be a godsend for our own well being. Finally, he claimed that evil (both natural and moral) is necessitated by the richness of life's complexity. Just as a painting requires contrasting hues and a musical composition some dissonance, so does the full-ness of life and the diversity of experience require some dark moments and flaws. As Leibniz observes, it would be very dull to own a thousand well-bound Vergils and to eat nothing but par-tridges.

Such explanations will appear to many as forced and superficial. Large consolation to someone racked with cancerous pain to be assured that into every life a little rain must fall or to be assured that the experience will count for much personal enrichment—if he sur-vives! We are reminded of Voltaire's satirical novel *Candide*, in which the hapless Candide falls from one outlandish and ridiculous evil into another, smiling all the while and maintaining that "this is the best of all possible worlds." There are, however, four explanations of evil that, though sometimes overlapping in some ways with those already presented, are worthy of greater attention. In every age, many have found them, in various forms, persuasive and helpful.

The first of these consists of an appeal to the goodness of the whole. On this view, evil (both moral and natural) is something that appears to exist only from our human, limited, finite point of view. If we could survey history and the universe *sub specie aeternitatis* ("under the aspect of eternity"), or from the standpoint of the whole, we would see that ultimately all things are interconnected and related so as to produce the greatest possible harmony, beauty, and good. This understanding of good and evil probably received its most emphatic expression in the ancient Greek philosophy known as Stoicism. Central to this philosophy was its conception of a divine *Logos*, or Reason, that directs the unfolding of the cosmos and history, a divine reason and purpose that encompasses all that exists and turns evil to good. This idea is explicit in the following stanza from Cleanthes' *Hymn to Zeus* (*c*. 250 B.C.):

> No deed is wrought upon the earth apart from thee, O God,
> Nor down the divine aethereal sky, nor in the sea,
> Save what the wicked do in their own unthinking.
> But you know how to equalize,
> To order things disordered, and the unlovely are lovely to you.
> Thus have you harmonized all into one, the evil with the good:
> Making the Reason of all to be one, eternal.[5]

In the Stoic's view, everything is governed by divine reason and law, and everything contributes, ultimately, to the ordered unity and goodness of the whole. The judgment that there is evil in the world follows simply from our ignorance of the whole, from our barbarous insensitivity to the rationality and purpose present in all things. From the standpoint of the all-embracing knowledge of God, on the other hand, all things are good and beautiful, all things reflect an ultimate order and purpose—even what, from our limited points of view, appears disgusting and pernicious. It behooves one,

---

[5]Cleanthes, *Hymn to Zeus* (my translation).

then, to attune the soul to the divine *Logos*, to appreciate the ultimate harmony of things, to cultivate a divine perspective. Such a
person is freed from the anxiety and fear that plague the ignorant,
for he or she has seen and has confidence in the rule of Reason. In
this sense, knowledge is salvation. Of course, there follows from all
of this the well-known Stoic doctrine of resignation to one's allot-
ted role. This idea received eloquent expression in Epictetus, a later
Stoic:

> Remember that you are an actor in a drama of such sort as the Author
> chooses—if short, then in a short one; if long, then in a long one. If it be
> his pleasure that you should enact a poor man, or a cripple, or a ruler, or a
> private citizen, see that you act it well. For this is your business—to act well
> the given part, but to choose it belongs to another.

And he urges us always to have ready at hand this short piece by
Cleanthes:

> Conduct me, Zeus, and thou, O Destiny,
> Wherever your decrees have fixed my lot.
> I follow cheerfully; and, did I not,
> Wicked and wretched, I must follow still.[6]

It may be no small problem for some readers to maneuver themselves into a Stoic view of things, with its optimism about the
world's nature and outcome, and certainly an unqualified denial of
evil would have to be judged as either hopelessly naive or the product of philosophical psychosis. Further, one might find it impossible
to accept any theodicy that subordinates personal good to an impersonal aesthetic scheme. This is to say nothing of the problem of reconciling a pervasive determinism (even a divine determinism) with
the moral necessity of free will, a problem never satisfactorily
resolved by the Stoics or by anyone else.

Nonetheless, this position reminds us that aside from Mill,
Hume, Goethe, and all those who seem bent upon exalting the problem of evil, there are others who find themselves overwhelmed by the
balance of harmony, beauty, and goodness in the world; and any

---

[6]Epictetus, *The Enchiridion*, 17 and 51, tr. Thomas W. Higginson (New
York: Macmillan, 1948).

teacher of religion will testify that in the classroom the least suggestion of Original Sin is shouted down with humanistic cries affirming
the basic goodness of humanity. There are some, then, for whom it is
not so much a problem of evil as a problem of goodness. Mill's outrage, quoted earlier may in fact be restated without any loss of its
original force: Not even on the most distorted and contracted theory
of evil that was ever framed by atheistic fanaticism can the government of nature be made to resemble the work of a being who is
unconcerned about the well-being of his creatures. And is not the
question "Whence is love, good will, harmony, and beauty?" every
bit as interesting and deserving of an answer as is Hume's "Whence
is evil?" Why is it any easier to account for goodness without God
than it is to account for evil with him? That the problem of evil gen-
erates more fury than the problem of goodness may be more a matter of psychology than of philosophy. At any rate, the Stoics represent a long tradition of reflective people who have felt constrained to
opt for a *Logos*, God, or some such, rather than an inconceivable
abandonment of the world and experience to a malevolent irrational.

Evil as Privation of Good

Another influential explanation of evil is that evil is nothing at all,
being but a privation or absence of being and goodness. The most
important version of this position derives from Platonism. In Platonic and Neo-Platonic thought, reality is conceived as a continuum
extending from absolute being to nonbeing. All things have being
in varying degrees, depending on their proximity to their common
source, the One or the Good. Just as the rays of the sun, shining
into the surrounding darkness, become more and more dispersed
and diluted with increasing distance from their source, so the being
and goodness (one and the same thing) of this world, being an
emanation of the divine, represent a falling away from or diminution of the absolute being and goodness—but this means the
inevitable presence in the world of a degree of nonbeing and evil,
that is, the absence of being and goodness. Try it again: Platonically
understood, the relative nonbeing and evil in the world manifests
itself as multiplicity and mutability, a kind of distortion and frag-
mentation of the divine unity and immutability; this distortion, in
turn, produces the vicissitudes of nature resulting in human misery

and the perturbations of the soul resulting in moral evil. For Platonism, then, the One or the Good is responsible for the relative being of the world, not its nonbeing; it is responsible for the degree of goodness in the world, not the evil.

We may state this still otherwise and in terms that recall one of Leibniz's arguments. The first move: Even an omnipotent God cannot do what is *logically* impossible; he cannot make a rock so big that he cannot lift it, he cannot make four-sided triangles, he cannot make things both to be and not to be at the same time and in the same respect, he cannot create something that he did not create, and so on. That God cannot do such things will sound startling or even offensive to some, but it has been affirmed by virtually all major thinkers, including St. Thomas, who expressed the idea in his well-known claim: "What involves a contradiction does not fall under the omnipotence of God." Does this not place a limitation on God? No. On the one hand, while it is true that with God all things are possible, four-sided triangles and other self-contradictory things are not actually *things*—they can't possibly be. On the other hand, it is clearly a perfection in God that he cannot, like us limited beings, do silly things, be irrational, or sin; such "limitations" actually point to God's power, don't they? And now the second move: If God cannot do what is logically impossible, then he cannot create something that possesses the full power of being that he himself possesses, for anything that God creates is by its conception dependent for its being and is therefore a relative being, not an absolute being. And since the being of creation is only relative, not absolute, it is lacking also in complete goodness; in other words, it is imperfect. This "metaphysical" evil is, then, necessarily attendant upon creation and is the ultimate source of all natural and moral evil. One can conceivably blame God for creating a world in the first place (another problem), but one can't blame God for creating a world with evil in it, for a created order that possesses God's own measure of being and goodness would be a logical absurdity.

In the Christian Platonism of St. Augustine (354–430) we find a variation on the Platonic theory of evil, though conceived quite differently. The Christian believes (as was mentioned in an earlier discussion) that God created the world not through an emanation of his own being but out of nothing, which means that the being of the world is fundamentally different from God's being. Evil in the world does not, therefore, reflect a diminution of God's being, but rather the diminution of a thing's *own* being brought about by sin, a concept foreign to pagan Platonism. Augustine's position on the nature of evil is a classic one in the history of philosophy and theology; let us consider it further.

Before Augustine's conversion to Christianity, he was a disciple of Manichaeism, a later version of the old Persian Zoroastrianism. The Manichaeans, like their Zoroastrian predecessors, held to an absolutely dualistic and materialistic conception of reality. There are two primordial realities, Light and Darkness, or Good and Evil, both conceived as material substances. The world and the human soul are the battlefields of these eternal powers, which are engaged in an endless struggle for supremacy. In time, however, Augustine became disenchanted with this crude materialism and especially with the Manichaeans' failure to explain the nature of good and evil, a problem that preoccupied him from his youth. After rejecting Manichaeism, Augustine discovered Platonism, which lifted his mind to incorporeal reality. As he testifies in his *Confessions*, addressing God, " . . . having then read those books of the Platonists, and thence been taught to search for incorporeal truth, I saw Thy invisible things, understood by those things which are made."[7] According to the Platonism that Augustine knew (actually the Neo-Platonism of Plotinus, a third-century Greek philosopher), this world is, as we have seen, suspended midway on a ladder of reality extending from being to nonbeing. This world is but an imperfect likeness of a transcendent realm of ideal realities presided over by the absolute One, the cause of all being, truth, and goodness.

Understandably, Augustine interpreted his discovery of Platonic philosophy as a providential preparation for his own reception of the Gospel. And it was in this spiritual view of reality that Augustine found a satisfying philosophical solution to the problem of evil: Evil is simply a privation or absence of being and goodness.

In any Platonic-type philosophy, being, truth, and goodness are viewed as commensurate, or more precisely, as different aspects of the same thing; that which is greatest in being is, therefore, greatest

---

[7]St. Augustine, *The Confessions*, tr. Edward B. Pusey (New York: Modern Library, 1949), p. 140.

in truth and goodness. It follows for the Christian Platonist that God, the supreme being, the one who says "I *am who I am*" (Ex. 3:14),[8] is the absolute and supreme good as well. Now because everything in the universe exists through the creative act of God (Augustine would be apt to Neo-Platonize this as the inevitable overflowing of God's creative fecundity), everything, by the sheer fact of its existence (and this includes even the Devil!), possesses some trace of God's own being and goodness. We naturally think of the recurring judgment in Genesis 1, "And God saw that it was good," and Augustine concludes, "All things that exist, therefore, seeing that the Creator of them all is supremely good, are themselves good." It must be noted, however, that though the natural world is good in its own way, it is only derivatively good and not supremely good. Augustine continues:

. . . because [created things] are not, like their Creator, supremely and unchangeably good, their good may be diminished and increased. But for good to be diminished is an evil, although, however much it may be diminished, it is necessary, if the being is to continue, that some good should remain to constitute the being. For however small or of whatever kind the being may be, the good which makes it a being cannot be destroyed without destroying the being itself.[9]

Still, because the world is *created*, its being and goodness are contingent, or mutable, or able not-to-be. This ability not-to-be is not itself evil, nor does it necessitate evil; it merely renders evil possible. The actual defection of the creature from God and the consequent vitiation of the creature's own nature are what Augustine understands by evil. This defection, in the case of humans, is an act of free will whereby one incurs guilt; hence Augustine calls it

---

[8]St. Augustine knew this text from the Latin Vulgate (*Ego sum qui sum*), which, though in the Old Testament was based on the Hebrew, was at this point clearly influenced by the translation of the Greek Septuagint (ἐγώ εἰμι ὁ ὤν). It was interpreted by St. Augustine and other medieval and scholastic thinkers as a self-designation of the Self-Subsistent Being. But these translations and subsequent "metaphysical" interpretations are not borne out by the original Hebrew ('*ehyeh* '*asher* '*ehyeh*), which suggests, rather, a dynamic conception of God.

[9]St. Augustine, *The Enchiridion on Faith, Hope and Love*, 12, tr. J. F. Shaw (Chicago: Henry Regnery, 1961).

malum culpae, "evil of guilt." Free will is a gift of God that enables the human to be a moral agent: ". . . no righteous act could be performed except by free choice of the will. . . . God gave it for this reason."[10] Sin, on the other hand, is the abuse of free will, the failure to will what is right, a rebellious turning aside from God's goodness:

The will . . . commits sin when it turns away from immutable and common goods, toward its private good, either something external to itself or lower than itself. It turns to its own private good when it desires to be its own master; it turns to external goods when it busies itself with the private affairs of others or with whatever is none of its concern; it turns to goods lower than itself when it loves the pleasures of the body. Thus a man becomes proud, meddlesome, and lustful.[11]

The evil will has, as Augustine describes it, not an efficient but a "deficient" cause.

Such passages as the preceding make it sound as if each individual is responsible for his or her own deficient will, or sin. From Augustine's later work comes the starker—and controversial—idea of *corporate* guilt, or, as the Puritan jingle had it, "In Adam's Fall we sinned all," an idea bound up with Augustine's teaching about the Fall or Original Sin, which has embraced everyone in its unhappy lot. Augustine carried on a fierce debate with Pelagianism, so called from its sponsor, Pelagius, a British monk contemporary with Augustine. Pelagius taught the cheery view that the individual is born in a sinless state and then freely chooses God or sin. Augustine, in opposition, maintained that Adam, the father of the race, freely chose sin, plunging not only himself but, through hereditary sin, all his descendants into moral bondage—some of whom, those elected by God, to be eventually redeemed. In the total Augustinian picture there is, thus, good news and bad news. The good news is that free will is a divinely bestowed good gift, a condition for authentic and moral humanity. The bad news is that the will, because of the original sin of Adam, is so mired in the desire for

---

[10]St. Augustine, *On Free Choice of the Will*, II, 18, tr. Anna S. Benjamin and L. H. Hackstaff (New York: Macmillan, 1964).
[11]*Ibid.*, II, 19.

base things that it cannot of its own power and apart from divine grace effectively will the good.[12]

There is more bad news. *Malum paenae*, "evil of suffering," follows *malum culpae*; it is the punishment consequent upon Adam's voluntary fall, or defection, from God and goodness. The generation and corruption of the created order are now experienced by fallen creatures in the form of suffering: plagues, famines, disease, accidents, and hardships in general. Thus God says to the fallen Adam that it is by the sweat of his brow that he shall eat, and to the fallen Eve that she will have pain in childbearing (Gen. 3:16, 19). *Quae causa infirmitatis nisi iniquitas?*, "What is the cause of the infirmity but iniquity?" What is the cause of *iniquity* remains an unanswered question. Although Augustine has explained (if he has) the *nature* of evil, he concedes that its ultimate *cause* is a mystery that lies hidden forever in the inscrutable human free will. Nonetheless, with his conception of evil as a privation of goodness, St. Augustine was confident that both moral and natural evil could be reconciled with the goodness and justice of God.

It must not be concluded from all of this talk about evil as the privation or absence of goodness that evil is for Augustine somehow *unreal*. Few have been more sensitive to the terrible reality of evil, sin, and suffering than Augustine. What is being denied, rather, is that evil has a positive existence or is, in Augustine's language, a substance. This philosophical understanding of evil does not at all lessen its existential urgency. Furthermore, the fact that the natural world and the human will represent only imperfectly the goodness of the Creator should give no occasion for blaming God. We ought rather, says Augustine, to marvel at the way in which God is able through suffering and evil to work his divine purposes and display his goodness in an even greater measure. The crucifixion of God's Son was at once both the epitome of evil and the occasion of God's

---

[12]With respect to his view of all humans as participants in Adam's sin, Augustine was no doubt influenced by his predecessor, Ambrosiaster, who appears to have been the first to advance it, mainly on the basis of the Latin Vulgate rendering of the last clause of Rom. 5:12, *in quo omnes peccaverunt* ("in whom all have sinned"), an interpretation not so easily derived from the original Greek, ἐφ᾽ ᾧ πάντες ἥμαρτον (probably "because all have sinned").

greatest blessing. Even the Fall turns out to be something over which the believer may exult: *O felix culpa!*, "O happy fault!"

The Augustinian solution (if that is the correct word) to the problem of evil raises, of course, one big question, namely, the truth of the Platonic metaphysics on which it is founded. We are reminded again that particular positions on the issues in this book are often intimately bound up with holistic views of reality and cannot be fully appreciated apart from a full understanding and appraisal of those views. More specifically, one might have problems with Augustine's doctrine of the Fall that functions so decisively in his explanation of evil. Whatever else Augustine might have thought about the Garden episode of Genesis 3, he clearly saw the Fall as a historical (if not literal) event. Whether we, reflecting on the Fall in light of recent historical, paleological, and Biblical criticism can accept a historical, before-and-after interpretation, and if not, whether the Augustinian position can be reconciled with some such theory as Paul Tillich's interpretation of the Fall (considered in a later chapter) as a transhistorical symbol of our abiding existential estrangement, are further questions worth raising.

Even more specific is the observation that human sin must have been predetermined inasmuch as God in his omniscience had foreknowledge of the Fall. But this involves a common misunderstanding. Although it follows, according to theologians like St. Augustine and St. Thomas, that if God foreknows *x*, then *x* will happen, it does not follow that *x* will necessarily happen because God foreknows it. In the case of the Fall, what God foreknows (by virtue of his immediate and eternal presence to all of history) is that Adam *in his freedom* chooses to sin. The Fall is no more determined by God's foreknowledge than it is by his postknowledge, or even by ours, for that matter. At least, this is one very old and standard explanation. The problem is, in fact, one of the thorniest in philosophical theology. Concerning the related question as to why God created humans, knowing full well that they would (whether inevitably or not) sin, Augustine's main response has already been given in the reference to *O felix culpa!*—a response that might or might not satisfy the contemporary, nonbiblically oriented person. Finally, many will judge Augustine's claim that all humans are punished for Adam's sin to be an outrage against our sense of justice, and we have already observed that this may not be the Biblical teaching anyway (note 12, above).

Before concluding this section, another attempt to rationalize the reality of evil might be mentioned to show that positions conceived to be entirely different may sound strikingly similar in their conclusions. We have already encountered F. R. Tennant's concept of the wider teleology, and now it will be seen that he has also a wider theodicy to go with it. Tennant rejected both the goodness-of-the-whole idea (on the grounds that if evil is an illusion, then the illusion is evil) and the Augustinian privation theory (on the grounds that through a linguistic sleight of hand it translates the concrete and positive manifestations of evil into an abstraction) and turns, as we might guess from our earlier discussion, to a thoroughly scientific and empirical analysis of evil.

We have seen that the several strands of natural processes, especially evolutionary development, are regarded by Tennant as divine instruments for the realization of human beings. Such processes, however, necessarily involve certain mishaps, accidents, and other unfortunate occurrences; natural evils are inevitable by-products of a created order inhabited by finite beings and characterized by natural processes. Moreover, are not the calamities and sufferings produced by nature often conducive to the purification and elevation of human values? As for moral evil, Tennant observes that there can be no moral goodness in a clock inasmuch as there is no moral goodness apart from autonomy and the possibility of evil. Thus free will is requisite to a moral being, as well as the full possibility of the misuse of that freedom resulting in sin. The natural and moral spheres converge, therefore, even with their imperfections and evils, upon the production of a developing moral consciousness, and thus upon the best of all possible worlds. To wish it otherwise is to wish for a world that isn't really a world.[13]

The Soul-Making Theodicy

We have, here and there, already touched on the third main proposal, what is sometimes called the "vale of tears" theodicy, or, to use a more upbeat term, the "soul-making" or "person-making"

---

[13]F. R. Tennant, *Philosophical Theology* (Cambridge, England: Cambridge University Press, 1928–30), II, Ch. 7.

theodicy. While not denying the awfulness of evil, this view claims that in the long run it is justified by its power to build, educate, purify, ennoble and perfect human beings, often at the individual level but always with respect to the race as a whole. And it has recently received a tremendous boost, thanks to John Hick, a contemporary English philosopher of religion, who taught for many years in the United States before returning, upon his retirement, to England.

One of Hick's most impressive achievements was his book *Evil and the God of Love*.[14] Hick provides an extended treatment of the Augustinian theodicy, along with extensive criticisms, and ultimately rejects it in favor of another ancient theodicy, and that of yet another (and even earlier) Church Father, Irenaeus, Bishop of Lyon (*c*. 130–*c*. 200). In fact, it is sometimes called the "Irenaean theodicy."[15] We may represent the Irenaean approach in terms of two main points. First, on the Augustinian view, humans were created perfect and then, through disastrous disobedience, fell away from God and plunged the race into misery. Irenaeus suggests a radically different picture. The human race is *being* created, and the Fall was rather like (in Hick's language) an understandable childhood lapse reflecting immaturity and weakness. Further, this is not only the experience of the whole race, it is also, in varying ways, the experience of each one of us—and some people never seem to grow up! This ongoing development, which Irenaeus represents as the continuing "workmanship of God," is apparent in the following:

> If . . . thou art God's workmanship, await the Hand of thy Maker which creates everything in due time; in due time as far as thou art concerned, whose creation is being carried out. . . . If, then, thou shalt deliver up to Him what is thine, that is, faith towards Him and subjection, thou shalt receive His handiwork, and shalt be a perfect work of God.[16]

---

[14]John Hick, *Evil and the God of Love*, rev. ed. (New York: Harper & Row, 1978).

[15]Summarized and restated in John Hick, "An Irenaean Theodicy," in Stephen T. Davis (ed.), *Encountering Evil* (Philadelphia: Westminster Press, 1981).

[16]Irenaeus, *Against Heresies*, IV, 39, 1–2, tr. Alexander Roberts and James Donaldson, in *The Ante-Nicene Fathers*, I (Grand Rapids, Mich.: Eerdmans, reprint, 1979).

Second, the total situation in which humans find themselves provides God-ordained experiences that challenge them on every side, and this, depending on their responses, instructs, cultivates, purifies, and perfects. The most obvious of these challenging experiences is that of evil, both natural and moral. We are all aware that the experience of suffering is often conducive to patience, understanding, sympathy, and the like. Specifically in reference to moral evil, Irenaeus observes,

. . . how, if [man] had no knowledge of the contrary, could he have had instruction in that which is good? . . . just as the tongue receives experience of sweet and bitter by means of tasting, and the eye discriminates between black and white by means of vision, and the ear recognizes the distinctions of sound by hearing; so also does the mind, receiving through the experience of both the knowledge of what is good, become more tenacious of its preservation, by acting in obedience to God.[17]

This is, says Hick, the basis of a theodicy that can best serve us today. It is coherent with and supported by contemporary perspectives while standing in a loose—often very loose—relationship to Biblical teaching, as well as the teaching of other religious traditions.

To begin with, the idea of a slow development of the human race, including false starts and detours, is coherent with the theory of biological evolution. Even on the most naturalistic view of evolution, it cannot be denied that what has been or is being produced is a uniquely intelligent being capable of ethical, religious, and social awareness. Of course, this emphasis on development, including moral development, is hardly compatible with the traditional Augustinian-type conception of the *Fall* of the human race. For Augustine our perfection lay in the past; for the soul-making theodicy it lies in the future. According to Hick, it is no longer possible even to speak, as Irenaeus did, of a childlike lapse. We must frankly abandon any notion of an actual historical Fall and use such language, if at all, to represent "the immense gap between what we actually are and what in the divine intention is eventually to be."[18] Closely connected to this is Hick's belief in a genuine eschatology

---

[17]*Ibid.*
[18]Hick, "An Irenaean Theodicy," p. 42.

(the end of history as we know it), certainly an interest that runs throughout the Biblical tradition. The notion that history has, as it were, a beginning, a middle, and an end, that everything is unfolding according to some divine plan and for a divine purpose, and that eventually "God will be all in all," is obviously relevant for an Irenaean theodicy. Hick adheres, in fact, to a conception of universal salvation, the idea that eventually everyone will be saved—but not before achieving a suitable stage of development, either in this life or one (or ones) beyond it.[19]

More philosophically, all of this is related to Hick's important concept of "epistemic distance." The idea here is that God has deliberately constituted things in such a way that his reality and his care for us would not be *too* apparent. An immediate, overwhelming, and unambiguous knowledge of God would not be what we ordinarily understand by authentic knowledge, with its risks, excitement, and, when appropriate, personal relation. The actual intellectual ambiguity in which we find ourselves *vis-à-vis* God makes for a hard-won knowledge and, for that reason, a knowledge of God all the more to be valued. Likewise, and closely related, an authentic relation to God can only be achieved on the basis of a kind of volitional ambiguity whereby the uncoerced individual, at a volitional distance from God, *freely* chooses to relate himself or herself to God. This idea will be addressed in the next section.[20]

In the meantime, the most obvious objection to all this should be addressed. It may be possible to understand how the human race is improved through hardship and suffering, and even how a single individual is often benefited. But it is considerably more difficult to understand when the individual in question is, say, an innocent child whose life is extinguished in the gas chambers of Auschwitz or someone whose life is irrevocably shattered by waves of devastating disease, torture, or sorrow. How is such a life even remotely benefited by the suffering? Are we not back to pointless suffering? Is it not often a matter of soul-*breaking* rather than soul-*making*?

Hick is sensitive to this problem, faces it squarely, and responds

---

[19] *Ibid.*, pp. 50ff.
[20] *Ibid.*, pp. 42ff.

in a manner that may or may not be satisfying: In a way that we can't yet fathom, the ultimate perfecting of souls is worth it. In a more venturesome response, Hick suggests that the soul-making process surely continues in the afterlife—instantaneous perfection at the resurrection, say, would render the present labors pointless. It is no accident that the world's great religions all posit some form of afterlife, and the Hindu image of reincarnation as well as the Roman Catholic doctrine of Purgatory offer a glimpse, perhaps, of the role of ongoing struggle beyond the present life. This is Hick's answer to the soul-breaking charge.[21]

With respect to the pointless-evil charge, an unexpected twist emerges. Evil is not, as it were, cut-to-order in accordance with the particular needs or deserts of people but, rather, is distributed with remarkable randomness. Even this, says Hick, is part of the plan and is conducive to personal development. For only in a world of unfairness, unwarranted suffering, and real victims are caring and loving attitudes developed—nobody feels sorry for one who had it coming. The haphazard and seemingly pointless visitations of evil thus heighten the ambiguity (epistemic distance again) of our situation but thereby can provoke greater virtue in the soul, giving such evil a point after all.[22] With respect specifically to the moral version of the pointless-evil problem, Hick himself admits that even if we can "see" the answer intellectually, we can't be expected to "feel" it emotionally. The answer involves two points, both of them familiar to us by now: free will and eschatology.

. . . the thought that humankind's moral freedom is indivisible, and can lead eventually to a consummation of limitless value which could never be attained without that freedom, and which is worth any finite suffering in the course of its creation, can be of no comfort to those who are now in the midst of that suffering. But while fully acknowledging this, I nevertheless want to insist that this eschatological answer may well be true. Expressed in religious language it tells us to trust in God even in the midst of deep suffering, for in the end we shall participate in his glorious kingdom.[23]

---

[21]*Ibid.*, pp. 50ff.
[22]*Ibid.*, p. 50.
[23]*Ibid.*, p. 49.

The Free-Will Defense

In several instances, we have already touched upon what is surely the most effective response at least to the problem of moral evil: the Free-Will Defense. Anyone can see immediately that this is an attempt to get God off the hook by an appeal to human free will. The general reasoning is this. God is to be thanked for the wonderful gift of free will, by which we are enabled to be authentic human beings and to stand in a genuine relation of love, trust, faithfulness, and obedience to him. Mere automata, who could not do otherwise than they do, are hardly *moral* creatures at all. The failure, misguidedness, and positive perpetration of evil is a problem with *our* exercise of free will, not God's. One of the most energetic recent attempts to bolster the Free-Will Defense is that of Alvin Plantinga. (Incidentally, Plantinga urges the distinction between a *theodicy*, which tries to show *why* God permits evil, and a *defense* against the argument from evil, which tries to show that evil is *compatible* with God.) He represents the hub of the reasoning this way:

A world containing creatures who are significantly free (and freely perform more good than evil actions) is more valuable, all else being equal, than a world containing no free creatures at all. Now God can create free creatures, but He can't *cause* or *determine* them to do only what is right. For if He does so, then they aren't significantly free after all; they do not do what is right *freely*. To create creatures capable of *moral good*, therefore, He must create creatures capable of moral evil; and He can't give these creatures the freedom to perform evil and at the same time prevent them from doing so. As it turned out, sadly enough, some of the free creatures God created went wrong in the exercise of their freedom; this is the source of moral evil. The fact that free creatures sometimes go wrong, however, counts neither against God's omnipotence nor against His goodness; for He could have forestalled the occurrence of moral evil only by removing the possibility of moral good.[24]

So far, so good—until someone wants to know why God couldn't have constituted people who are free *and* who always freely

---

[24]Alvin Plantinga, *God, Freedom, and Evil* (Grand Rapids, Mich.: Eerdmans, 1974), p. 30.

choose the good. This is the point of J. L. Mackie's well-known question and answer:

If God has made men such that in their free choices they sometimes prefer what is good and sometimes what is evil, why could he not have made men such that they always freely choose the good? If there is no logical impossibility in a man's freely choosing the good on one, or on several occasions, there cannot be a logical impossibility in his freely choosing the good on every occasion.[25]

But the "incompatibilist" (one who believes that free will is logically incompatible with determinism) not only has an intuition that there is something surely wrong in the idea that God can so *constitute* us that we always freely choose the good, he or she may be able to show it. It is true that there is no logical contradiction in the proposition

(1) All people always freely choose to do good.

But there is a contradiction in the proposition

(2) God so constitutes all people that they always freely choose to do good

because that entails (1), plus the proposition

(3) No one can do otherwise than to do good.

which is incompatible with (1).[26] Furthermore, Plantinga asks, how can God bring into being a world in which people freely always choose the good when such a world can't exist apart from those people who actually freely choose the good? The Mackie-type claim is, thus, incoherent; what it asks for is logically impossible!

John Hick, as we have seen, is also an advocate of the Free-Will Defense, but takes a somewhat different approach. He is doubtful

---

[25]J. L. Mackie, "Evil and Omnipotence," in Basil Mitchell (ed.), *The Philosophy of Religion* (London: Oxford University Press, 1971), p. 92.

[26]I originally represented the reasoning in this way in my *Questions That Matter: An Invitation to Philosophy*, 3rd ed. (New York: McGraw-Hill, 1992), p. 364.

that the Plantingian maneuvers just recited are decisive against the Mackiean challenge. Hick invokes Newton's First Law of Motion: A moving body will continue in uniform motion unless interfered with by an external force. By analogy, says Hick, we can imagine a perfectly good being who, though formally free, in a "morally frictionless environment" (no temptations, no stress), would continue forever on the same moral course. Even so, it is not a "morally frictionless environment" in which we find ourselves, and that is because—back to the soul-making theodicy—hard-won virtues are intrinsically more valuable than those created ready-made. And even though it would be logically possible for God to create people who consistently and freely do what is right by one another, it is not logically possible for God to constitute people so that they freely stand in a relation of love, trust, and obedience to *himself*:

The authentic fiduciary attitudes are . . . such that it is impossible—logically impossible—for them to be produced by miraculous manipulation: "it is logically impossible for God to obtain your love-unforced-by-anything-outside-you and yet himself force it" [John Wisdom].
    . . .It would not be logically possible for God so to make men that they could be guaranteed freely to respond to Himself in genuine trust and love. The nature of these personal attitudes precludes their being caused in such a way.[27]

Evil and the Absurd

If anything is common to the several positions we have just surveyed, it is a confidence in the ultimate intelligibility of things. Not everyone shares this confidence, and some have seized upon evil (especially suffering) as a reflection, rather, of the ultimate irrationality and absurdity of existence. This approach is characteristic of existentialism, at least in its atheistic variety, at least in its heyday in the 1950s and 60s. Space does not permit a full exposition of atheistic (or humanistic) existentialism, but neither is it possible to present the existentialist position on evil without at least a cursory consideration of some of the central concepts of this philosophy.

---

[27]Hick, "An Irenaean Theodicy," pp. 273ff.

Most of these thinkers are agreed in their rebellion against the more or less traditional idea that all of history and life takes place, as it were, in a big box, with its stable sides, top, and bottom providing fixed points of reference. According to one dominant strain of traditional philosophy, an existing thing is determined to be what it is by something outside and anterior to it. We might distinguish the existence of a particular dog from its essence or essential nature, which somehow determines and explains the particular dog: why it is shaped thus, why it has a furry coat, a tail, and barks. In this way, essences are prior to their particular existing embodiments. This view of reality is most obvious in Platonic philosophy, with its belief in a transcendent world of ideal and eternal "Forms" or essences or archetypes that cause and order all existing things, though it is true generally of all those philosophies that seek in one way or another to impose a rational structure on the world.

According to the existentialist Jean-Paul Sartre, whom we encountered in Chapter 5, there is no God, all things are possible, and the responsibility for the universe falls on humanity itself. There is no God, no big box, no ultimate frame of reference, no absolute and eternal truths, no anterior essences—only individual, existing persons, doomed to pick their way through an ambiguous and meaningless existence, doing what they can to give it some essence or meaning. In this way, "existence precedes essence," the closest statement in existentialism to an official doctrine. To put it another way, as Sartre himself did, "subjectivity must be the starting point."[28] The point of departure for all authentic philosophizing must be the existing individual cast into a world that is, on the face of it, meaningless and absurd.

The idea of the absurd figures strongly in existentialist literature. It suggests, of course, something more profound than the observation that life seems at times to be no more than a dull and pointless routine. It suggests, rather, that existence itself is meaningless. Any attempt to explain the universe must be in terms of existence. But existence, the fundamental category, is absurd. Therefore the confrontation with existence and the discovery of oneself as an existing being is, as the German existentialist Martin Heidegger

---

[28]Jean-Paul Sartre, "Existentialism," tr. Bernard Frechtman, in *Existentialism and Human Emotions* (New York: Citadel Press, 1957), p. 13.

expressed it, "forlornness," or, to use the title of one of Sartre's novels, "Nausea." It is despair. Thus the existentialist preoccupation with Nothingness (Heidegger: *das Nichts*; Sartre: *le néant*; Tillich: Nonbeing) is not so much an ontological or metaphysical concept as it is a value concept expressive of the existentialist's sense of isolation and powerlessness in the midst of an alien universe.

Closely related is the existentialist rejection of the view that the human mind resembles a big machine, and all we have to do is drop in a nickel and grind out the answers to all the philosophical problems of the ages. For the existentialist, most traditional philosophical thinking, with its elaborate proofs and scholastic distinctions, is academic and irrelevant. Though not usually considered an existentialist, Robert Frost in his poem "A Masque of Reason" reflects the ludicrous element in the presumptuous attempt to grasp intellectually the enigma of suffering. At one point in the poem, which is a satire on Job's suffering, Job asks God why he has been allowed to suffer, to which God replies,

"I'm going to tell Job why I tortured him
And trust it won't be adding to the torture.
I was just showing off to the Devil, Job,
As is set forth in chapters One and Two."

In other words, ask a stupid question and you get a stupid answer. Or, as Job himself responded to God,

"Twas human of You. I expected more
Than I could understand and what I get
Is almost less than I can understand."[29]

The traditional formulas are dead. The philosophers' attempts to explain evil have proved empty. The universe is absurd.

But what then shall we do? Sartre urges us to meaningful decision making and commitment, for only in responsible commitment can authentic living be found and a human essence evolved. Albert Camus represents a variation on this Sartrean theme. He asserts, in

---

[29]Robert Frost, "A Masque of Reason," in *The Poetry of Robert Frost*, ed. Edward Connery Lathem (New York: Holt, Rinehart, & Winston, 1945).

a way, that the solution to the problem of evil is to see that it has no solution, and he shifts our attention to the question of how or in what manner we are to live in view of this fact. In his essay "The Myth of Sisyphus," Camus thus directs himself to the most urgent of issues, the meaning of life, and asks the ultimate existential question, namely, whether suicide is not perhaps a legitimate response to absurdity. The answer is, No:

One of the only coherent philosophical positions is . . . revolt. It is a constant confrontation between man and his own obscurity. It is an insistence upon an impossible transparency. It challenges the world anew every second. . . . That revolt gives life its value. Spread out over the whole length of a life, it restores its majesty to that life. To a man devoid of blinders, there is no finer sight than that of the intelligence at grips with a reality that transcends it. The sight of human pride is unequaled. . . . It is essential to die unreconciled and not of one's own free will. Suicide is a repudiation. The absurd man can only drain everything to the bitter end, and deplete himself. The absurd is his extreme tension, which he maintains constantly by solitary effort, for he knows that in that consciousness and in that day-to-day revolt he gives proof of his only truth, which is defiance.[30]

Camus says, in effect, that whatever we do in the face of absurdity, we must not yield to the temptation of suicide, for that is exactly what it wants us to do. We must not give in. On the contrary, we must struggle against it with all the passion we can muster, thereby letting it know that it has not conquered us. (One cannot help but note with what frequency such words as "revolt," "challenge," "confrontation," "struggle," and "defiance" occur in Camus' writings.) It turns out, then, that while the point is to live without resignation to the absurd, without illusion, and without hope, Camus concludes, paradoxically, that precisely therein lies our hope. Our dignity and meaning lie in our unyielding resolve against the absurd. Camus' is a life-affirming pessimism.

In this way, "'The Myth of Sisyphus' . . . attempts to resolve the problem of suicide . . . without the aid of eternal values," it "declares that even within the limits of nihilism it is possible to find the means to proceed beyond nihilism," and it invites us "to live

---

[30]Albert Camus, *The Myth of Sisyphus and Other Essays*, tr. Justin O'Brien (New York: Vintage Books, 1955), pp. 40f.

and to create, in the very midst of the desert." For as in the case of the mythological Sisyphus, who was doomed by the gods to spend eternity rolling a huge stone up a hill, only to have it roll back down, "the struggle itself toward the heights is enough to fill a man's heart."[31] Or as Dr. Rieux, a character in Camus' novel *The Plague*, says:

> "... since the order of the world is shaped by death, mightn't it be better for God if we refuse to believe in Him and struggle with all our might against death, without raising our eyes toward the heaven where He sits in silence?"
> Tarrou nodded.
> "Yes. But your victories will never be lasting; that's all."
> Rieux's face darkened.
> "Yes, I know that. But it's no reason for giving up the struggle."
> "No reason, I agree. Only, I now can picture what this plague must mean for you."
> "Yes. A never-ending defeat."
>
> .   .   .
>
> "Who taught you all this, doctor?"
> The reply came promptly:
> "Suffering."[32]

But it is crucial to appreciate that if Sisyphus and Rieux are existential heroes, it is because they are, as Camus says, *conscious*. They live in full awareness of their wretchedness before the absurd. This consciousness is opposite to the everyday sleep of the everyday person who, caught up in the wheel of everyday trivia, is oblivious to the malignant absurdity that engulfs existence, and it is a consciousness that issues in action and involvement.

In all of this it is clear that, for Camus, life may be lived all the better if there is no meaning, no *Logos*, no God, no box. For one thing, the existential person will refuse to be indifferent to evil and suffering. Camus himself said as much in his brief comment to a group of Dominican monks: "I share with you the same revulsion

---

[31]*Ibid.*, pp. v, 91.
[32]Albert Camus, *The Plague*, tr. Stuart Gilbert (New York: Modern Library, 1948), pp. 117f.

from evil. But I do not share your hope, and I continue to struggle against this universe in which children suffer and die."[33]

The Appeal to Majesty and Mystery

We have mentioned several solutions (or at least responses) to the problem of evil and have seen that these can be reduced, generally, to two fundamental though essentially different approaches. First, there are those who, dominated by an optimistic intellectualism, believe that if only we concentrate our critical faculties we can, to some extent, understand evil and reconcile it with God or at least with a rational universe. On the other hand, there are those who, struck by the unintelligibility of existence, choose to relegate evil to the domain of the enigmatic and irrational. Each of these approaches, proffered in every generation, probably reflects something very important about the human psyche: its desire for meaning and intelligibility and its frustration with its own limits.

What is the consensus of the ages? From the epic of Gilgamesh to the tragedians of Greece to Shakespeare to Dostoevsky, confidence in the good has not been eclipsed by the mystery of evil. Certainly this is the position of the Bible, which has dominated the thinking of the Judeo-Christian culture.

The writers of the Bible do not shrink from treating evil, nor do they entertain any illusions about it. The most scathing indictments of human nature in all of its perversity and depravity are found in the Judeo-Christian Scriptures, and, of course, the perennial problem of innocent suffering receives classic expression in the book of Job. Yet, for all of its realism about evil, the Bible delivers no coherent, articulate, and ready-made solution. Even though God finally speaks, in the book of Job, he never answers the question "Why do the righteous suffer?" Rather, he contrasts the learned discourses of Job and his friends with the authority that shrouds his own divine majesty—sort of like Captain Ahab in *Moby Dick*, who says, "I do not give reasons, I give orders!"

---

[33]Albert Camus, *Resistance, Rebellion, and Death*, tr. Justin O'Brien (New York: Modern Library, 1960), p. 53.

Then the Lord answered Job out of the
    whirlwind:
"Who is this that darkens counsel by words
    without knowledge?
Gird up your loins like a man,
    I will question you and you shall declare to me.

"Where were you when I laid the foundation
    of the earth?
Tell me, if you have understanding.
Who determined its measurements—surely you know!
    Or who stretched the line upon it?
On what were its bases sunk,
    or who laid its cornerstone,
when the morning stars sang together,
    and all the heavenly beings shouted for joy?

"Or who shut in the sea with doors,
    when it burst forth from the womb?—
when I made the clouds its garment,
    and thick darkness its swaddling band,
and prescribed bounds for it,
    and set bars and doors,
and said, 'Thus far shall you come, and no farther,
    and here shall your proud waves be stopped'?"

. . .

And the Lord said to Job: "Shall a faultfinder
    contend with the Almighty?
Anyone who argues with God, let him answer it."
                                   (Job 38:1–11, 40:1–2)

Throughout the Bible there is a recurrent emphasis on the
divine transcendence and mystery. Moses was not permitted to look
upon the face of God. Again,

". . . my thoughts are not your thoughts,
    nor are your ways my ways," says the Lord.
"For as the heavens are higher than the earth,
    so are my ways higher than your ways
    and my thoughts than your thought."
                                   (Isa. 55:8–9)

And St. Paul exclaims, "O the depth of the riches and wisdom and
knowledge of God! How unsearchable are his judgments and how

inscrutable his ways!" (Rom. 11:33). On the other hand, for the Biblical writers, the mystery never gives way to despair. They are possessed of an unshakable confidence in the ultimate purposefulness of the universe and of history, a confidence born of their conviction that, in the words of the great hymn that opens the Gospel of John,

> In the beginning was the Word,
> And the Word was with God.
>
> All things came into being through him,
> And apart from him nothing came into being.
>
> What has appeared in him was Life,
> And the Life was the Light of men.
>
> And the Light shines in the Darkness,
> And the Darkness cannot overcome it.
>
> (John 1:1a–b, 3–5)[34]

And the same Paul who speaks of the unsearchableness of God's judgments also writes, "We know that in everything God works for good with those who love him, who are called according to his purpose" (Rom. 8:28). Even Job himself, though consumed with suffering, cried out his faith:

> ". . . I know that my Redeemer lives,
>   and that at the last he will stand upon the earth;
> and after my skin has been thus destroyed,
>   then in my flesh I shall see God,
> whom I shall see on my side. . . ."
>
> (Job 19:25–26)[35]

---

[34]My translation. The origin and meaning of the Johannine Christological title "Word" (λόγος) is one of the great problems of Biblical scholarship. On my view, the title originated in the Johannine community itself and represented the judging, healing, redeeming, and sanctifying revelation of God in Christ. "Life" (ζωή) in the Johannine literature always means the spiritual and salvific life granted to believers by the incarnate Word.

[35]It is difficult to rid the interpretation of "Redeemer" of certain overtones, thanks to George Frederick Handel. The Hebrew *go'el* is more appropriately translated as "vindicator," and though it may refer here to a heavenly or divine being, it more likely refers to some human (perhaps kinsman) expected to exonerate Job. It is also controversial whether there is reflected in this passage a conception of resurrection.

We may be reminded, in conclusion, that whereas the few positive disproofs of God's existence have usually been based on evil (most attacks are in fact leveled against the theistic arguments rather than against God himself), it would appear that none have succeeded in showing an actual *formal* or *logical* contradiction between the essential tenets of theism and the reality of evil. This failure suggests, of course, that like other issues we have encountered, the problem of evil versus God cannot be decided on purely rational, deductive, or scientific grounds but is, for the atheist no less than for the theist, bound up with a general way of reading the world, a total confrontation, interpretation, and feeling for the whole of things. As we observed in an earlier context, surely there is a lesson in the fact that so many intelligent and insightful people disagree about the most obvious facts of experience.

9

The Soul and Immortality

Almost everyone has, at one time or another, experienced the anguish and the hope of Job's question: "If a man die, shall he live again?" (Job 14:14). For many the idea of finality is a torment, and, as Pascal says, "The immortality of the soul is a matter which is of so great consequence to us, and which touches us so profoundly, that we must have lost all feeling to be indifferent as to knowing what it is."[1]

Plato or Paul?

Before the rise of philosophy (about 600 B.C.), the Greeks had only a vague, pessimistic idea of the hereafter. In Homer, for example, the soul is a shadowy something that leaves the body at death and is transported across the gloomy river Styx to the House of Hades, where it squeaks and flits about indefinitely in the dank darkness of the underworld. No wonder Achilles, when visited by Odysseus in the underworld, lamented:

> I would rather as a hireling serve
> A needy man without much wealth,
> Than rule all the perished dead.[2]

---

[1]Blaise Pascal, *Pensées*, no. 194, in *Pensées and the Provincial Letters*, tr. W. F. Trotter and Thomas M'Crie (New York: Modern Library, 1941).
[2]Homer, *Odyssey*, XI, 489ff. (my translation).

The Old Testament Sheol (place of the departed) appears to be little better than the Greek Hades.[3] But in time, all of this underwent a radical reformulation, and the picture of the soul and the hereafter that we, in turn, have inherited is (more often than not) a confused mixture of elements drawn from both Greek philosophy and the New Testament.

The classical Greek concept portrays the soul as something essentially different from the body and superior to it. This dualistic idea is reflected in Hesiod's *Theogony*, was passed along by the Orphics and the Pythagoreans, and finally received eloquent philosophical expression in Plato's *Phaedo*. In this Platonic dialogue, which ostensibly relates the last moments of Socrates with his disciples before his execution, Socrates explains that he does not fear death but, in fact, desires it. The reasoning is that the highest and most essential activity of the soul is the pursuit of knowledge, though as long as the soul is imprisoned in the body, it is continually distracted from its proper pursuit by the requirements of the body and the distracting cares of this life. Furthermore, in this life, knowledge is only imperfectly accessible, owing to the deficiency of the senses. Only in the hereafter, when the soul is released from the body into the presence of absolute truth, can it enjoy complete knowledge and uninterrupted happiness. Socrates concludes:

It seems that so long as we are alive, we shall continue closest to knowledge if we avoid as much as we can all contact and association with the body, except when they are absolutely necessary; and instead of allowing ourselves to become infected with its nature, purify ourselves from it until God himself gives us deliverance.[4]

Very different from the Platonic conception of the immortality of the soul is the Pauline doctrine of the resurrection of the body. This latter receives its fullest treatment in the fifteenth chapter of I Corinthians, where, among other things, St. Paul says (vss. 42–44, 51–55):

---

[3]Though one should note Jesus' use of the Old Testament in connection with his belief in the resurrection in Mark 12:18–27.

[4]Plato, *Phaedo*, 67A, tr. Hugh Tredennick, in *The Last Days of Socrates* (Baltimore: Penguin Books, 1954).

What is sown is perishable, what is raised is imperishable. It is sown in dishonor, it is raised in glory. It is sown in weakness, it is raised in power. It is sown a physical body, it is raised a spiritual body. . . . Lo! I tell you a mystery. We shall not all sleep, but we shall all be changed, in a moment, in the twinkling of an eye, at the last trumpet. For the trumpet will sound, and the dead will be raised imperishable, and we shall be changed. For this perishable nature must put on the imperishable, and this mortal nature must put on immortality. When the perishable puts on the imperishable, and the mortal puts on immortality, then shall come to pass the saying that is written:

> "Death is swallowed up in victory."
> "O death, where is thy victory?
> O death, where is thy sting?"

The radical difference between the New Testament idea of the resurrection of the body and the Greek idea of the immortality of the soul reflects their very different concepts of reality and human nature. The Greek debasement of the body and elevation of the soul follows from a more or less dualistic understanding of things: The body belongs to the mundane, corporeal, dark, and evil sphere, eternally juxtaposed to the sphere of the intelligible and spiritual world of light, the proper home of the spiritual soul and the place to which it seeks desperately to make its escape. The Bible, on the other hand, represents the world as a good creation of God, and the body, not a thing to be despised, is called by St. Paul "a temple of the Holy Spirit" (I Cor. 6:19). Death is the consequence of sin and represents a hostile invasion of evil into the good and natural sphere; it is not a natural and friendly thing to be embraced with Socratic equanimity, but rather a horror and a tragedy that causes one to sweat, as it were, great drops of blood. Yet death is an enemy that will be finally defeated in God's gracious gift of a new creation (when the perishable puts on the imperishable and all things are made new), which has already been anticipated and indeed made possible in the resurrection of Jesus Christ. It is important to emphasize that the resurrected body is not a body like that of the raised Lazarus (John 11), resuscitated only to die once more, but a body like the resurrected Christ's—changed, reconstituted, re-created, and glorified.

Closely related to this is the Bible's unwillingness to separate body and soul. It is true that the New Testament writings emphasize that there is something more to a person than the body (in one passage St. Paul distinguishes between body, soul, and *spirit*—as if we didn't already have enough problems), but any honest reader must concede that the primary emphasis in St. Paul and throughout the New Testament is upon the *unity* of the human being: body and soul, outer and inner, both created by God, both good, and both together constituting full humanity.

St. Paul's notion of a "spiritual body" is not easy to grasp, and the Biblical idea of the eventual re-creation and glorification of the body is hardly a subject for philosophical speculation or demonstration. When St. Paul called the resurrection a "mystery," he meant that it was a divine secret now revealed, something that could be appreciated only in light of the total Biblical teaching concerning God's sovereignty and purposes. Nevertheless, the Christian idea of resurrection has had a widespread and profound influence in every age; its inspiration is, for example, apparent in John Donne's famous lines:

> At the round earths imagin'd corners, blow
> Your trumpets, Angells, and arise, arise
> From death, you numberlesse infinities
> of soules, and to your scattered bodies goe,
> All whom the flood did, and fire shall o'erthrow,
> All whom warre, dearth, age, agues, tyrannies,
> Despaire, law chance, hath slaine, and you whose eyes
> Shall behold God, and never tast deaths woe.[5]

Proofs for Immortality

Aside from the question of resurrection, the Greco-Christian view that we somehow survive death and live on in the hereafter has occupied a fairly secure position in Western thought. The list of philosophers, scientists, and poets who have affirmed the soul's immortality is impressive indeed, perhaps bearing out Cicero's observation that " . . . somehow or other, there is inherent in the mind a forecast of times to come, and this is especially the case and

---

[5]John Donne, *Holy Sonnets*, VII.

most readily exhibits itself in the highest characters and the loftiest souls."[6] Even the skeptic Voltaire, who set out to destroy Christianity, could not but admit that we are profoundly indebted to the New Testament for its teaching concerning the future of the soul. And though the idea of immortality, like the idea of God, gripped people even before they were able to devise arguments for it, they did not hesitate to devise the arguments when they were finally able to do so. Three different approaches are apparent in Plato, St. Augustine, and Kant.

Actually, Plato offered a whole series of proofs for the immortality of the soul. He argues, for example, that in the sphere of things that come into being and pass away, every state is generated out of its opposite: the small from the great and the great from the small, the weak from the strong and the strong from the weak, the cold from the hot and the hot from the cold, waking from sleep and sleep from waking. It would seem to follow, then, that just as death is generated out of life, so likewise life must be generated out of death; otherwise in this one instance, nature will be, as Socrates says, limping or lopsided. Furthermore, were not all things generated out of their opposite states, all natural processes would eventually cease altogether, including the phenomenon of life—something quite incompatible with the observed fact of a continuing cycle of living and dying.

Plato observes, again, that even in this life we discover in our minds such concepts as absolute equality. Where do we get these concepts? Surely not from this world, because there is not a single instance in the entire sensible world of absolute equality or absolute anything: Everything grasped through sense experience is at best relative, a fluctuating approximation of its absolute and immutable essence. Plato answers that we must have acquired the idea of equality, for example, in a former state wherein the soul existed, prior to its embodiment in this world, in the immediate presence of the absolute essences or, as he called them, "Forms"; this knowledge was "forgotten" at birth but later "recollected" through a kind of association of ideas when the soul, peering out through prison bars of the body, was confronted with sensible and relative counterparts

---

[6]Cicero, *Tusculan Disputations*, I, 15, tr. Robert Black, in *The Basic Works of Cicero*, ed. Moses Hadas (New York: Modern Library, 1951).

of the Forms. Plato believed that only on the hypothesis of the pre-existence of the soul could innate knowledge be explained.[7]

Neither of these, however, should be mistaken for Plato's main proofs, spread out over many pages of the *Phaedo* and focusing on his belief in the soul's immateriality. Given the difference between the body and the soul, and given the spiritual nature of the soul, it is not possible that the soul could ever die. By "death" we usually mean the dissolution of a thing or the scattering of its parts. A flower is said to die when it wilts, fades, and crumbles into dust; a person is said to die when the soul is separated from the body; the body is said to die when it is corrupted and its elements are dispersed. But how can the soul die? It is not physical, it has no parts, there is nothing to be dissolved or separated. The soul cannot die, for it is by its nature simple, noncomposite, spiritual: If, through the practice of philosophy, the soul has kept itself pure from the contaminations of the body, then it "can have no grounds for fearing that on its separation from the body it will be blown away and scattered by the winds and so disappear into thin air, and cease to exist altogether."[8] Also, life is an essential attribute of the soul. That is, it is the very nature of the soul to live, just as it belongs to the essence of 3 to be odd. And since life is eternally incompatible with death, the soul can no more die than 3 can admit evenness. But though there can be no such thing as a dead soul, can't the soul perhaps simply cease to exist at the approach of death? The answer is that if the soul cannot admit death, then it is deathless or immortal and thus also imperishable. The soul, then, is a spiritual reality, and its essence is to live. From this it follows, says Plato, that the soul is indestructible.[9]

Another classical proof for the soul's immortality was provided by St. Augustine. Augustine, too, was enamored of incorporeal truth, abiding above both our mutable senses and minds, an absolute and unchanging light to which all rational people assent and by which the truth or falsity of all judgments may be (and will be in the end) illuminated. In fact, he devoted the whole of his *Against the Academicians* to variations of the *reductio ad absurdum* that one cannot even deny the reality of truth without presupposing

---

[7]Plato, *Phaedo*, 69Eff.
[8]*Ibid.*, 84B.
[9]*Ibid.*, 102Aff.

it, as when the skeptic asserts, "There is no truth," thereby implying that his own statement, at least, is true. Augustine further stressed the eternal necessity of some truths, for example, mathematical truths: At all times and in all places it is absolutely true that 3 plus 7 equals 10—something even a fool could hardly deny. From the inexorable givenness of such truths, Augustine believed that it is possible to prove both the existence of God and the immortality of the soul.

Briefly stated, his argument for God is that unless eternal truths are purely subjective and relative (which by their conception is impossible), there must exist for them an eternal *locus* from which they derive, namely, the infinite mind of God who is the Eternal Truth itself.[10] One may recognize in this *a priori* reasoning an epistemological counterpart to Rashdall's version of the Moral Argument; we might, in fact, call it the Epistemological Argument for God. Augustine believed also that from the reality of truth it is possible to formulate a demonstration of the soul's immortality. For if knowledge "exists anywhere, and cannot exist except in that which lives; and if it is eternal, and nothing in which an eternal thing exists can be non-eternal; then that in which knowledge exists lives eternally."[11] The body belongs to the sensible world and is eventually corrupted, along with everything else in it. But the mind's activity lies in the intelligible world; its aim is incorporeal truth. And since the mind must share in the nature of that which actualizes it, the mind must be, like truth and knowledge, itself immaterial, spiritual, and eternal. Augustine's debt to Platonic philosophy should be obvious.

A very different proof is offered by Immanuel Kant. As we have seen, Kant rejected all of the traditional theistic arguments on the grounds that "theoretical reason" has no application beyond what is given in experience, and he presented a new argument, the Moral Argument, according to which it is necessary to postulate God as a condition of moral experience. Now we may add that the immortality of the soul is also, for Kant, a postulate of moral experience, built into moral experience as one of its conditions.

---

[10]St. Augustine, *On Free Choice of the Will*, II, 12ff.
[11]St. Augustine, *On the Immortality of the Soul*, 1, in *Concerning the Teacher and On the Immortality of the Soul*, tr. George G. Leckie (New York: Appleton-Century-Crofts, 1938).

According to Kant, in a moral universe the actualization of the *summum bonum*, the "highest good," must be a real possibility. No single rational being (the only kind of being capable of moral experience), nor all collectively, are able to achieve the highest good. Such an achievement requires the complete conformity of our will to the moral law, but this would involve a degree of holiness of which we limited beings are totally incapable, as we know only too well. All that is possible for limited beings like ourselves is an endless progress from a lower to a higher worthiness to receive the *summum bonum*. And an infinite progress is possible for us only if we possess an infinitely enduring existence; thus, Kant reasons, our souls must be immortal. There is a further matter. In a truly moral universe, all goodness must sooner or later be rewarded and evil punished, something that obviously does not happen in this life. It follows that rational beings must somehow survive death, for only on that supposition is possible the complete actualization (at least as seen from the standpoint of the Infinite Being who grasps our enduring progress as completed) of the happiness or misery that Kant believed inevitably follows upon keeping or breaking the moral law.

In this way, immortality is required if morality (as it displays itself in this life) is to be rational or consistent with itself. Apart from immortality, the moral law either (1) is degraded by indulging our personal desires and convenience, winking at our moral failures and achievements; or (2) it becomes a suffocating impossibility, an unattainable and therefore an unreal ideal. Kant concludes: ". . . the highest good is practically possible only on the supposition of the immortality of the soul, and the latter, as inseparably bound to the moral law, is a postulate of pure practical reason."[12] Thus again, what we cannot attain through "theoretical reason" we can attain through "practical reason."

These proofs rest plainly on important assumptions. Whether a contemporary will find such arguments persuasive will surely depend on one's own philosophical mood and frame of reference. Proofs inspired by Plato can hardly hold any force for someone unwilling to accept the hypothesis of absolute and incorporeal truth

---

[12]Immanuel Kant, *Critique of Practical Reason*, tr. Lewis White Beck (Indianapolis, Ind.: Library of Liberal Arts, 1956), p. 127.

or, for that matter, unwilling to acknowledge any nonempirical reality whatsoever. Kantian proofs clearly rest on the belief in objective value, but we have seen already that this itself is a subject of philosophical debate and the source of a major split among philosophers.

More specifically, traditional arguments for immortality have been challenged along the following lines. First, from a physiological standpoint, it would appear that what we call the mind is intimately and causally bound up with bodily functions, especially those of the brain. Some hold, in fact, that the *self* is just the continuity of one's thoughts and memories (if neither my mind nor my memory survive, what would make me think that *I* as a distinct personality have survived?), and that these are exclusively a matter of stimuli, brain cells, and chemical reactions. Second, the idea of the self as simple, distinct, and continuing may be incompatible with psychological and psychoanalytic findings concerning mental disintegration and the phenomenon of multiple personalities. Finally, and more philosophically, the charge is made that the concept of a disembodied soul makes for linguistic difficulties. Person-words (for example, "I," "you," "he," "someone") are intelligible insofar as they refer to concrete embodiments of physical and mental characteristics, personal histories, and so on. A disembodied soul, on the other hand, is not an object that may be pointed out: It neither wears a tie nor shakes hands, and it is otherwise radically different from anything that "he" or "someone" usually refers to. What could "disembodied soul" *mean?*

Nevertheless, many contemporary thinkers appear to have no trouble identifying with traditional metaphysical systems, nor do they seem much troubled by physiological, psychological, or analytic challenges such as those just mentioned. One example is the late French philosopher Jacques Maritain. He first rejects that noble but uninspiring view of immortality according to which we shall all live eternally in the contribution we have made to posterity. It would be, Maritain says, a supreme delusion to seek in this concept of immortality "any adequate fulfillment of that irrepressible aspiration to survival which inhabits the depths of our substances."[13] He then proceeds to fashion his own version of the Platonic-Augustin-

---

[13]Jacques Maritain, *The Range of Reason* (New York: Scribner, 1952), p. 54.

ian proof. In order for there to be genuine knowledge at all, the intellect must be capable of rising above the purely material or sensible dimension of things and grasping their immaterial essences, for the knowable is that which abides unchangeably, unconditioned by the imperfections and relativities of matter. This means that the intellect too, commensurably with its object, must be immaterial or spiritual in nature; because the intellect is a faculty of the soul, the soul too must be spiritual; and from the spirituality of the soul, Maritain deduces its immortality:

A spiritual soul cannot be corrupted, since it possesses no matter; it cannot be disintegrated, since it has no substantial parts; it cannot lose its individual unity, since it is self-subsisting, nor its internal energy, since it contains within itself all the sources of its energies. The human soul cannot die. Once it exists, it cannot disappear; it will necessarily exist forever, endure without end.[14]

It would appear, then, that in some philosophical and theological circles, at least some of the traditional proofs for immortality continue to be very much alive.

Paranormal Experiences

Others, products of our scientific age, have become disenchanted with philosophical proofs for immortality and have sought instead a more empirical evidence for their belief in the soul and the afterlife. Such evidence has been more and more forthcoming from the investigations sponsored by "psychical research," or, as it is now more commonly called, "parapsychology." Understandably, there has been widespread suspicion of such investigators because they are so often associated with the occult, including weird things such as ghosts and séances. The days are gone, however, when one could scoff and sneer at talk about phenomena such as extrasensory perception and perhaps even disembodied spirits. The Society for Psychical Research, founded in London in 1882 and presided over by an impressive list of notable people including psychologists, philosophers, and scientists, has done much to make these subjects both prominent and respectable. In recent years, psychical research

---

[14]*Ibid.*, p. 60.

has become a center of serious scientific study and will clearly have to be taken more seriously in the future.

According to believers in extrasensory perception (ESP) and psychokinesis (PK), literally, "mental movement," one mind can operate upon or move another mind, thing, or event (or vice versa) without any aid whatever from the five senses. Telepathy, clairvoyance, and precognition are examples of ESP. In telepathy one mind is said to communicate certain ideas to another mind through mental activity alone; clairvoyance is the ability to perceive things not present to the senses; precognition is the ability to perceive and predict future events. The most notable pioneer in this area, J. B. Rhine, published extensive accounts of his telepathic experiments (conducted in the 1930s at Duke University), including results that reflected staggering odds against chance occurrences.[15] The results of other experimenters have been equally spectacular. Of course, such findings have come under the scrutiny of skeptics, and the inevitable statistical questions have been raised. Nevertheless, the growing consensus of responsible researchers is that the evidence for ESP and PK must be reckoned with.

The question of otherworldly spirits (a second concern of parapsychology) is, at this stage, more dubious. But even here one should be cautioned against a premature out-and-out rejection. C. D. Broad, a well-known philosopher of science, wrote in 1924 of his confidence in the psychical evidence for survival:

I do presuppose that the careful work of the Society for Psychical Research has elicited a mass of facts which may fairly be called "supernormal," in the sense that they cannot, if genuine, be explained on the usual assumptions of science and common-sense about the nature and powers of the human mind. And I do assume that a great many of the facts that come up to the extremely high standard of evidence required by the Society are "genuine," in the sense that they have been correctly reported and that they are not simply due to fraud or self-deception. I assume this on the basis of a fairly careful study of the literature; of a knowledge of the kind of persons who have controlled the policy of the Society and taken part in its investigations; and of some investigations of my own.[16]

---

[15]J. B. Rhine, *Extra-Sensory Perception* (Boston: Society for Psychical Research, 1935).

[16]C. D. Broad, *The Mind and Its Place in Nature* (London: Kegan Paul, Trench, Trubner & Co., 1925), p. 514.

It may be of interest, further, to quote an account of a more recent, firsthand experience by the celebrated Biblical translator J. B. Phillips. Phillips, who describes himself as "incredulous by nature, and as unsuperstitious as they come," ventures his encounter with the late C. S. Lewis:

C. S. Lewis, whom I did not know very well and had only seen in the flesh once, but with whom I had corresponded a fair amount, gave me an unusual experience. A few days after his death, while I was watching television, he "appeared" sitting in a chair within a few feet of me, and spoke a few words which were particularly relevant to the difficult circumstances through which I was passing. He was ruddier in complexion than ever, grinning all over his face and, as the old-fashioned saying has it, positively glowing with health. The interesting thing to me was that I had not been thinking about him at all. I was neither alarmed nor surprised nor, to satisfy the Bishop of Woolwich, did I look up to see the hole in the ceiling that he might have made on arrival! He was just *there*—"large as life and twice as natural." A week later, this time when I was in bed, reading before going to sleep, he appeared again, even more rosily radiant than before, and repeated to me the same message, which was very important to me at the time.[17]

For myself, what is most striking about this account is that it was sworn by a man of such integrity and unquestioned good sense.

The claim for the individual's survival of death got a terrific boost in 1975 with the publication of the instant best-seller *Life After Life*, by Raymond A. Moody, M.D.[18] This book is filled with case histories of individuals who have claimed that while subjected to some physically traumatic experience (heart surgery, drowning, injury resulting from an automobile accident, and the like), they actually died and then came back to tell about it. This in itself would not be remarkable—the world is full of kooks and liars— were it not for two facts.

---

[17]J. B. Phillips, *Ring of Truth* (New York: Macmillan, 1967), p. 117. The Bishop of Woolwich was the late J. A. T. Robinson, who, in his *Honest to God* (Philadelphia: Westminster Press, 1963), had pooh-poohed spatial references to God, for example, as being "up there."

[18]Raymond A. Moody, *Life After Life* (New York: Bantam Books, 1975).

First, independently of one another, they tell strikingly similar stories about what it's like on the other side, or, at least, what it's like to go there. These accounts often include (1) a distinct noise, variously characterized as buzzing, whistling, Japanese wind bells, a sort of music, and so on; (2) the sensation of being drawn through a narrow enclosure, variously described as a tunnel, trough, funnel, or cylinder; (3) the awareness of possessing a "spiritual" body, though accompanied by a sense of weightlessness and (especially paradoxical) timelessness; (4) the experience of being drawn to an increasingly bright, indescribable light endowed with personality and able to communicate reassuringly by a sort of thought transference; (5) an instantaneous but nonetheless vivid review of one's whole life, in some cases with great detail, and in others the highlights, sometimes the images appearing in chronological order and sometimes all at once; and sometimes (6) the experience of approaching a limit or border of some kind—a fence, body of water, door, or line. That so many are able to relate such similar experiences—independently of one another, and also insisting that the experience can't really be put into words—is remarkable, to say the least. But it is no more remarkable than the second fact. Many have "returned" bearing knowledge they couldn't possibly have acquired except in a disembodied state. A good example is the man who, upon regaining consciousness on the operating table, informed those present that there was a quarter sitting on top of the light fixture attached to the ceiling! To all this it should be added that in a subsequent book, *Reflections on Life after Death*,[19] Moody considered further and more religious aspects of the experience, such as "the City of Light," "judgment," and "the realm of bewildered spirits."

Naturally, many explanations for such experiences have been advanced, as Moody himself noted: supernatural (which invoke God or Satan), naturalistic (pharmacology, physiology, neurology), and psychological (dreams, hallucinations, delusions). Such explanations are, as you might guess, found wanting by Moody. Like-

---

[19]Raymond A. Moody, *Reflections on Life After Death* (New York: Bantam Books, 1977).

wise, the obvious charge that those who have such experiences are merely projecting onto the screen, as it were, their cultural and religious biases has been more recently addressed by Melvin Morse's *Closer to the Light*.[20] This book documents the near-death experiences of children, which, though largely free from cultural determinants, turn out, nonetheless, to be of the same cloth as those adult experiences studied by Moody. Still, it is not for nothing that these experiences are cautiously called *near*-death experiences. The fact that these people "got back" shows that their connection with this sphere was not completely broken and that they were not dead—in the sense of *dead* dead. And thus, whatever fascination these experiences may hold (and that may be a lot), in order to construe them as evidence for the real survival of the soul, it may be necessary to mix in a good helping of speculation.

The evidence of parapsychology and near-death experience is, of course, especially agreeable to those who would like to meet the scientist on the scientist's own empirical ground. Some have insisted, for example, that inasmuch as such research has scientifically established the reality of things like ESP and disembodied spirits, it has overthrown the materialist theory of human personality. Others hesitate at this point, for they see that the sword is two-edged: The materialist may argue just as forcefully from the same evidence that materialism is simply more subtle and that the materialist horizon of things is simply more distant than we had surmised. At any rate, the statistical analyses and testimonials proffered by parapsychology and near-death researchers are subject to the same incompleteness and tentativeness that plague all scientific claims. Further, is the picture of the soul being painted by such investigations really relevant from a *religious* point of view? Most theologians would probably balk at any attempt to ground the reality, personality, and survival of the soul in the obscure evidence drawn from this approach. Still, who questions that there are, after all, more things in heaven and earth than are dreamt of in our philosophy?

---

[20]Melvin Morse, *Closer to the Light*: *Learning From Children's Near-Death Experiences* (New York: Villard Books, 1990).

Mind and Body

If you're only interested in the fun stuff in this chapter, you might as well stop right here. What follows is not nearly so exciting as talk about resurrection, ESP, ghosts, and near-death experiences. On the other hand, questions pertaining to personal survival in the here-after are clearly inseparable from questions about the nature of the soul or self, its relation to the body, the meaning of "mind," free will versus determinism, and so on. To these issues we now turn in the attempt to consider some theoretical underpinnings to the topic of the soul and immortality.

Most people are convinced that they have a body and that they have a soul (though they may prefer to call it by some other name), and that these are essentially different from one another. The body is thought to be physics and chemistry, whereas the soul is conceived as transcendent and spiritual, incapable of being weighed or dissected or in any way grasped by the senses. Of course, the belief that the soul transcends the space-time world is for many people closely related to the idea of life after death. If, after all, the soul is independent of the body, why should it not survive the death of the body?

This persistent view of the soul and its survival has its roots in René Descartes, who argued more emphatically than anyone else in the history of philosophy that mind (he used "mind," "soul," "spirit," and "self" interchangeably) is one thing and matter is another. Beginning with his celebrated intuition, *Cogito ergo sum* ("I think, therefore I am"), Descartes believed that through a kind of introspective immediacy he could grasp directly his own enduring mind or soul:

I concluded that I was a thing or substance whose whole essence or nature was only to think, and which, to exist, has no need of space nor of any material thing or body. Thus it follows that this ego, this mind, this soul, by which I am what I am, is entirely distinct from the body and is easier to know than the latter, and that even if the body were not, the soul would not cease to be all it now is.[21]

---

[21]René Descartes, *Discourse on Method*, IV, in *Discourse on Method and Meditations*, tr. Laurence J. Lafleur (Indianapolis, Ind.: Library of Liberal Arts, 1960), p. 25.

According to Descartes, the first thing of which I can be absolutely certain is that I exist and that I am a "thinking substance." He then proceeds to deduce the existence of another kind of reality, matter, or "extended substance." These two substances underlie all reality; everything in the cosmos, including human beings, is reducible to mind and matter.

With his dualism of mind and matter Descartes laid the foundation for many modern philosophies, but he also posed a most vexing problem: the mind-body problem. If we believe with Descartes that the mind is one thing and the body is another—essentially different substances—then how do we get them back together again? And we must get them back together again if we are to explain their obvious causal relation to one another. Clearly, our mental states depend on our bodily states as, for example, when we become depressed by being repeatedly beaten over the head. Similarly, psychosomatic illnesses show that bodily states may be caused by mental states. But how can there exist such a causal relation between body and mind if they are two absolutely different substances with nothing in common?

Descartes' immediate successors inherited from him the mind-body problem and found themselves hard pressed to provide a solution. Malebranche, another French thinker, suggested occasionalism, the doctrine that on the occasion of a physical sensation God causes the appropriate idea to occur in the mind, and vice versa. In this way there is always an appropriate and predictable correspondence between mental and physical states. Whereas Malebranche attributed the agreement between mind and body to the immediate intervention of God, Leibniz's doctrine of a preestablished harmony declares that God so ordained mind and matter from the beginning that thoughts and sensations would always agree, just as two clocks, wound up and synchronized, would always tell the same time. More likely is the double-aspect theory of the Dutch philosopher Spinoza. According to this view, mind and matter are "attributes" of a single underlying substance, providing through parallel mental and physical states two manifestations of the one reality.

One of the most obvious moves is that of the materialist who simply denies that the mind exists as anything different from matter. The only thing that really exists is matter in motion, and mind turns out to be a configuration of energy or, at best, an "epiphenomenon," a mere by-product of physical and chemical processes. The idealist, on the other hand, reverses this position, saying that mind is the only reality and all sensible things are in some way ideas or configurations of mental activity.

Probably the most common solution (at least, over the years) is interactionism. This position (which was Descartes') holds that though the mind and body are essentially different from one another, there must be, nevertheless, some kind of necessary though obscure causal relation between them. Descartes had said that the mind must be intimately joined to the body, and he even identified the exact place where matter and mind are transformed into one another—the pineal gland! Aside from Descartes' questionable physiology, this explanation simply begs the question by pushing it a step backward. In fact, any version of interactionism ultimately poses all over again the very difficulty that it attempts to explain, namely, how two different substances with no common *nexus* can interact.

Nonetheless, interactionism can't simply be laughed off the stage. The interactionist does have a problem explaining the causal relation of mind and matter (whether in the pineal gland or elsewhere), but then we have already seen that *any* causal relation is a far from simple matter and that the critic may be wise not to push this objection too far lest it backfire. Further, the image of some sort of unbridgeable chasm fixed forever between mind and matter is itself probably misleading. It suggests that the mind is another "thing" standing in a kind of spatial relation to the body, which is exactly what the mind-matter dualist denies; there can hardly be a literal gap between two things if one of them does not even occupy space. On the other hand, not even the interactionist denies that there is *some* sense in which the mind, whatever its nature, exists in time and is localized in space: I am very sure that my mind exists now rather than 200 years ago and that it is present in this room rather than someplace down the hall.

Or am I? David Hume believed that we have no knowledge of our own minds whatever, at least no rationally derived knowledge. We saw in Chapter 3 that for Hume there can be no knowledge of reality except what is disclosed through the data of sense experience, and that this, in turn, led him to abandon causality as a metaphysical principle. Now we must prepare for the collapse of a second pillar of traditional philosophy, the concept of *substance*.

Philosophers like Descartes and Locke were certain that just as there must be some material substance (from the Latin *substantia*, literally, "that which stands under") upholding the physical qualities of sensible objects, so must there be a mental substance—mind— that underlies mental activities such as thinking, doubting, willing, and remembering. After all, they reasoned, qualities and activities can no more exist apart from a substance than a predicate can exist without a subject. But according to Hume's phenomenalism, there is no reason for thinking that there is anything more to the table than its perceived qualities: rectangular, brown, smooth on top, and so on. There is no evidence or necessity for some mysterious, underlying material substance; the table is merely a collection of sensible qualities, or at least that is as much as we can know. Hume applies the same reasoning to mental substances as well. He charac- terizes the position of his opponents:

There are some philosophers, who imagine we are every moment inti- mately conscious of what we call our SELF; that we feel its existence and its continuance in existence; and are certain, beyond the evidence of a demon- stration, both of its perfect identity and simplicity. . . . To attempt a farther proof of this were to weaken its evidence; since no proof can be deriv'd from any fact, of which we are so intimately conscious; nor is there any- thing, of which we can be certain, if we doubt of this.[22]

But, as we should expect by now, Hume does doubt it. He argues that it is simply not possible to plumb the depths of con- sciousness and confront at last an underlying self or "I." At least it was not possible for Hume:

If any one upon serious and unprejudic'd reflexion, thinks he has a different notion of *himself*, I must confess I can reason no longer with him. All I can allow him is, that he may be in the right as well as I, and that we are essen- tially different in this particular. He may, perhaps, perceive something sim- ple and continu'd, which he calls *himself*; tho' I am certain there is no such principle in me.[23]

All that can be discovered introspectively is a passing parade of per- ceptions: love, hatred, pain, pleasure, hot, cold, and so forth. In

---

[22]David Hume, *A Treatise of Human Nature*, ed. L. A. Selby-Bigge (Oxford, England: Clarendon Press, 1888), p. 251.
[23]*Ibid.*, p. 252.

fact, says Hume, in an important statement, a man *is* simply a "bundle or collection of different perceptions."[24] With Hume's analysis, the concept of substance vanishes into thin air, and all possible talk about mental substance or the soul vanishes with it.

Another and more recent view rejects altogether such talk about mental substances as involving a "category mistake," a concept introduced by the analytic philosopher Gilbert Ryle. A category mistake is the mistake of applying a concept within a conceptual system to which it is inappropriate. For example, says Ryle, if a visitor comes to the university campus and asks to see the library, it is a simple matter to point to the library and say, "There it is"; or, if he asks to see the administration building, to point to it and say, "There it is." But if the visitor then asked to see the *university* it would be clear that he mistakes a university for something like a library or a science building, something that can be pointed out, rather than an organization of colleges and schools. According to Ryle's logical geography of mental concepts, the traditional dogma of the "ghost in the machine" rests on the same kind of a mistake: "It represents the facts of mental life as if they belonged to one logical type or category (or range of types or categories), when they actually belong to another."[25]

Though the origins of the category mistake antedate Descartes, it was he, says Ryle, who foisted it on the modern mind. Himself a man of science, Descartes was naturally influenced by the concepts of Galileo's mechanics. And though he contended for the real difference between mind and matter, he understood both of these within the same framework, namely, the categories of thing, stuff, attribute, state, process, change, cause, and effect. Ryle represents Descartes' thinking: "Minds are things, but different sorts of things from bodies; mental processes are causes and effects, but different sorts of causes and effects from bodily movements. And so on."[26] Ryle believes that our troubles began when Descartes called mind a "thing" or "substance." The mind-body problem is a pseudoproblem, a problem of language rather than reality.

---

[24]*Ibid.*, p. 190.
[25]Gilbert Ryle, *The Concept of Mind* (London: Hutchinson, 1949), p. 16.
[26]*Ibid.*, p. 19.

And, this clarification having been achieved, what emerges for Ryle as the proper concept of mind? Answer: a set of "dispositions." By this Ryle means those desires, inclinations, convictions, habits, moods, and so on that have no real meaning, except as inseparably linked to and expressed by bodily states such as speaking, gesticulating, and listening. With this, Ryle claimed to be pushing a view of the person that is conceptually meaningful, largely because the person is now publicly accessible. At the same time, he denied that the view was a behavioristic or materialistic one (more on this in a moment), a denial that for many fell flat. Similar, and still more recent, is the strategy of "functionalism," the idea that the nature of something is best gotten at not in terms of what it is made of but in terms of, well, its function. If asked what a coffee pot is, your answer would hardly consist simply in an enumeration of its elements: plastic, ceramic, metal, rubber, wires, prongs, and so on. Rather, you would have to explain how all of these are put together, how they relate, what they do—how they produce coffee. Likewise in the case of mind. An adequate conception of mind would have to account for the actual give-and-take (a complex causal relation) constantly going on between differing mental states, and between mental states and the external environment—the active processing of sensory input and behavioral output, as it were. As with Ryle, this picture of mind is a radical alternative to the old substantialist and ghost-in-the-machine picture. And, aided and abetted by innovative work in psycholinguistics, cognitive science, and cybernetics, the non-Cartesian pictures continue to be refined.

Man a Machine?

For many, what is *not* possible is a materialistic reduction of the person—including mind—to physical states pure and simple. Such a view, as old as philosophy itself, found recent and renewed expression in the Identity Thesis, the view that mental states (thoughts, desires, sensations) are identical to brain states (gray matter, electrochemical reactions, alpha waves). For all its simplicity, this equation involves big problems indeed. We can only suggest, by means of a few questions, what some of the problems are. First, a logical problem: I can be mistaken, responsible, blameworthy, or praiseworthy, but how can this be said of my *brain*? My thoughts may be mistaken, but can my *brain* be mistaken? I may be reprimanded, but should my *brain* be reprimanded? Then, too, even if (I say, if) the brain is a condition for our sensations such as those of red, hunger, anger, and sweetness, these sensations themselves are obviously not, even in principle, exposable by the surgeon's knife, are they? Finally, and closely related, what about memory? Isn't your continuity of memories an essential part of your self-identity? Would you still be *you* if someone else's memories were substituted for your own up to this moment? Or would you be interested in dying and going to heaven if you wouldn't remember it was *you*? But memories aren't physical things in the brain to be observed along with synapses, cells, and nerve tissue, are they? No wonder that many regard the materialistic solution to the mind-body problem as a cure that's as bad as the disease. But it gets even worse.

One of the corollaries of traditional materialism is the belief in a complete causal determinism, the belief that anything that happens can be explained entirely by means of antecedent causes. This would mean that one's mental states and decisions, no less than one's physical makeup, are explained by factors over which one has ultimately no control, and that one is, therefore, merely an elaborate machine.

Two points before proceeding. First, determinism is not to be confused with the belief in causality. According to the Principle of Causality, everything that comes into being is caused; but according to determinism, everything that comes into being is caused such that *it could not have been otherwise*. Second, it should be noted that most philosophers would distinguish between determinism and the more extreme mechanistic determinism. Mechanistic determinism conceives of the universe as a gigantic machine governed by a fixed and finite number of causal laws such that if we could know the exact condition of every detail in the universe at any point in time, we could, theoretically, predict the exact condition of the whole universe for any time in the future. Many would claim that whereas mechanism is incompatible with teleology or purpose, determinism is not. Nevertheless, any version of determinism holds that human choices and decisions are completely determined, and for our purposes, that is the important point.

One of the starkest examples of the determinist—indeed, mechanist—vision is that of the sixteenth-century French physician/metaphysician Julian Offray de La Mettrie. All it takes is matter and motion:

. . . since all the faculties of the soul depend to such a degree on the proper organization of the brain and of the whole body, that apparently they are but this organization itself. . . . Given the least principle of motion, animated bodies will have all that is necessary for moving, feeling, thinking [etc.]. . . .

Let us then conclude boldly that man is a machine, and that in the whole universe there is but a single substance differently modified.[27]

A recent, and quite different, example is that of the late behaviorist B. F. Skinner, whose book *Beyond Freedom and Dignity* was all the rage in the 1970s. Skinnerian behaviorism teaches that there is nothing to the human being but behavior (in principle completely observable), and that this is exhaustively determined from the inside through genetics and from the outside through environment. This is seen to warrant a "technology of behavior," a manipulation of environmental and possibly genetic factors in the interest of producing a better human species. But it means also proceeding "beyond freedom and dignity" in the sense that the traditional ideas of human autonomy and responsibility must be discarded.[28]

And that's just the problem. However enormous the empirical evidence for determinism may appear to be, it is, for many, unable to withstand the indisputability of two facts or values essentially involved in human reality: moral experience and cognitive experience.

Take moral experience first. We do not hold machines morally responsible for their actions. We may kick them and curse them, but we do not blame or punish them. Similarly, if man is a machine, however complicated and sophisticated, then the idea of moral responsibility becomes meaningless. If, then, we take moral experience seriously, we must believe that something in the human reality (or about it) transcends the mechanism and determinism of purely empirical processes. There must be *free will*. It is difficult to give a positive account of just what is involved in the concept of free will or indeterminism, but no one means by it that the will can operate in a vacuum or independently of conditions. What is denied is that

---

[27]Julian Offray de La Mettrie, *Man a Machine*, tr. Gertrude C. Bussey et al. (La Salle, Ill.: Open Court, 1912), pp. 18, 89, 140–141.

[28]B. F. Skinner, *Beyond Freedom and Dignity* (New York: Bantam Books, 1972), passim.

given a set of conditions, a *certain* decision must be made; a particular choice may be caused, and yet not be determined.

The idea that there can be no genuine morality apart from free will has a very good pedigree, having been defended by a number of major philosophers—Kant, for example.

Kant believed that freedom of the will must be postulated in order to account for moral experience. We saw previously that Kant was a firm believer in the "moral law within," a fundamental sense of duty or "ought." He now emphasizes that the implementation of the moral law requires that the will somehow rise above the morally blind determinism of the natural world, for "ought implies *can*." Of course, it will have to be admitted that all scientific research favors (more accurately, presupposes) a complete causal determinism, even though physics has abandoned the billiard-ball model of things and causality in science is not what it used to be. But for Kant, the data of moral experience are as real and undeniable as the data of sense experience, and we are driven, therefore, to the conclusion that there must be more to reality than what appears in the phenomenal world. To accept a complete causal determinism extending even to thinking and willing would be to exclude oneself from the world of moral discourse and responsibility.[29] Kant's famous trilogy of moral postulates is now complete: God, Immortality, and Freedom.

Of course, the "self-determinist" turns this reasoning upside down by insisting that one can be held morally responsible for one's actions only if they are determined—determined by the person's own character. If someone were suddenly seized by a momentary and uncontrollable spasm of his arm and struck you in the face, you would not hold him morally responsible for the act, for it hardly reflected his intention or attitude. On the other hand, you would most certainly hold him morally responsible if you judged that his act was the product of his real character, that is, was caused by his deliberation, disposition, and intention. According to self-determinism, then, I can be held morally accountable for my acts only if they reflect the person that I am, only if they are determined by my character. Though there is on the surface a plausibility about this position, two rather obvious questions may be raised. First, has not the

---

[29]Immanuel Kant, *Foundations of the Metaphysics of Morals*, tr. Lewis White Beck (Indianapolis, Ind.: Library of Liberal Arts, 1959), pp. 64ff.

self-determinist simply defined the problem away by identifying genuine freedom with self-determinism and then announcing that freedom is compatible with determinism? Second, is it not the case that those features of our own character (choices, desires, attitudes, interests) are themselves the product of external causes over which we have no control? Are we not who we are because of biological constitution, religious training, education, and innumerable other factors? Upon closer examination, then, the self-determinist appears to take back with one hand what is given with the other, and the real problem of determinism and morality remains.

Now turn to rational or cognitive activity. This too is often cited as evidence for the transcending nature of human beings. We observed a moment ago that we do not blame machines or hold them morally responsible; similarly, though we plug them in and program them, we do not reason with them. (A person who seems to be reasoning with a computer is, of course, actually reasoning with the computer's logical system, which is the invention of human intelligence.) The possibility of knowledge and meaningful discourse suggests that cognitive experience also transcends the contrived and blind responses of the causally determined: There is an obvious difference between the reasons for a position and its causes. Thus the doctrine of the determinist is even self-refuting. For the determinist intends that the statement "All things are causally determined" should be taken as a piece of meaningful discourse, but if all things are indeed causally determined, then that statement too is causally determined and therefore of no more cognitive significance than if uttered by someone drugged and "out to lunch." In sum, if human beings are truly rational and moral, they cannot be reduced to a mere bundle of inclinations being bounced about in an environmental pinball machine.

It might be objected, as in our discussion of the Moral Argument, that neither physics-and-chemistry language *nor* transcendence language are adequate to the full, manifold, and complex character of human reality, that they pose false alternatives, that both languages plus many others represent equally real and important dimensions of that reality. But whatever may follow from this broader conception of human nature, it remains that we are compelled to acknowledge dimensions of our experience that cannot wholly be explicated by the categories employed by the behavioral or physical sciences. And this, if nowhere else, is the point at which a philosophical discussion of the soul may begin. On the other hand, we seem now to be a long way removed from Donne's religious certainty:

> One short sleepe past, wee wake eternally,
> And death shall be no more; death, thou shalt die.[30]

---

[30]Donne, *Holy Sonnets*, X.

10

God and Language

It is frequently remarked that the task of the theologian nowadays is not to show that the statement "God exists" is true, but to show that it is even intelligible. Of course, not all religious language is problematic. There is, for example, nothing more or less troublesome about the statement in the Nicene Creed that "he suffered under Pontius Pilate" than about many other statements. Nevertheless, religious language does have, in many respects, peculiar problems. The Scripture says, "the Lord's hand is not shortened, that it cannot save," but God does not have hands, does he? We read that the serpent in the Garden beguiled Eve to sin, but do we take that story seriously? The answer is probably both Yes and No. When we say that God is good, do we mean that he is good like this or that or anything in this world? Would not the Christian continue to assert that "God loves us" in spite of all evidence to the contrary? And some, though they ordinarily strain to free themselves of contradiction, nonetheless have no trouble affirming (as the *Augsburg Confession* expresses it) that Christ "took on man's nature in the womb of the blessed virgin Mary. So there are two natures, divine and human, inseparably conjoined in the unity of his person, one Christ, true God and true man. . . ."[1] Clearly, there is something special about a kind of discourse that cultivates and even thrives on

---

[1]*Augsburg Confession*, III, in *The Book of Concord*, tr. and ed. Theodore G. Tappert (Philadelphia: Fortress Press, 1959), p. 29.

such paradoxes and ambiguities. It should cause no wonder that religious language constitutes still another problem that has long preoccupied philosophical theologians.

The *Via Analogiae*

One of the most influential interpretations of religious language was suggested by St. Thomas Aquinas. Having demonstrated the existence of God, Thomas sought to establish certain of the divine attributes, an enterprise that fills long sections of his *Summa Theologica* and *Summa Contra Gentiles*. But how is it possible to know or to say of a reality that infinitely surpasses us that it is one, incorporeal, good, and wise? In fact, how is it possible to say anything at all about it? The answer (at least for a long line of Christian thinkers) lies in the *via negativa* and the *via affirmativa*, the "way of negation" and the "way of affirmation."

Negative theology has always been regarded by theologians, especially those of a mystic bent, as an effective means to a knowledge of the divine nature. According to the way of negation (sometimes called the "way of remotion"), it is possible to ascend to a knowledge of some things about God by stripping away or removing from the concept of God all that is inappropriate to it. Approaching God (as Thomas says we must) indirectly through sense experience, we can never know the divine substance as it is in itself, but we can at least know what it is not and therefore, through systematic remotion, approximate more and more to a positive (though ever incomplete) knowledge of what it is:

Now, in considering the divine substance, we should especially make use of the method of remotion. For, by its immensity, the divine substance surpasses every form that our intellect reaches. Thus we are unable to apprehend it by knowing *what it is*. Yet we are able to have some knowledge of it by knowing *what it is not*. Furthermore, we approach nearer to a knowledge of God according as through our intellect we are able to remove more and more things from Him.[2]

---

[2]St. Thomas Aquinas, *Summa Contra Gentiles*, I, 14, tr. Anton C. Pegis (Garden City, N.Y.: Image Books, 1955).

We can establish, for example, that God must be infinite (not finite), immutable (not changeable), incorporeal (not material), and simple (noncomposite). Whereas the *via negativa* in this way moves our knowledge of the divine nature forward by denying to it certain features found in sensible reality, the *via affirmativa* allows us to predicate of God other features, such as wisdom and goodness, positively and affirmatively.

This brings us to a crucial (if not the essential) doctrine of Thomistic philosophy, the doctrine of the *analogia entis*, the "analogy of being." Reflecting again the influence—if not the terminology—of Aristotle, Thomas explains that our positive talk about God is neither "univocal" nor "equivocal," but "analogical."

We speak univocally (literally, "naming in one way") when we apply a word with the same meaning to different things. Thus when we say, "Peter is a man, and James and John also," we predicate exactly the same thing of James and John as we do of Peter. Here we are using the word "man" univocally. But when we say, "God is good," are we predicating "good" univocally of both God and created things? Obviously not. God cannot be good in exactly the same way that Peter, James, and John are good. Any good with which we are acquainted here in this world is at best a pale reflection of the infinite goodness of God. And because there is a great gulf fixed between the Creator and created things, concepts like being, goodness, and wisdom cannot bear exactly the same meaning, or be used univocally, in reference to both God and creatures.

Then, is all talk about God equivocal? We speak equivocally (literally, "naming in like ways") when we employ a single word but intend completely different meanings, as when we use the word "pen" to mean at one time an instrument for writing and at another time a place for pigs. (And thus in logic the "fallacy of equivocation" is the fallacy of shifting the meaning of a word or phrase in the course of an argument.) Whereas it may be true that when we say, "God is good," we do not intend that he is good in exactly the same way that we are good, we surely do not intend either that his goodness is wholly unlike and completely unrelated to our own. Though there may be a great gulf fixed between God and his creatures, it is not that great. If God so transcends our concepts that they have no application to him at all, then all knowledge of God and discourse about him would be impossible. In this way, our concepts like being, goodness, and wisdom do not apply to God and creatures entirely equivocally, or in an altogether different way.[3]

We speak about God, therefore, neither univocally nor entirely equivocally, but analogically. The creature is the effect of the Creator. The world stands in a real relation to God and bears his imprint, as every effect necessarily bears something of the perfection of its cause. Thus, however imperfectly represented in space and time, something of the divine nature is preserved and reflected in the natural world. Thomas summarizes both sides of this situation when he says:

> Sensible things, from which the human reason takes the origin of its knowledge, retain within themselves some sort of trace of a likeness to God. This is so imperfect, however, that it is absolutely inadequate to manifest the substance of God. For effects bear within themselves, in their own way, the likeness of their causes, since an agent produces its like; yet an effect does not always reach to the full likeness of its cause.[4]

The natural world, and we ourselves, may not be wholly like God, but neither is it wholly unlike him. Creatures, by the fact that they *are*, resemble God who is Being Itself, and analogical predication is based on just this resemblance. Thomas believed that we can acquire, through experience of God's creation, ideas of perfections such as being, goodness, and wisdom. Moreover, we can by analogy affirm these perfections of God:

> whatever is said of God and creatures is said according as there is some relation of the creature to God as to its principle and cause, wherein all the perfections of things pre-exist excellently. Now this mode of community is a mean between pure equivocation and simple univocation. For in analogies the idea is not, as it is in univocals, one and the same; yet it is not totally diverse as in equivocals; but the name which is thus used in a multiple sense signifies various proportions to some one thing. . . .[5]

---

[3]*Ibid.*, I, 32f.

[4]*Ibid.*, I, 8.

[5]St. Thomas Aquinas, *Summa Theologica*, Part I, Qu. 13, Art. 5, in *Basic Writings of St. Thomas Aquinas*, ed. Anton C. Pegis (New York: Random House, 1945), I.

Certainly, therefore, when Thomas speaks of "analogy" he does not mean likeness pure and simple, nor does he have in mind the use of metaphor wherein there is no real likeness at all. When we say metaphorically that God is a fortress, we do not mean that God is really a fortress, but when we say that God is good, we mean that he is really good. That is, Thomas' idea of analogy involves a real metaphysical relation and resemblance of creatures to God. Even so, this idea is a bit more complicated than one might at first think. Actually, there is considerable discussion concerning the exact nature of Thomas' doctrine of analogy, though it appears that the most fundamental meaning of analogy in Thomas is that of "proportion." The perfections that exist in the sensible world divided and multiplied exist in God supereminently or most excellently, and the predication of perfections is necessarily relative to the subject's mode of existence: As we are good in a finite way, so is God infinitely good; as we are wise in a finite way, so is God infinitely wise. In this way, creatures exhibit relatively and proportionately the perfections that exist infinitely in God. It should be noted, however, that what is epistemologically prior is metaphysically posterior. The term "good" as we *know* it applies first to creatures and second to God, whereas in *fact* goodness exists primarily in God and only derivately or secondarily in creatures.

It should not be thought that the predication of many attributes to God (such as one, simple, good, and wise) does violence to the divine simplicity. We identify and label the divine nature in a plurality of ways because we necessarily approach God through the world of nature in which the being of God is, as it were, refracted and seen under different and varying lights; something of the divine being is reflected in the goodness that we creatures know, in the wisdom that we know, and so on. If we were able to know God as he is in himself (which is impossible), then we would, of course, see that the divine attributes converge into one, identical with the simple and divine nature that is God.[6]

Thomas' doctrine of analogy is more than a conception of language. It is a metaphysical doctrine of the unity of God and the world in terms of a proportion between the being of the Creator and the being of creatures. Nonetheless, the doctrine also illumi-

---

[6]St. Thomas Aquinas, *Summa Contra Gentiles*, I, 31.

nates the meaning of religious discourse. Though it does not allow us to say anything more or anything less about God than we did before, it does clarify *what* we are saying—and are not saying. On the other hand, it should be noticed that since Thomas's *via analogiae* depends upon a real likeness between creatures and God resulting from God's creative causality, it therefore depends upon the success of his Cosmological Proof.

Theology as Meaningless

At the opposite extreme from St. Thomas is the view (born of a modern climate) that discards theology entirely, claiming that we can say nothing about God and related matters because all such talk is, quite literally, meaningless.

This is the position of Logical Positivism, a philosophical movement that had its roots in the Vienna Circle, a group of thinkers who banded together in the 1920s with a common interest in a new and radical empiricism seasoned with a strong dash of linguistic analysis. These thinkers (Moritz Schlick, Rudolf Carnap, Herbert Feigl, Kurt Gödel, Frederick Waismann, and others) saw themselves as following in the tradition of David Hume, who, as we have seen more than once, rejected metaphysical knowledge as groundless, reducing all knowledge to self-evident analytic truths and empirically derived synthetic truths:

If we take in our hand any volume; of divinity or school metaphysics, for instance; let us ask, *Does it contain any abstract reasoning concerning quantity or number?* No. *Does it contain any experimental reasoning concerning matter of fact and existence?* No. Commit it then to the flames: for it can contain nothing but sophistry and illusion.[7]

Another empiricist having somewhat to do with the shaping of Logical Positivism was the French philosopher and sociologist Auguste Comte, who over the years 1830–1842 published a work in six volumes entitled *Philosophie Positive*. Comte's thesis was that several evolutionary stages are discernible in the history of philoso-

---

[7]David Hume, *An Enquiry Concerning Human Understanding*, ed. L. A. Selby-Bigge, 2nd ed. (Oxford, England: Clarendon Press, 1902), p. 165.

phy, and that just as the mythological stage gave way to the theo-logical and the theological to the metaphysical, so now must the metaphysical stage yield to the scientific. Philosophy, if it is to enjoy the same kind of advance and unanimity in its inquiries that the sci-ences have achieved, must abandon its speculative or metaphysical concerns and adopt a thoroughgoing empirical methodology. Phi-losophy must, in other words, become scientific. The Vienna Circle bore also the imprint of Ludwig Wittgenstein, who, along with Russell and Moore, contributed much to the shaping of British ana-lytic philosophy. Wittgenstein himself worked out an empirical-ana-lytic rejection of metaphysical problems as linguistic bubbles, con-cluding his *Tractatus Logico-Philosophicus* with the quasi-mystical aphorism, "What we cannot speak about we must consign to silence."[8]

Out of the Vienna Circle came the celebrated "Verification Principle," the watchword of Logical Positivism. The Verification Principle has been variously expressed and many times modified, but its essence is this: A statement has literal meaning if and only if it is either analytic or (at least in principle) empirically verifiable. Or, to express it otherwise, a proposition is meaningful, that is, pos-sesses truth-falsity status, only if one knows what kinds of situations would have to exist in order for its truth or falsity to be shown. If a statement is not even in theory empirically verifiable (the only kind of verification the Logical Positivists allow), then it is cognitively vacuous and meaningless. The Verification Principle reflects at once an interest in linguistic analysis, a radically empirical criterion of meaningfulness, the judgment that speculative philosophy and metaphysics have been the source of philosophical confusion, and a desire to rescue philosophy from its traditional and allegedly abortive state.

Where does this leave propositions like "God exists?" For the Logical Positivist, such statements are *meaningless*. This is not to say that "God exists" is simply irrelevant or unimportant, as in "That was a meaningless experience." Instead the statement "God exists" is, for the Logical Positivist, literally without meaning, literally non-sensical; it holds no more cognitive significance than "Creech creech." And so it is with all traditional speculative or metaphysical

---

[8]Ludwig Wittgenstein, *Tractatus Logico-Philosophicus*, tr. D. F. Pears and B. F. McGuinness (London: Routledge & Kegan Paul, 1961), p. 151.

statements such as "The soul is immortal," "The world had a beginning in time," and "Everything that exists is an imperfect copy of an archetypal ideal."

This position was given classic expression in A. J. Ayer's influential *Language, Truth and Logic* (1936), the first chapter of which bears the revealing title "The Elimination of Metaphysics." He begins, as he says, "by criticising the metaphysical thesis that philosophy affords us knowledge of a reality transcending the world of science and common sense."[9] Specifically on the question of God, Ayer argues that it is not even possible to be an atheist. The atheist says, in effect, "The statement 'God exists' is meaningful, that is, it is either true or it is false, and I think that it is false." For Ayer, however, the statement "God exists" is neither true nor false, because there is not even in principle any way of verifying it. The statement is cognitively empty and nonsensical. The same is also true of the agnostic. He or she cannot say, "I do not know if the statement 'God exists' is true," without assuming that it may be true, whereas according to Ayer it can be neither true nor false. The whole of theological discourse is, in this way, relegated to the realm of meaninglessness and nonsense.[10]

Furthermore, Ayer argues, even if such statements *were* meaningful, we still could not provide any demonstration of God's existence in the manner of traditional philosophers like St. Thomas or Descartes. The reason is that the Verification Principle, with its purely empirical criterion of meaningfulness, excludes any possibility of synthetic *a priori* propositions, that is, propositions whose truth is known independently of sense experience but that inform us, nonetheless, about reality. This means, echoing Hume, that every meaningful statement is either an analytic tautology (like "All barking dogs bark") or an empirical generalization (like "All swans are white"). Thus the premises of any theistic argument must be either analytic or empirical. And because we can get no more out of a conclusion of an argument than is already contained in the premises, the conclusion, too, must be either analytic or empirical. If the conclusion is analytic, it is an uninformative tautology; and if

---

[9]Alfred Jules Ayer, *Language, Truth and Logic*, 2nd ed. (London: Gollancz, 1946), p. 33.
[10]*Ibid.*, pp. 115f.

the conclusion is empirical, its truth can only be probable. In either case, the existence of God cannot be proved with demonstrative certainty.[11]

The critics of this position immediately saw that it was self-refuting: The Verification Principle itself cannot be empirically verified and is, therefore, meaningless on its own showing—something the Logical Positivists could never quite get over. (Similarly, Hume's own principle, quoted earlier, should be committed to the flames inasmuch as it fails its own criterion of meaningfulness!)

In the introduction to the second edition of *Language, Truth and Logic*, Ayer, who did not want his Verification Principle to be construed as either an empty tautology or a mere empirical generalization, answered rather lamely that it was intended as a "definition" and a "methodological principle." Others responded that we should no more expect the Verification Principle to judge its own meaningfulness that we would expect a weighing machine to weigh itself. Of course, both of these defenses played into the hands of the critics, for both admit that there is at least one statement (the Verification Principle itself) that is nontautologous and nonempirical, yet cognitively meaningful. John Wisdom notes: "The fact is, the verification principle is a metaphysical proposition—a 'smashing' one if I may be permitted the expression."[12] Smashing aside, the Logical Positivists' intent to pigeonhole meaningful knowledge exclusively in terms of empirical verification was even more philosophically intolerant than the traditional approaches they sought to reject.

A more popular criticism charges that Logical Positivism is, perhaps, both arbitrary and unimaginative from an epistemological standpoint. As one philosopher observes, ". . . it seemed extraordinary to have to exclude a vast area of language from what could be admitted as meaningful and significant; and even odder that people still continued to use 'meaningless' jargon."[13] Certainly it is misguided from an existentialist standpoint. Whereas positivistic or

[11]*Ibid.*, pp. 114f.

[12]John Wisdom, *Philosophy and Psychoanalysis* (Oxford, England: Blackwell, 1953), p. 245. For one of the very earliest criticisms along the above lines, see A. C. Ewing's important article, "Meaninglessness," *Mind*, 46 (1937). It should be noted that Ayer made several adjustments in his position in the Introduction to the second edition of *Language, Truth and Logic*.

[13]Ian T. Ramsey, *Religious Language* (New York: Macmillan, 1957), p. 13.

"scientific" philosophy emphasizes that the only meaningful questions are those that fall within the domain of the scientific method and empirical investigation, the existentialists, on the other hand, insist that the most meaningful and urgent questions are those that lie *beyond* the domain of the scientific method. (We see, however, that these are two very different conceptions of meaningfulness, the former cognitive and the latter existential.) Kierkegaard has already warned us that the more "objective" a truth is, the less interest it holds for the subjectively existing individual, and Paul Tillich charges that although Logical Positivism "can be interpreted as the justified distrust of an interference of emotional elements with cognitive statements," it may also be interpreted as "the desire to escape problems which are relevant to human existence."[14]

Even Ayer, toward the end of life, claimed to have had an honest-to-goodness near-death experience that left him philosophically shaken.

The Falsification Debate

Notwithstanding the success or failure of the logical positivist rejection of metaphysics and theology, the nature of religious language continues to be a very lively issue in philosophical theology. In the next section, we will consider an existentialist interpretation of religious language; for the moment, we must pursue a bit further the question of its cognitive status. Legion are the positions and moves that have been proposed concerning the logical and empirical placing of religious discourse. Whereas the older issue centered on the question of verifiability, one of the subsequent approaches has centered on the further question of "falsifiability." This received its best-known and sort of inaugural statement in "Theology and Falsification," a discussion by three British analytic thinkers: Antony Flew, R. M. Hare, and Basil Mitchell. The Flew-Hare-Mitchell debate, along with a response by John Hick, represents, then, at least one very important and recent slant on the significance (or nonsignificance) of religious statements.

---

[14]Paul Tillich, *Theology of Culture*, ed. Robert C. Kimball (New York: Oxford University Press, 1959), p. 172.

A favorite point of departure for what might be called "falsification approaches" was John Wisdom's parable of the garden, and it is with this parable that Flew begins:

> Two people return to their long neglected garden and find among the weeds a few of the old plants surprisingly vigorous. One says to the other, "It must be that a gardener has been coming and doing something about these plants." Upon enquiry they find that no neighbor has ever seen anyone at work in their garden. The first man says to the other "He must have worked while people slept." The other says "No, someone would have heard him and besides, anybody who cared about the plants would have kept down these weeds." The first man says "Look at the way these are arranged. There is purpose and a feeling for beauty here. I believe that someone comes, someone invisible to mortal eyes. . . ."[15]

And so the parable goes on, the first man insisting that there is evidence in the garden for the existence of some kind of a gardener, though he continually modifies his idea of the gardener in order to accommodate the second man's evidence to the contrary. Finally, after both men have examined the evidence, pro and con, for a gardener the first man concludes, "I still believe a gardener comes," and the second man, "I don't." According to Flew, the original, fine, brash hypothesis of the gardener has died by inches, the "death by a thousand qualifications." Similarly, we may begin with a meaningful concept but so qualify it, step by step, that the final result bears little or no relation to what we originally started with; in fact, what we are left with may be nothing at all. For example, the gardener that the first man continues to believe in has, in the last analysis, no more significance than an imaginary gardener or even no gardener.

Now, says Flew, theological utterances appear to have a peculiar weakness for death by a thousand qualifications. Take the statement "God has a plan." On the face of it this seems to be a genuine, meaningful, factual assertion. Consider, however, that the man who

[15]Antony Flew (with R. M. Hare and Basil Mitchell), "Theology and Falsification," in Antony Flew and Alasdair MacIntyre (eds.), *New Essays in Philosophical Theology* (London: SCM, 1955), p. 96. Though Flew provides his own version of the parable, this quotation is actually from Wisdom's version in "Gods," *Proceedings of the Aristotelian Society*, New Series, 45 (1944–45), p. 191.

asserts that "God has a plan" would be likely to assert it no matter what. That is, there is probably no evidence, no conceivable set of conditions, that could cause him to deny that God has a plan. A tornado destroys part of a community and the qualification process begins: "Our church and our parishioners remained untouched, witnessing to God's protection of the faithful"; "The tornado destroyed our church and killed several of our parishioners, displaying that God's inscrutable plan requires at times even the suffering of the faithful"; "God has a plan, but. . . ." Thus it turns out that "God has a plan" may be so eroded away with qualification that the result is not a genuine assertion at all. Any statement that is compatible with every conceivable situation does not assert anything about any particular situation and is, therefore, not even in theory falsifiable. And if a statement cannot even in principle be shown to be false, then it cannot be shown to be true either, which means that it has no truth-falsity value, which means that it has no cognitive value, which means that we are back to "Creech creech." Statements like "God has a plan," "God created the world," and "God loves us" may be, according to Flew, as vacuous as the gardener who turned out to be nothing at all. Or at least until someone can say what would have to occur to constitute their disproof.[16]

To this challenge Hare responded simply that Flew is right in judging that religious statements are not assertions of fact. But what are they then? Hare says they are *bliks,* a word he coined to suggest the nonverifiable, nonfalsifiable, nonfactual, though nonetheless very real and deeply rooted feeling we have concerning the truth of some things. Hare asks us to consider his own parable:

A certain lunatic is convinced that all dons want to murder him. His friends introduce him to all the mildest and most respectable dons that they can find, and after each of them has retired, they say, "You see, he doesn't really want to murder you; he spoke to you in a most cordial manner; surely you are convinced now?" But the lunatic replies "Yes, but that was only his diabolical cunning; he's really plotting against me the whole time, like the rest of them; I know it, I tell you."[17]

---

[16]Flew, "Theology and Falsification," pp. 96ff.
[17]Hare, *ibid.*, pp. 99f.

The moral of this story is that the lunatic has a *blik* about dons, though, more important, he has a wrong (in fact, an insane) *blik* about dons. The nonassertional character of *bliks* aside, clearly there is a difference between right *bliks* and wrong *bliks*, and it is important to have the right *bliks*. From our belief that our cars will not disintegrate as we careen down the freeways, to our conviction that tables continue to exist when unperceived, to our confidence in the promise of a friend, our lives are filled with *bliks*, and it obviously matters a great deal whether you think that dons are trying to murder you!

In spite of it all, therefore, *bliks* appear to have some cognitive status, even though Hare himself does not spell this out; they bear upon the truth of things and can be mistaken. But what, then, is the logical status of these peculiar beliefs—unarguable, but so essential to our lives? Where Flew erred, says Hare, is in taking *bliks* as *explanations* of something. *Bliks* (for example, "God has a plan") are not themselves explanations of anything, though taken together they constitute a view of the world, a feeling about the way things are, that in turn makes explanation possible. *Bliks* cannot be verified or falsified because they are themselves the elemental ideas that make possible the verification and falsification of other ideas.[18]

It would appear that Hare is right. On both the practical and intellectual planes, one cannot function without *bliks*; they are constitutive of one's *Weltanschauung*, or image of the world. For the religious person to abandon the belief, say, that the world is created and sustained by Almighty God would require that his or her whole way of seeing the world be remodeled. Since *bliks* are at once determinative of and the products of the sum total of our experiences (sensory, intellectual, emotional, aesthetic), it is often the case that we cannot deny them without, in a way, denying ourselves at the same time. Why one should hold a certain *blik* to begin with, or how one is to decide between competing *bliks*, are questions that remain. Perhaps the notion of *conversion* has some relevance at this point. At any rate, we find ourselves confronting once again a fact of intellectual experience that we have encountered in one form or another throughout our discussions: the presence of the nonrational. Notwithstanding our desire for completely rational justifica-

---

[18]*Ibid.*, pp. 99ff.

tion, our positions are usually shot through and through with non-rational elements that, though nonrational, appear to be inevitable, relevant, and even necessary for our understanding of the world.

Mitchell answered Flew differently, maintaining that religious statements are genuine assertions even though they cannot be conclusively verified or falsified. As we might expect, Mitchell enlists the help of a third parable to make his point. Let us imagine, he says, that during a war in an occupied country a resistance fighter meets a Stranger who impresses him deeply. The Stranger tells the partisan that he, the Stranger, is also on the side of the resistance. Thus the partisan is won over by the Stranger, who then urges the partisan to trust him no matter what happens. The partisan leaves the meeting confident in the sincerity and truth of the Stranger. But the Stranger is sometimes seen in enemy uniform handing over patriots to the occupation powers. Because the partisan is still convinced of the Stranger's sincerity, he now interprets the Stranger's present actions as part of a secret resistance maneuver. When he asks for help from the Stranger, sometimes he receives it and feels grateful for the confirmation of his belief; at other times, his request is not granted and he thinks to himself, "The Stranger knows best." And so the partisan goes on clinging to his conviction in spite of appearances to the contrary.

The important difference between Hare's parable and Mitchell's is that Hare's lunatic allows nothing to count against his *blik* that dons are trying to murder him, whereas Mitchell's resistance fighter admits that many discrepancies do seem to belie his faith in the Stranger. And if there is evidence that counts against the truth of the statement "The Stranger is on our side," then this statement has (whatever the case with *bliks*) truth value and it qualifies as a genuine assertion, even though there may be no *conclusive* verification or falsification of it; and (whatever the case with *bliks*) it does explain some things, at least in the eyes of the resistance fighter. Similarly, the believer does allow certain evidence, like the fact of evil and suffering, to weigh against the belief that "God has a plan" (a genuine assertion that helps explain the way things are), though never *decisively*. And is this not, after all, what is often meant by "having faith?"[19]

---

[19]Mitchell, *ibid.*, pp. 103ff.

Furthermore (though Mitchell does not suggest this), "The Stranger is on our side" would, in fact, be conclusively verified or falsified when the war was over. This is the point of John Hick's concept of "eschatological verification"—and still another parable. (That Hick saw his position as an answer to the Flew-Hare-Mitchell discussion is evident from the title of his own article: "Theology and Verification.")

Hick invites us to consider two men walking together down a road. One man believes that the road leads eventually to a Celestial City; the other man believes that the road leads nowhere. Along the way, both men experience times of refreshment and times of hardship, and both men find it possible to interpret their experiences, the bad as well as the good, as consistent with their different beliefs about their ultimate destination. Thus, as Hick says, during the journey the issue between the two men—like that of Flew's garden watchers—is not an experiential one; they have no argument about their experiences along the way, but rather about their ultimate destination.

And yet when they do turn the last corner it will be apparent that one of them has been right all the time and the other wrong. Thus, although the issue between them has not been experimental, it has nevertheless from the start been a real issue. . . . Their opposed interpretations of the road constituted genuinely rival assertions, though assertions whose status has the peculiar characteristic of being guaranteed retrospectively by a future crux.[20]

Of course, it will be noted that if the road leads nowhere, then there is no hope of refuting the one man's claim that it leads to a Celestial City. Similarly, some theological statements, like "The soul is immortal," by their nature can never be falsified: If we die and that is the end of the matter, then we will not be there to observe whether that is the end of the matter. On the other hand, we know what it would be like for the soul to survive death, that is, we know what empirical difference it would make. Such statements are, therefore, potentially verifiable in the future—eschatologically—and that is enough to ensure their nature as genuine descriptive asser-

---

[20]John Hick, *Faith and Knowledge*, 2nd ed. (Ithaca, N.Y.: Cornell University Press, 1966), pp. 177f. Hick's position was first published as "Theology and Verification," *Theology Today*, 27 (1960).

tions. Their meaning is not symbolic, not ceremonial, not emotive, but factual: ". . . the existence or non-existence of the God of the New Testament is a matter of fact, and claims as such eventual experiential verification."[21]

Hick, of course, opened a new front on the question, and his position was answered in a variety of counterattacks. Kai Nielson responded, for example, that Hick reasons in a circle, inasmuch as the eschatological verification of Christian theological propositions requires already the meaningfulness of those very propositions. To use Hick's examples, the truth of "God exists" may be confirmed in the postmortem state in which we, in our resurrected bodies, discover the fulfillment of God's purpose for us, or in which we experience a communion with God through Christ, God's Son. But clearly, the possibility of such experiences, involving God's purposes or involving Christ (the divinely "anointed") or God's Son, presupposes already the meaningfulness of God-talk.[22] To this, George Mavrodes responded that the criticism applies equally to all verification-talk: We cannot ask what evidence is relevant for the verification of any statement whatsoever unless we first know what that statement means. Mavrodes concluded that the verificationists are more confused about the meaning of their language than are the theologians, and he recommended that theologians proceed with business as if nothing had happened:

Theologians have no logical reason to be troubled by the current state of the philosophical challenge to the meaningfulness of God-talk. Perhaps at a later time some philosopher will formulate such a challenge in some coherent way. But until then theologians will probably be justified in devoting the major part of their attention to the more substantive problems of their discipline.[23]

---

[21]*Ibid.*, p. 193. One might note also I. M. Crombie's earlier version of the idea of eschatological verification in his contribution to the Flew-Hare-Mitchell discussion, reprinted as Part Two of "Theology and Falsification," in Flew and MacIntyre, *New Essays in Philosophical Theology*, pp. 109ff.

[22]Kai Nielsen, "Eschatological Verification," *Canadian Journal of Theology*, 9 (1963).

[23]George Mavrodes, "God and Verification," *Canadian Journal of Theology*, 10 (1964), p. 191.

And Alvin Plantinga argued that Flew's original falsification-challenge—which started the whole thing—was itself ill-conceived.[24]

No doubt a more charitable estimation of verificationism could be provided. But even so, on what possible grounds could a cogent verificationism commend itself to us in competition with other approaches? Would it not in the end find it necessary, like the older Positivism, to appeal rather dogmatically to the nature of things and the nature of knowledge, and to take a rather narrow view, at that?

Symbol, Poetry, and Metaphor

Most people are naturally inclined to view religious statements (such as "God loves us") as *cognitive* statements; that is, they take them as being informative, as describing some factual situation or other (such as "Sirius is 8.7 light years away"), and therefore as having truth-falsity status. But we have now seen that whereas the cognitive significance of religious statements has been defended by some (for example, St. Thomas), it has been challenged by others (Flew). On this latter view, such statements are not statements at all; they convey no factual meaning; they make no claim about reality whatsoever. Somewhere in between these two are those views which take religious propositions as being cognitively meaningful but which locate their significance outside of their literal truth or falsity. That is, a claim may be factually false and yet convey or support what is ethically, symbolically, or poetically true.

Some of the attempts to recover the significance of religious language by shifting to a nonliteral interpretation have been sponsored by the analysts-empiricists themselves. One of the most successful of these is contained in R. B. Braithwaite's *An Empiricist's View of the Nature of Religious Belief*. In place of the Verification Principle, Braithwaite substitutes what may be called the Use Principle: The meaning of a statement is disclosed in the way it is used. On inspection it turns out that religious utterances are used by the religious person to express an intention to adopt a certain behavioral policy or to live in a certain way (for example, in a Christian

---

[24]Alvin Plantinga, *God and Other Minds* (Ithaca, N.Y.: Cornell University Press, 1967), pp. 157ff.

way, with its practice of love and so forth) and as support for the determination to carry through in that policy. These moral intentions are, in this way, related to a story or group of stories (for example, the stories about Jesus) that are "entertained" as the empirical or factual—though not necessarily historical or true—basis of the intention, and that cumulatively suggest that policy or way of life. The essence of religion, he says, lies in its exhortation to a life of love, and the great religions differ only, therefore, in their ritual practices and, more important, in the different stories (or sets of stories) entertained as the empirical foundation of their moral teaching.

Braithwaite summarizes his position:

A religious assertion, for me, is the assertion of an intention to carry out a certain behavior policy, subsumable under a sufficiently general principle to be a moral one, together with the implicit or explicit statement, but not the assertion, of stories.[25]

Braithwaite believes that this understanding of religious assertions possesses the advantage of, among other things, doing justice both to the religious person's demand that his or her beliefs be taken seriously and to the empiricist's demand that religious discourse be factually grounded.

In fact, however, it may be asked whether Braithwaite does justice to either of these. First, the religious person's beliefs usually (depending on the person) extend beyond a mere "entertaining" of hypothetical stories. Rather, one may conceive of oneself as a participant in a real drama involving the Christ who "for us men and for our salvation, came down from heaven . . . was made man . . . was crucified . . . suffered . . . rose again. . . ." More than a lifestyle or a behavioral policy of love, it may be for the believer a matter of salvation and hope, and hope that is dependent upon real occurrences. It may be Braithwaite himself who does not take religious belief seriously enough.

Second, if Braithwaite's position does justice to the empiricist's demands, it does so at too great a price, for, as was just suggested, the real stuff of religious conviction (depending on the religion) is

---

    [25]R. B. Braithwaite, *An Empiricist's View of the Nature of Religious Belief* (Cambridge, England: Cambridge University Press, 1955), p. 32.

hardly exhausted in what can be empirically apprehended. That Jesus of Nazareth lived, that he taught certain things, that he was crucified under Pontius Pilate around the year 33 A.D., and even that he was raised from the dead may be taken as factual, empirical information, even if untrue. But that the *Logos* was in the beginning, that he was God, that all things were made by him, that he was the light of men, and that he himself became a man and atoned for the sins of the world cannot be empirically apprehended, though it is the foundation of Christian belief and hope. Furthermore, in his reduction of the great religions to essentially the same concern for the moral life, Braithwaite underestimates their differences. The story of the Gospels and the story of the *Bhagavad-Gita*, for example, involve very different theologies, very different conceptions of salvation, and make quite different points. It would appear that the situation of the religious believer may be considerably richer than Braithwaite has allowed.

The interpretation of religious language as symbolic (Braithwaite preferred the more neutral "story" to "myth" or "symbol") has always been popular, and not even the staunchest fundamentalist would deny the presence of symbolism in the Bible. Surely one of the most notable attempts to express the symbolic meaning of Christianity is that of the German-American theologian Paul Tillich (1886–1965).

Tillich's concept of the religious symbol is inseparable from his concept of faith. According to Tillich, faith is not merely an intellectual affair, as in an intellectual assent to revealed truths; nor is it merely a volitional matter, an act of the will; nor is it to be identified with emotion or feeling. To identify faith with any one of these (and it has, in fact, been identified with each) is a distortion of its true nature. Faith, rather, involves the total person, the sum of one's faculties; it is "a centered act of the total personality" (I once heard Tillich characterize the human being as "a multi-dimensional unity") affirming that which is grasped as holding ultimate significance. In two words, faith is "ultimate concern." But faith is idolatrous when it affirms something as ultimate that is not really ultimate, for example, the nation, wealth, and social prestige. For Tillich what is really ultimate, the Ground of Being, cannot itself be something that exists alongside other things; rather, it lies infinitely beyond the reach of the finite concepts that designate ordinary realities—the "God above God." In this way, the nature of genuine faith itself requires the transformation of idolatrous concepts into symbols:

That which is the true ultimate transcends the realm of finite reality infinitely. Therefore, no finite reality can express it directly and properly. . . . Whatever we say about that which concerns us ultimately, whether or not we call it God, has a symbolic meaning. . . . The language of faith is the language of symbols.[26]

Tillich is eager to answer anyone who is disappointed to learn that religious language turns out to be "only symbolic." There is a difference between a sign and a symbol, a recurring idea in Tillich's works. Whereas signs and symbols both point to something beyond themselves, symbols (whether artistic, political, or religious) participate in that to which they point; they share in the dignity and honor of what they represent. Further, as in art and music, symbols disclose new levels of reality otherwise inaccessible to us and unlock corresponding dimensions of the soul. Finally, because symbols are projections of the collective unconscious and hold significance only insofar as a community (unconsciously) accepts and responds to them, they are born and they die; they are never invented or wilfully discarded. Let us, then, never say, "only a symbol" but rather "not less than a symbol."[27]

Underlying Tillich's view of the significance of religious symbols is his view of the human as an estranged being. This latter idea is actually the point of departure for Tillich's whole existential theology. The phrase "existential anxiety" expresses Tillich's appraisal of the human situation. We are beings who live continually under the threat of nonbeing. In the anticipation of death, we are confronted with our finitude. Our sense of guilt reflects our deviation from our essential nature, what we ought to be. And hope is lost in the experience of meaninglessness. We find ourselves, therefore, estranged from our own being, suffering existential anxiety.

It is precisely these existential dimensions of the human and this state of anxiety that religious symbols address. For example, the mythical symbolism of the creation story speaks to our sense of fini-

---

[26]Paul Tillich, *Dynamics of Faith* (New York: Harper & Row, 1957), p 44.
[27]*Ibid.*, pp. 41ff.

tude; it testifies that we are not alone, that we are creatures, that we have been created, and that we thus participate in the inexhaustible depth of reality. Let us then take courage and affirm ourselves in the infinite Ground of our being. In this way, the symbol of creation gives us the "courage to be"—the title of one of Tillich's works—even in the face of the ever-present threat of nothingness. Or again, central to many religions are the symbols of the fall and salvation, along with a multitude of closely related symbols. The symbol of temptation, as Tillich says, expresses the anxiety of existential decisions. Adam and Eve symbolize our situation of being confronted with the decision between "the dreaming innocence of Paradise and achieving self-realization in knowledge, power, and sex." Their fall symbolizes this transition to existential self-actualization. (Of course, the essential human state "before" the fall is not conceived here as a literal state in time, but rather as the potentiality for authentic existence that is present in every stage of human development; nor is the "transition" a literal or historical transition but rather a statement about the tragic-universal character of existence.) The symbols of the demonic represent the "feeling of being possessed by structures of self-destruction." And salvation symbols like redemption, regeneration, and Christ speak mythologically of our "passionate quest" in our existential situation.[28]

Such, for Tillich, is the power and significance of religious symbols as they confront us with the reality and the urgency of our existential plight. In reference to the symbol of the Fall he says: "It is a genuine description of man's predicament here and now and should not be vitiated by the absurdities of literalism."[29]

Tillich's analysis of religious symbolism gives rise to several problems. First, and recalling a problem with Braithwaite, one may wonder if Tillich's thoroughgoing symbolic interpretation can be squared with the starkly empirical-historical elements that seem, at least in part, constitutive of Christianity. Many would freely grant, say, the mythic and symbolic character of the stories of the creation and the Fall but would insist on a literal, bodily resurrection of Jesus from the dead. In fact, it might be argued, it is precisely the

---

[28]Paul Tillich, "Existential Analyses and Religious Symbols," in *Contemporary Problems in Religion*, ed. Harold A. Basilius (Detroit: Wayne State University Press, 1956), pp. 42ff.

[29]*Ibid.*, p. 50.

presence of these empirical-historical elements that both identifies the distinctive features and content of the Christian story and prevents it from slipping into a pipe dream with no relation to any objective reality, or to anything that has actually happened, or to anything that could make an actual difference with respect to our relation to God.

Further, as the ultimate reality to which all religious symbols point, Being Itself may turn out to be (quite opposite to Tillich's intent) both a theologically and a religiously empty concept. If nothing nonsymbolic can be affirmed about Being Itself, then we may legitimately wonder how any theology can justify itself as more adequate than another. Bare Being Itself, without any elaboration or qualification, can hardly serve as a criterion for theological (symbolic) discussions and appeals. Moreover, if *all things* by their nature participate in the Ground of Being, then it is devoid of the distinctive character and demand that it alone can inspire worship and commitment. We are, in fact, at the opposite extreme from both the distinctive Wholly Otherness of Otto's numinous and the particularity of Kierkegaard's object of faith. According to Tillich, the First and Great Commandment is a symbolic translation of ultimate concern. But whereas I might feel suitably constrained to love the Lord my God with all my heart, with all my soul, and with all my mind (Matt. 22:37–38), I might have some difficulty experiencing such devotion and excitement towards an impersonal and general Being Itself. Certainly we would be left cold if Billy Graham were to conclude one of his evangelistic broadcasts with the benediction, "And may the Ground of Being bless you real good!"

Another view that sees the meaningfulness of religious language in its essentially noncognitive function is that of George Santayana (1863–1952). Santayana was a romantic and a poet as well as a philosopher. He believed that the poetic and imaginative impulse, cultivated in accord with intellection or ideation, contributes an essential element to understanding and life, and that these two together—imaginative impulse and ideation—constitute the essence of human activity. This twofold activity is, in turn, manifest in every sphere of human endeavor, as is suggested in the five volumes of Santayana's *The Life of Reason*, which bear the individual titles *Reason in Common Sense, Reason in Art, Reason in Science, Reason in Society,* and *Reason in Religion.*

That religion belongs essentially to the Life of Reason (the seat of ultimate values) is apparent from its projection of ideals and its shaping of moral aspirations. But although it aims at the ends of the rational life, it does so by means of an imaginative activity similar to that of the poet:

Religion remains an imaginative achievement, a symbolic representation of moral reality which may have a most important function in vitalising the mind and in transmitting, by way of parables, the lessons of experience.[30]

On the relation of religion to poetry, Santayana goes so far as to claim that

religion and poetry are identical in essence, and differ merely in the way in which they are attached to practical affairs. Poetry is called religion when it intervenes in life, and religion, when it merely supervenes upon life, is seen to be nothing but poetry.[31]

It is clear, then, that religion functions not on the plane of literal truth (Santayana says that religions may be better or worse but never true or false), and two important observations follow from this. First, the traditional conflict between science and religion is a wholly misguided one. Since religion has nothing at all to say about the factual world, it can hardly oppose the truths of science. It is understandable, however, that the problem arises. Religion has always had a tendency to misunderstand its own true nature, arrogate to itself the role of pronouncing literal truths, and harden into a dogma about the way things are rather than be a "struggling force" for the sake of what ought to be. The sooner we recognize the moral (not factual) and symbolic (not literal) character of religious expression, the better will it be for religion's relation to other disciplines, especially the sciences. On the other hand, and second, we must not allow the positive contribution of the religious-poetic imagination to become obscured by the contradictions and confusions of religions:

[30]George Santayana, *The Life of Reason: Reason in Religion* (New York: Scribner, 1905), p. 12.
[31]George Santayana, *Interpretations of Poetry and Religion* (New York: Scribner, 1900), p. v.

Nor have we any reason to be intolerant of the partialities and contradictions which religions display. Were we dealing with a science, such contradictions would have to be instantly solved and removed; but when we are concerned with the poetic interpretation of experience, contradiction means only variety, and variety means spontaneity, wealth of resource, and a nearer approach to total adequacy.[32]

Yet another view, and one that brings us somewhat more up to date in the continuing discussion, is that of Sallie McFague. The basic idea is apparent from the title of her very influential book, *Metaphorical Theology*. Her contribution draws at once on Biblical studies, church history, and literary theory, all of which she synthesizes with a feminist theology.

The problem, says McFague, is to steer a middle course between religious language that is idolatrous and religious language that is irrelevant. The possibility of idolatry arises from the failure to reckon with religious relativity and plurality—an unmistakable deliverance of our contemporary consciousness. In the one case (idolatry) one tradition of images for God gets absolutized. This means, on one hand, a preoccupation with the propositions and literal meaning of Scripture ("The Bible is the Word of God") and, on the other hand, a retreat in the face of competing or pluralistic perspectives into dogmatism and exclusivism. In the other case (irrelevance) a tradition of images for God is discarded as meaningless (in the existential sense) because, first, its Sunday-School familiarity has long since lost its "punch," as with a creed cited by rote, and, second, and more important, it has become increasingly recognized that the world addressed, say, by the Bible, with its particular and peculiar cosmology, psychology, ethics, and social-political institutions, is not *our* world. It is the latter that is especially off-putting (an understatement if there ever was one) to feminist theologians like McFague. The Biblical tradition and Christian history are shot through-and-through with a patriarchalism that not only isn't any longer viable, but is morally and politically offensive.

The task is to "revitalize" religious language in the spirit of the "Protestant sensibility" (McFague is completely upfront with respect to her own and emphatically Protestant perspective). This sensibility is recognized by its open, tentative, iconoclastic, challenging, spirit—just think of the word "Protestant." And what

---

[32]Santayana, *The Life of Reason: Reason in Religion*, p. 13.

method of expressing and interpreting religious language embodies this spirit? The *metaphorical*. Let us be clear, though, that this is neither analogical interpretation (St. Thomas) nor symbolic (Tillich). Both of these operate, in one way or another, with a kind of dominant strain of unity or commonality that runs through everything and thus connects us, and our religious language, with the divine. Metaphor, however, understood not as a mere poetic ornament but in its full literary and communicative power, involves a *tension*. A metaphor implies both similarities and dissimilarities; it emphasizes neither easy continuities nor radical discontinuities; it contains the whisper, "it both is and isn't.":

> Most simply, a metaphor is seeing one thing *as* something else, pretending "this" is "that" because we do not know how to think or talk about "this," so we use "that" as a way of saying something about it. Thinking metaphorically means spotting a thread of similarity between two dissimilar objects, events, or whatever, one of which is better known than the other, and using the better-known one as a way of speaking about the lesser known.[33]

"God is a mighty fortress" is both true *and* false. "God is our Father" is both true *and* false. Now, to make McFague's long story short, is not this approach—the metaphorical approach—exemplified throughout the Biblical literature with its numerous and various representations of God? Is it not employed by Jesus himself, who not only taught parables of the Kingdom (the "root" metaphor), with their contrasts, surprises, and reversals of meaning, but who might be represented as a "parable" *himself*? And is it not faithful to the Protestant sensibility which seeks to open up and challenge?

Of course, some "Protestant sensibilities" might be raised against McFague herself. Here we can only generalize along several lines of criticism. First, some would surely object that they hardly recognize themselves in her characterizations (not to say caricatures) of, say, Catholics and Protestants. Some of these, usually Catholics, will be dumbfounded to hear that their sacramental view of the world has been dismissed as no longer credible. Closely

---

[33]Sallie McFague, *Metaphorical Theology: Models of God in Religious Language* (Philadelphia: Fortress Press, 1982), p. 15.

related, others will accuse McFague as being entirely too controlled by a criterion of what is or is not relevant—an absolutizing, indeed, of current sensibilities. In fact, in a strange way she claims that very little is normative in the Biblical tradition, except for the principle that very little is normative. And, speaking of the Bible, she draws upon certain strains of contemporary New Testament scholarship without indicating that they are not the only ones or even the dominating ones.

For both Tillich and Santayana, religious expression conveys us beyond the world of ordinary experience to the realm of ultimate concern (Tillich) or to the inspiration of moral life (Santayana). For McFague, it provides an arena for the constant renewal of our images of God. Scientific and literal discourse is, of course, appropriate to one kind of situation, but it seems not to be the situation in which we are compelled to ask the questions that matter most.

In this postpositivist time, it seems incredible to have once thought that meaningful discourse could so simply be sifted through an analytic—*a priori*/synthetic—*a posteriori* linguistic sieve. Even the later Wittgenstein, with his notion of many legitimate "language games" (the total fabric of speech forms, situation, and behavior) has contributed to a new interest in the richness and diversity of domains and kinds of discourse, each with its own principles and its own purpose. Not the least of these is religious discourse. And we may conclude with Ian T. Ramsey's observations that religious language is necessarily an odd one, commensurate with the oddness of the religious situation itself, and that

the central problem of theology is how to use, how to qualify, observational language so as to be suitable currency for what in part exceeds it—the situations in which theology is founded.[34]

---

[34]Ramsey, *Religious Language*, pp. 42f.

Postscript: On Finding the Cat

In the Preface, we mentioned the allegation that philosophy looks for a black cat in a dark room when no cat is there, but that theology finds the cat anyway. By now, some readers are surely persuaded o the accuracy of this characterization, though, many of us find our selves captured by these disciplines, with no apparent means o escape.

Two observations are in order. First, and echoing Kierkegaard, the obscurity and elusiveness of this enterprise is exactly what one should expect. And it is, in fact, a hopeful sign because it signals that (at least in this case) we are on the track o the really big and important issues. It's the trivial or ultimately unimportant questions that can be neatly disposed of in a scien tific or objective way and commended for universal assent. It's the most important questions, the ones that bear upon us as existing individuals, that are fraught with doubt, confusion, uncertainty risk—and passion.

The second observation reflects the tenor of the whole book as advocating a historical approach to the enterprise. Although everyone necessarily experiences the world from the standpoint o a personal and historical situation and cannot be condemned for not being a god, a wider historical awareness liberates one from the imprisonment of the moment. Ancient Heraclitus said, "It' the mark of a foolish person to get all excited over every new idea." Philosophical and theological understanding comes, rather through a confrontation with and reflection on the insights, ideas experience, and wisdom of the broad sweep of a whole tradition As is chiseled in stone above the entrance to Norlin Library at the University of Colorado: "He who knows only his own generation remains always a child."

In the meantime, Plato summarizes our predicament when, in his dialogue *Phaedo*, Simmias poses the alternatives:

. . . either [one] must learn or discover the truth about these matters, or if that is impossible, he must take whatever human doctrine is best and hardest to disprove and, embarking upon it as upon a raft, sail upon it through life in the midst of dangers, unless he can sail upon some stronger vessel, some divine revelation, and make his voyage more safely and securely.[1]

---

[1]Plato, *Phaedo*, 85c, tr. Harold North Fowler (London: Heinemann, 1914).

Bibliographical Note

As was stated in the Preface, most of the positions considered in these chapters may be found in my book of readings, *Philosophical/Religious Issues: Classical and Contemporary Statements* (Englewood Cliffs, N.J.: Prentice-Hall, 1996). This volume contains a full representation of the classical and contemporary approaches to the problems of philosophical theology, as well as extensive, annotated bibliographies on each topic. A second, and shorter, collection of readings may be mentioned: Ed. L. Miller (ed.), *Believing in God: Statements on Faith and Reason* (Englewood Cliffs, N.J.: Prentice Hall, 1996).

Further discussion of the theistic arguments may be found in Donald R. Burrill (ed.), *The Cosmological Arguments: A Spectrum of Opinion* (Garden City, N.Y.: Doubleday, 1967), and Alvin Plantinga (ed.), *The Ontological Argument* (Garden City, N.Y.: Doubleday, 1965). In addition, one should note both the April and July 1970 issues of *The Monist*, vol. 54, which are devoted entirely to contemporary treatment of the theistic arguments. On the topic of God and morality, see the readings in Paul Helm (ed.), *Divine Commands and Morality* (Oxford, England: Oxford University Press, 1981). A useful selection from mystical literature, along with helpful introductions, is provided in Walter T. Stace (ed.), *The Teachings of the Mystics* (New York: New American Library, 1960). On the problem of evil, see the several contributions and critical interchanges in Stephen T. Davis (ed.), *Encountering Evil: Live Options in Theodicy* (Atlanta: John Knox Press, 1981). On the soul and immortality, see the readings in Paul Edwards (ed.), *Immortality* (New York: Macmillan, 1992).

Other collections of essays may be mentioned that bear more generally on issues of religious epistemology. Extremely influential for analytic-style debates in the second half of the twentieth century and covering a variety of topics are the discussions in Antony Flew and Alasdair MacIntyre (eds.), *New Essays in Philosophical Theology* (London: SCM Press, 1955). More recent developments and angles are represented in Alvin Plantinga and Nicholas Wolterstorff (eds.), *Faith and Philosophy: Reason and Belief in God*, (Notre Dame, Ind.. University of Notre Dame Press, 1983); Robert Audi and William J. Wainwright (eds.), *Rationality, Religious Belief, and Moral Commitment: New Essays in the Philosophy of Religion* (Ithaca, N.Y.: Cornell University Press, 1986); R. Douglas Geivett and Brendan Sweetman (eds.), *Contemporary Perspectives on Religious Epistemology* (New York: Oxford University Press, 1992); and C. Stephen Evans and Merold Westphal (ed.), *Christian Perspectives on Religious Knowledge* (Grand Rapids, Mich.: Eerdmans, 1993).

Individual works of merit that range over the standard problems, but from differing standpoints, include E. L. Mascall, *He Who Is* (London: Libra Books, 1943), which represents a modern Thomistic approach; James F. Ross, *Philosophical Theology* (Indianapolis, Ind.: Bobbs-Merrill, 1969), an attempt to illuminate the traditional Thomistic approach by the light of language philosophy; Alvin Plantinga, *God and Other Minds* (Ithaca, N.Y.: Cornell University Press, 1967), a logical and critical scrutiny of the theistic arguments, the problem of evil, issues in verification and falsification, and so forth; likewise, from a very different (pluralistic) standpoint, John Hick, *An Interpretation of Religion: Human Responses to the Transcendent* (New Haven, Conn.: Yale University Press, 1989).

In addition, treatments of specific themes may be noted. A recent and sympathetic approach to the theistic arguments may be found in Richard Swinburne, *The Existence of God* (Oxford, England: Clarendon Press, 1979); an unsympathetic approach (written somewhat in answer to Swinburne) is J. L. Mackie, *The Miracle of Theism: Arguments For and Against the Existence of God* (Oxford, England: Clarendon Press, 1982). For another critical treatment of the theistic arguments and related issues (hefty and more recent), see Richard M. Gale, *On the Nature and Existence of God* (Cambridge, England: Cambridge University Press, 1990). Specifically for an Ontological Argument, see Alvin Plantinga, *God, Freedom and Evil* (New York: Harper and Row, 1976), Part 2. On the Cosmological Argument, see William Lane Craig, *The Cosmological Argument from Plato to Leibniz* (New York: Barnes & Noble, 1980), and William Rowe, *The Cosmological Argument* (Princeton, N.J.: Princeton University Press, 1975). On the Teleological Argument, see Thomas McPherson, *The Argument from Design* (London: Macmillan, 1972). On the Moral Argument, see H. P. Owen, *The Moral Argument for Christian Theism* (London: Allen & Unwin, 1965).

Old but standard treatments of religious experience include William James, *Varieties of Religious Experience* (New York: Longmans, Green & Co., 1902), and Evelyn Underhill, *Mysticism* (London: Methuen, 1911). More recently, see R. C. Zaehner, *Mysticism: Sacred and Profane* (Oxford, England: Clarendon Press, 1957); William Alston's sympathetic treatment, *Perceiving God: The Epistemology of Religious Experience* (Ithaca, N.Y.: Cornell University Press, 1991); John Hick, *Faith and Knowledge*, 2nd ed. (Ithaca, N.Y.: Cornell University Press, 1966); John Hick, *Evil and the God of Love*, 2nd ed. (New York: Harper & Row, 1978); John Hick, *Death and Eternal Life* (San Francisco: Harper & Row, 1976); C. J. Ducasse, *Nature, Mind and Death* (La Salle, Ill.: Open Court, 1951); Ian T. Ramsey, *Religious Language* (New York: Macmillan, 1957).

On related topics, see John Baillie, *The Idea of Revelation in Recent Thought* (New York: Columbia University Press, 1956); Ronald Nash, *The Concept of God* (Grand Rapids, Mich.: Zondervan, 1983); William P. Alston, *Divine Nature and Human Language* (Ithaca, N.Y.: Cornell University Press, 1989); Paul Davies, *God and the New Physics* (New York: Simon & Schuster, 1983); C. S. Lewis, *Miracles* (New York: Macmillan, 1947).

For a book similar to the present one but more analytic (in the loose sense) in its discussion of the topics and somewhat more oriented to recent and current angles, see Brian Davies, *An Introduction to Philosophy of Religion*, 2nd ed. (New York: Oxford University Press, 1993). Davies also provides an extensive, annotated, and up-to-date bibliography. Special mention should be made of the multivolume *Encyclopedia of Philosophy*, ed. Paul Edwards (New York: Macmillan, 1967), which contains entries and bibliographies (now somewhat dated) pertaining to the ideas and thinkers considered in this book. Also, one should attend to the continuing parade of articles (sometimes technical) to be found in *Faith and Philosophy*, the journal of the Society of Christian Philosophers.

Index

Note: f = following page; ff = following pages; n = footnote